AN IRISHMAN
ABROAD

AN IRISHMAN
ABROAD

Growing up with unity and division in an Anglo-Irish family

Tarka King

UNICORN

First published by Unicorn
an imprint of the Unicorn Publishing Group LLP, 2023
Charleston Studio
Meadow Business Centre
Lewes BN8 5RW

www.unicornpublishing.org

10 9 8 7 6 5 4 3 2 1

ISBN 978-1-911397-25-0

Cover design by Matt Wilson
Typeset by Vivian Head

All photographs from the author's collection unless stated otherwise.

Printed in Malta by Gutenberg Press Ltd

Contents

For my wife Jane
and in memory of Bourke Cockran,
a fellow Irishman abroad

Prologue

The funeral took place in 2016, two months before the British vote on whether to leave or stay in the European Union. In his 100th year my Uncle Jack had died in his bed at Castle Leslie, the mid-Ulster family home lying just in the Republic, with fellow Knights of Malta coming to make their farewells, along with a broad Ascendancy remnant representation of those who had made it to the 21st century. The ceremony over, the coffin made its way down the aisle and out into the April sunshine, where a horse-drawn hearse waited. There a surge of locals moved forward to shake hands and express condolences during the short pause while the undertakers went about their work of loading.

A man appeared among the throng who I'd not seen in years and did not recall ever having actually conversed with. He took my hand, said something polite about my late uncle and then, I guess skilfully, judging how much time he had before the procession moved off, launched straight into asking if I'd consider renting an 'auld shed at the foot of the field with two gates'. I asked why he was interested in a corner of my old farmyard and he replied, nodding his head in the direction of the Northern Ireland border about a mile away, 'Well, if this Brexit thing was to come off we'd all be back in business.' The horses' hooves began to clatter, announcing the imminent departure of the cortège to Jack's final resting place, and I terminated the conversation with a smile, accompanied by a fairly strong jab to the man's rib-cage so my words, 'This time I'm in the frame, OK?' would not be taken light-heartedly.

The rest of the day was normal in that after the committal there was a reception for all on the big house lawn. However, the memory of the incident outside the church with the smuggler still lingered and so, in the evening, I took the time to go down to the old farmyard alone and quietly wander up from the rusting barns to 'the field with two gates'. There, in the fading light and standing in Co. Monaghan, I had a view of Caledon House across the border in Co. Tyrone and the trees surrounding Tynan Abbey in Co. Armagh, both not more than two miles distant as the crow flies but across an invisible social gulf wider than America's Grand Canyon. The disused railway running parallel to the bed of the derelict Ulster canal I'd first encountered aged seven, the restoration of which was still a burning passion, was also within sight, but the significant fact trumping all was the hedge at the bottom of the field where it marked the juridical boundary between the Republic of Ireland and Northern Ireland. In the middle of it beside a rusty well there was a gate. On the other side of the gate lay a track that led nowhere other than into a neighbour's farm – nothing special about this, other than that he was a cattle dealer by trade and beneath the track's coating of mud lay steel girders capable of supporting laden lorries. We both used the well as a reserve for watering stock in dry weather.

As I leaned on the gatepost, memories came back of wild moonlit nights herding mature bullocks weighing almost a ton each from the yard to the gate up the hill. They would be let out into the big, lush pasture glistening with dew. Usually it was after a long ride in a cattle truck and so they'd take off in an immediate mad gallop to circuit the field. We'd call it the 'lap of honour' as they raced round the perimeter encompassing the 36 acres. The funny thing was that the gate at the far side would be open and there would not be a beast in the field in the morning. But that was all back in the 1970s, now so very long ago. From where I was standing a couple of chaps from a nearby village had once opened up with a 12.7 mm machine-gun aimed at Caledon House, with some bullets finding their target and knocking cow-pats of plaster off the walls. A white bungalow was also just visible through trees where the occupant, an Ulster Volunteer Force member, had received an untimely doorstep execution by an opposing paramilitary force that hadn't had far to reach from the Republic. Behind it tall trees marking the site of yet another terrible happening stood against the darkening eastern sky like tombstone sentinels.

I began to think back to other days in that same field. There was a hollow in its centre which provided a perfect killing ground when deerstalking, and along a bit from where I was standing a little bank was just right for lying on to take a shot. Early one morning I'd watched a fallow buck suitable for culling casually make its way into the field through a hedge that actually defined the border with the North and wander towards the safe target area. When the rifle's crosshairs could neatly bracket the animal's heart zone I had eased off the safety catch and prepared to fire once it stood still. At that moment two army helicopters had risen in the air from the police station a mile to my right and, like giant overladen bumblebees, had begun their clattering journey towards the next stop at Caledon. Knowing the route they would take, which lay along the bottom of the field before me, I had wondered if by chance one of my Army Air Corps friends from earlier times might be in a pilot's seat. Safety pushed to 'on', the rifle bolt had been slid back, bullet ejected and scope adjusted for long-range spotting – it was not detachable. Once the lead helicopter was in the crosshairs magnification had been increased until heads were clearly visible. For a second or two memories of chums from another world and time had come to mind. (One claimed to hold the altitude record for a helicopter over Northern Ireland and another had been awarded an MC for extracting troops under fire and somehow managing to fly them to safety with his helicopter's tail rotor more or less shot off. I'd last seen them both years before when serving in the Household Cavalry at the eastern end of the Mediterranean.) Then the craft had banked behind some trees and disappeared. I reloaded the rifle, only to discover the buck too was gone. It had been a Sunday. Drizzle began to fall and it was time for breakfast. That evening the 6 pm news had announced that HRH Prince Charles had paid a visit by air to the RUC at Middletown and Caledon police stations.

Here I was, decades later, still looking at that wonderfully rural scene but threaded through and through with extraordinary historical linkages. Mother, father, grandfather were all part of the colourful agrarian tapestry in front of me. The view was deceptive, though, as on either side of it lay two entirely separate legal, educational, financial and taxation systems, police forces, postal and health services, with even water and electricity supplies differing in pressure and voltage. The calibration of the humble kitchen pipe was based on the imperial standard and the inch in the Republic, while in the North measurement was calibrated in millimetres. All this invisible difference lay silently hanging in the air as rooks cawed nearby in some tall ash trees, having flown the same divide over from Caledon to roost in the old oak wood behind.

It was time to return to the big house and the remainder of the day's event, but as I turned away more and more memories began to dance about over the chapter of accidents that had led to my becoming and then surviving as cattle farmer here in the centre of Mid-Ulster's bandit country, hotfoot from serving as an officer in the British Army. Images flitted by, landing briefly but then taking off again, one memory quickly replaced by fragments of another – the image of civil rights leader Bernadette Devlin's angry face taken from a Syrian newspaper decorating my bedroom wall in Damascus in 1972; the despair in a young blood-spattered woman's eyes in Cambodia as she cradled a child twitching in its last spasms of life still haunted me; being kissed expansively by an ex-Soviet minister who had once been Kazakhstan's champion pugilist; explaining the roots of Winston Churchill's First Nation American ancestry to the wartime Japanese Emperor Hirohito's younger brother – all drifted in and out of focus.

As I reached the farmyard the reverie should have come to an end, only it didn't. What if a vote in favour of Brexit did actually come to pass – what would happen then? The prospect seemed as likely as shaking hands with the man on the moon – the real question was why the old smuggler had emerged from decades of obscurity with an assumption that I was worth approaching so directly about 'the yard'. For 40 years I'd been embedded in the local community as what might be described as a co-operative landowner with a strategically important border property. Though the family could be branded as classically Anglo-Irish, a relationship with the grass-roots peasantry was historic and close, reaching back centuries to 'the Fighting Bishop'. Bishop John Leslie had opposed Cromwell's forces for the entire period of the Commonwealth's existence and then purchased Glaslough in 1662 with the compensation handed to him by the King for his consistent Royalist support. He wasn't a 'Planter', guilty of dislodging an unwilling indigenous landowner, and this had become a key factor centuries later at the rise of Irish Nationalism.

My American grandmother had taken up residence in the big house in 1921 as the Irish war for independence from Britain raged, only to be followed by the Civil War which erupted over whether the emerging state should remain a member of the British Commonwealth or not. Her husband, Shane, my grandfather, later Sir Shane Leslie, had rejected his Protestant heritage to become a dedicated Nationalist campaigner, working closely with Eamonn de Valera and Michael Collins in the years from 'The Rising' in 1916 up to the Treaty and independence. His heart was broken by the final outcome and partition, but the upside was a legacy of the family being thoroughly rooted in the formative years of the new 'Free State'. For him the now defunct Ulster canal was a strong physical link with the past, and twice he'd walked me as a small boy along a remnant of its towpath while describing the waterborne society that had once existed.

But the smuggler's confidence in approaching me so bluntly wasn't based on that either – rather more to do with the way he understood me. Like schooling a young horse, the man had detected a line of communication not requiring words, just a sort of sense of what needed to be imparted using eyesight alone. Over the years good fortune had played a part in survival, in that twice I'd suddenly been bearded by strangers in the village pub with the question 'Where were you on Bloody Sunday?' Each set-up had come totally without warning, conducted by interrogators, not people I knew. Pints had flowed beforehand to disarm, and hesitation would have been fatal. It was obvious my British ex-serviceman's reaction to the question concerning the Derry massacre in 1972 was being studied as closely as the answer. Had I been implicated in military activities of any kind in Northern Ireland at any time it would have been game over, as after a few pints it is difficult to be other than that which you are. Hesitation implying guilt of some sort was being looked for, but luckily sheer fate had given me an indisputable ace card to play and each time it had worked.

Six years spent serving in the British Army in the 1970s had not exactly prepared the way for taking on a rundown farm on the Ulster border, but I'd survived. The earlier years at an English public school and while fooling around London on the fringes of the deb scene had been harder – an effort had to be made to fit in but a subconscious off-key echo always remained. In conversation with Jim the smuggler no such tension existed. What lay behind it all?

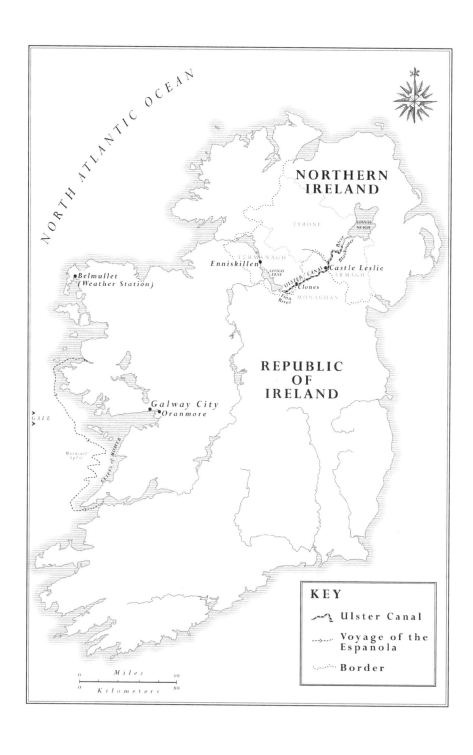

NORTH ATLANTIC OCEAN

NORTHERN
IRELAND

TYRONE

LOUGH
NEAGH

River
Blackwater

FERMANAGH

Enniskillen

LOUGH
ERNE

ULSTER CANAL

Castle Leslie

ARMAGH

Belmullet
(Weather Station)

Clones

MONAGHAN

Finn
River

REPUBLIC
OF
IRELAND

Galway City
Oranmore

GALE

Mainsail
Split

Cliffs of Moher

KEY

Ulster Canal

Voyage of the
Espanola

Border

Miles
0   50

Kilometers
0   80

1
Youth in Ireland

Where I grew up probably had relevance, as my earliest years were largely spent playing about along the shore of Galway Bay in the west of Ireland. Stormy seas smashing in windows, wild seals, the smell of rotting weed and the shrieks of gulls formed the backbone of childhood memories. Hotfoot on this came religious worries, fear the world would end in 1964 and, almost as bad, Co. Kerry might beat Galway and win the annual All-Ireland Gaelic football match. The first person's name to register outside my immediate family was that of Archbishop the Rev. Dr McQuaid. I didn't understand who or what he was but every daily news bulletin broadcast in English on the radio after the Irish version would start with a summary of his latest decrees. I only took notice because they sometimes made the girls who minded me weep – all were reduced to tears when the Archbishop deemed nylon stockings sinful; girls were banned from being allowed to accept lifts on bicycles from boys – even to Mass – and should only socialise with them at priest-supervised parish dances etc. The Archbishop appeared to be the nation's ruler, the ultimate authority to be feared as a god-like figure.

The single beacon of joy and excitement was the voice of Michael O'Hare, the radio commentator whose amazingly fast delivery held everyone in thrall on a Sunday when inter-county All-Ireland Hurling and Gaelic football matches took place. His clarity of voice and ability to create an atmosphere of continuous unfolding drama were totally gripping, whatever the occasion. (I was in the viewing box at the Canal Turn at Aintree when Foinavon won the Grand National in 1967 and O'Hare's eye-witness commentary of the great pile-up made history.)

At the end of the Second World War my mother, an authoress known as Anita Leslie, had fallen in love with and taken on the task of restoring a ruined castle, a 12th-century tower on the Atlantic seashore by a village called Oranmore in the west of Ireland. Two wartime friends arrived to help and work began. Later in life one, Peter, a retired army colonel, was to become a close friend; the other, Bill, a retired submarine commander, married my mother in 1949 and I was born later the same year. Materials in Ireland were scarce and much had to be fashioned by hand from locally sourced wood and stone but by 1948 the place was vaguely habitable.

A trans-Atlantic single-handed yachting race venue with a big prize had come up for Bill at the time my mother's pregnancy was due to run its course, so it fell to Peter to look after her when the moment came. Another yacht race came up, Bill won it, sold the boat well and, with the proceeds, bought a small farm near the castle. A thatched cottage was built on-site so he could set out to fulfil a burning ambition to be an organic farmer and repair his health, which had been partially wrecked by 15 years in submarines. The peace and quiet of 'the Cottage' enabled my mother to step back into her career as a writer, while I remained in the castle minded by Peter and various visiting relatives.

As an infant my cot was in the 'double-arrow-slit' cell located up in the 12th-century part of the tower and one evening a visiting godmother, Diana Daly, proved to be just that by asking for me to be produced for inspection. Peter collected me from my wicker basket and carried me down to the 'Great Hall'. When he returned with me 30 minutes later it was to find the basket on the floor squashed flat by what turned out to be a wheelbarrow-load of plaster that had fallen from the ceiling, indicating a truly close shave with death.

Time went by and my sister Leonie arrived, introducing an increased demand on the logistical front. A job came up for Peter in the Bahamas in 1953 and he left. Even at my age of only four his departure inflicted an acute sense of loss on me and my emotions tightened to form an inner survival core. Time passed and the castle's spartan conditions were found to be not ideal for raising small children, so we moved to Bill's cottage with two orphaned sisters from the village recruited as minders. We would be lulled to sleep at night by the sound of Atlantic gales blowing from the ocean beating rain against the windowpanes or, if it was a still night, the Banshee-like screams of vixens seeking mates in a nearby wood as the mournful light of a distant lighthouse blinked weakly against closed blinds.

Oranmore Castle was let and, aged five, my education began with primary classes at the local convent. Boys and girls separating at six, the next stage was the all-male village national school under Mr O'Sullivan, known locally as 'the Master', who had taken up the teaching post in 1924. He was a devout Catholic and an ardent Nationalist, with a fixation that the British prime minister Bonar Law (P.M. 1922–23) was largely responsible for all Ireland's woes. He had approximately 60 boys aged 6 to 14 under his charge in one room, about half of whom walked to school barefoot. Religion and a particular view of Irish history dominated everything. His *bête noire* was the partitioning of the island in 1924, seconded by the ruthlessness of Oliver Cromwell in the 17th century. Most of the time was spent lining up to be whacked for the wrong answer to some question.

The parish priest visited occasionally to grill all on the catechism. He too would thrash with a hazel stick of his own. In the yard welts were compared and I felt strongly that mine were usually deeper and redder. Bill was the only Protestant in the locality, so when 'the Master' let forth tirades against the Church of Ireland, accusing it of being a remnant left over from the dark and terrible times the country had suffered under British rule, life in the playground afterwards could become awkward in the extreme. His utterances – 'When the Devil stalked the land he took shelter behind the doors of its chapels' or 'Always run past a Protestant church or he might come out and grab you or trip you up with his tail' – took a bit of living down, but on one occasion when he said all Protestants had tails 'but kept them down their trousers so you might not see them' something snapped. When a hard teasing followed that day I used fists to fight my corner – there was no alternative – and found it worked. Fortunately I was right-handed, but those not so lucky had a hard time of it in class. Somehow, being 'kithoag' was deemed sinful, and anyone caught attempting to write with his left hand had it soundly walloped.

There was one issue the Master was not able to resolve in all the years I attended his school. Some of the boys never ever spoke to others, even during games. There was an invisible but identifiable social division marked by the occasional de-bagging in the bushes behind the playground. The problem harked back to the Irish Civil War of the

1920s. The school's catchment area straddled the Galway–Dublin main road, which had previously been a boundary line between the different areas of support in the years when Michael Collins and De Valera were at loggerheads over the issue of the emerging nation remaining within the Commonwealth. All I really knew was that it was not wise to utter the words 'Sinn Féin' too loudly, even as a boyish prank. A sense of unfinished business of some sort lingered in the air, silent but distinct.

Once a year after Easter someone from the Christian Brothers would come to the school to question the 'leavers', the top class made up of 14-year-olds who were in their last year of state education but mostly still struggling to read. Our rural establishment was deemed too low-life for Jesuit talent-spotters searching for potential priesthood recruits. The brighter boys were picked out for further education by the 'priest recruiters', the rest being allowed to return to their family farms. Amazing speech impediments, cross-eyes, peculiar breathing and twitching handicaps would appear in the run-up to the selection process, much to the amusement of all us lesser mortals.

Every six months an old black steamer too large for the Galway dock anchored in the bay for a day to collect passengers for the crossing to Boston. In the weeks running up to its arrival Canon Kenny's sermons at Mass turned to the evils and temptations of foreign life and the vital necessity of remaining close to one's parish priest wherever one ended up, in order to keep going to confession. It was a time of excitement and sadness in the weeks leading up to departure for those losing a family member. In the evening or night the ship sailed, leaving a melancholy trail of smoke to tint the sky for a day or two.

In 1958, in a holiday period shortly after the warning on the evils of Protestantism, my parents took me to London and an excursion to Chartwell for lunch, an invitation arising through our family connection. Aged nine, I found the going hard, as I was the only child at the table. Lady Churchill was in bed with a case of shingles, so there was no kind old lady to spot my frustration when my mother became preoccupied 'talking war' with the other grown-ups. Knowing no better, I began to seek opportunities to join in the conversations which, to me, sometimes appeared a little silly. When a reference to a 'cat's pyjamas' formed the reply to the oldest man's question, 'How is your book going, Monty?' I'd instantly demanded to know the cat's location, which didn't go down well. Another excited interruption was made when 'Rebecca', the name of one of my schoolfriend's sisters, was mentioned. More dark looks and a long wagging finger in my face was waved by the book's writer. When Bill began to talk about an 'amorous prawn' I asked what 'amorous' meant and dived into telling the finger-wagger I knew how to find lots of prawns in rock pools back at home. At the end of lunch the old man made his way slowly to an electric lift and the rest of the party headed for some stairs leading to the floor below and the drawing room. The temptation to ride in a lift cage was too much for me and as the mesh doors were being drawn shut I slipped in, spotting that there was just room for the two of us. As it began to descend slowly, looking down through his half-moon glasses the old man asked, 'Well, how do you find Monty?' Pondering for a moment on why I felt irritated by the finger-wagger and deducing what I thought the problem might be, I replied, 'Does he have a tail he keeps down his trousers?' The old man began to laugh and a tear ran down one cheek. He was still laughing when the lift stopped and my mother, with an unfamiliar expression on her face, reached in and whisked me out of it.

Years later Bill explained that the reason for the invite to lunch with Winston and Montgomery was twofold. He had been involved in squeezing German supply lines to North Africa with submarines based at Malta, and had been amazed at the quality of intelligence being supplied to brief patrol commanders, enabling repeated deep incisive blows to be made against Rommel's supply lines. Montgomery wanted to tie up some loose ends about how the 10th Submarine Flotilla had managed to keep going so effectively during the prolonged period of siege. My mother had worked in an intelligence capacity for Montgomery's boss, General Alexander, the younger brother of her immediate Irish neighbour, the Earl of Caledon, who lived literally next door in Ireland and had known her all her life. As an ambulance driver and organiser of hospital train movements, her direct contact with fighting men fresh from fields of battle enabled vital raw intelligence to be gleaned on morale, knowledge of enemy weaponry, strengths and weaknesses. Alexander had kept her close to avoid staff officers editing information during the North African and Italian campaigns, using their neighbourly relationship as an excuse, but Winston had not understood the subtlety of the connection. Through her the exposure of a sensitive security leak known as 'the Amorous Prawn' had been turned to the Allied advantage in a brilliantly executed ruse to lead the German armoured troops badly astray just before El Alamein.

The next year there was a family expedition to the Bahamas as guests of Peter's. In 1953 an old friend of his from wartime Palestine, the Earl of Ranfurly, had been appointed Governor. 'Dan' wanted someone he could trust to get to the bottom of an unsolved murder dating back to 1943, when the Duke of Windsor was Governor, and he had recruited Peter in 1954. Happy childhood memories of him had faded slightly but inexplicable pangs of emotion caused by his departure still flickered and made the thought of the coming island holiday thrilling beyond belief.

On reaching the semi-developed island of Andros, where Peter was managing a pineapple-growing enterprise, Leonie and I wasted no time in making local friends and going native. One great sport was hunting land crabs, which lurked everywhere, and one evening while stalking a particularly large one I found myself under a window through which the grown-ups could be heard conversing in hushed tones. They were discussing a murder and who might have done it. Peter was heard saying that he 'had covered the ground for Dan and all lay at the Duke's door', with something about 'Royal Prerogative' being a brick wall. My mother asked for an explanation as to 'why all the feathers?' It seemed an odd sort of conversation and it was better to focus on hunting the crab, which eventually made a bolt for freedom.

I knew the man we usually stayed with, after crossing from Ireland to Liverpool on the overnight ferry, was a Duke, but his being on Andros playing about with feathers didn't make much sense. It transpired that Peter had obeyed Governor Ranfurly's instructions to discreetly get close to Harold Christie, the main suspect, who had benefited from the murder of Sir Harry Oakes, with the aim of seeing if there was anything more to be learned so that the case could be closed. Peter had ended up becoming employed by Christie for some years but nothing new relating to the murder case came to light. On Christie's death Peter was appointed his estate executor and was himself left sufficient funds to be able to retire back to Ireland and buy a house outside Oranmore near the castle.

On our return from the Bahamas it was back to the village school and a new pony, Quicksilver. Actually, he was a very old pony, but great at climbing walls rather than jumping them, which made me popular leading others over large obstacles out hunting – the only form of county social life that existed.

My Uncle Jack had inherited the Castle Leslie Estate at Glaslough in Co. Monaghan in 1945, but his health never recovered from five years of incarceration as a prisoner of war, and by 1954 he was exhausted. That year the family home was made over to my mother and so, for me at the age of five, it became the place where I thought my future lay. Soon after handover a plea for help in restoring the Glaslough village Catholic church roof of St Mary's had materialised and one fund-raising answer was to have the pleasure grounds surrounding the house thrown open for fêtes in the summer. Fancy-dress parades and dancing competitions were held, but the highlight was wonderful ongoing battles between teams of dwarfs decked out in blue and green shirts who set about each other with sticks. Any who bolted from the fracas were just caught and thrown back into the ring, to great cheers from the crowd.

This annual fiesta to help the church finances was supplemented dramatically in 1962 when a sudden embargo on the export of eels from Northern Ireland came into force. The family solicitor in the town came to my mother, stating that an approach had been made by a respected local cattle trader, who wished to rent the old steam-engine water-tank in the farmyard. Some of Michael McNally's associates were declared as 'colourful', but he felt sure the income would be forthcoming and could go towards the church repairs. The end client appeared to be a Mr Kray of east London, who was a big operator in the jellied eel market, and the embargo had caused an acute spike in the trade. Many of the locals were skilled catchers and had gone to work in the county's rivers and streams, but there was a shortage of secure storage prior to transit to the UK. The old tank fitted the need perfectly as it still held water, and I was to benefit greatly years later from the goodwill earned at the time.

During my mother's nine-year reign as chatelaine of the Glaslough estate, Bill supported her in the struggle to make sense of what was basically a financial basket-case. He just about succeeded – by 1963 the farm was out of debt, with the land fenced and stocked with three herds of pedigree Black Angus cattle.

But, for me, Glaslough was for the Easter and summer holidays. I remained at Oranmore National School during term time and grew up largely with friends who lived nearby in a small cottage on the seashore. We would always walk back to their house after class, playing about as we went. Around 6 or 7 pm I'd be picked up and taken home for food and bed. On Sundays us boys would sometimes find a way of getting to the Town Hall cinema in Galway after Mass if there wasn't a match on or if the weather was bad. We would bring an air pistol with us for the Westerns so as to be able to join in when there were shoot-outs. At Bill's funeral in 2012 one whispered he 'still had the gun'.

A particular incident occurred in those early years which impacted heavily on my trust of adults and my sense of self-preservation. Soon after I was taken to a performance of *Peter Pan* a wartime submariner friend of Bill's came to stay. He'd lost a hand and his arm was fitted with a hook that split to hold instruments like knives. I might have been too young for the pantomime as I hadn't enjoyed it, and when this rather gruff man who I was convinced was Captain Hook appeared in the house one evening, I was quite terrified. It seemed my parents were totally unaware of his real identity and had been deceived by his false charm. To me survival depended on having an escape route ready when he appeared in the night – I was convinced he was going to come in through the window. The bedroom door-frame was doctored with carpet tacks until the lock didn't close properly and could be opened with just a pull. Sister Leonie was oblivious to the crisis, but my sense of fear knew no bounds – there was nobody to turn to for help. Survival itself depended on my own ability to escape any danger that materialised, and the one comfort was having a fast exit to fall back on when the moment came. A sense of the need for self-reliance was born that night that bored its way right down into my psyche, never to depart.

As I grew older, friends were made in Glaslough and I learned to drive a senior cousin's go-cart up to the village, where a few circuits round the houses were possible. Becoming the proud owner of a full-sized bicycle led to expeditions over the border for penny bangers, which would then be tied in bunches and chucked fizzing through the swing doors of the local public house. It seemed innocent fun at the time. The sport advanced in later years to borrowing cars that had been parked outside the castle by guests coming to stay for the night. A boy not much older than me worked in the house lighting fires, washing dishes and carrying bags to bedrooms. This duty meant we knew which cars would not be needed for the evening and therefore free. Automobile door and ignition locks were simple mechanisms to unpick if keys were not to hand. There were two dance halls at a distance of about five miles and it was the time of winklepicker shoes, Brylcreem, sticking-out dresses and 11- or 12-piece show bands belting out rock and roll. Car sorted, we'd drive up to the village to load as many as could fit in before heading either across the border to Middletown or up winding roads to Carrickroe, buried in the foothills of Slieve Beagh. No alcohol, dusty naked lightbulbs hung from ceilings, but there was fantastic live music to lift the soul. The occasional police checkpoint with guns and torches was encountered but we never got into trouble and, as the cars were always left exactly where they had been, we were never found out. Early social life was just that, playing about with village boys in Oranmore and Glaslough. The trappings of Anglo-Ireland didn't land on my shoulders as my mother and Bill were totally buried in their own lives of writing, fox-hunting and farming. As long as Leonie and I appeared happy, we were pretty well left to do what we wished.

During the early autumn months my mother would painstakingly drag me out of bed at 4 am to go cubbing, which meant watching young hounds being taught how to hunt by their peers. The effort was worth it as the natural beauty of a receding mist over turloughs (lakes) and the sight of early sunlight on bushes white with hoarfrost never failed to impress. These early morning escapades had begun when, aged seven, I was put on an elderly pony called Micky, harnessed with leading reins held by my mother, who ran along on foot. All went well until a hunting meet at Athenry, when she fell into conversation with a distinguished-looking gentleman wearing a fedora hat and sporting a neat moustache. Somehow, the leading reins became unclipped, setting Micky free to wander off through the mêlée of horses and chattering grown-ups. A state of absolute terror and panic only subsided when he began to respond to the reins in my hands and halt when requested. Words of encouragement from surrounding adults then spurred me on to make him move around through the mass of horseflesh gathered in the town square, to seek out some friends to whom I now wished to show off. Finally, returning to my mother, who appeared not to have noticed my absence, I was introduced to the wearer of the fedora hat. He meant nothing to me at the time, but years later we were destined to meet again, under very different circumstances.

In the same year, 1956, a lady immaculately turned out, riding side-saddle with top hat and veil, appeared on the hunting scene. Lady Christabel Ampthill seemed to be a friend of my mother's and in the following spring when the hunting season was over she called at the house, driving a Dormobile caravan, to ask me to go camping for the weekend. We drove off into the wilds of Co. Clare to look for stumps of ruined castles. She wanted to buy one but could not understand a word of the local dialect, so had me along as interpreter. The far west of Ireland was a fairly undeveloped area in those days, with unmetalled roads, little signage other than that erected by the British Automobile Association, and few shops. I don't remember that she had a map and the main guiding line seemed to be to keep as close as possible to the coastline. As spring turned into summer the weekend jaunts penetrated further and further into the lost lands of briars and undergrowth that comprised most of Co. Clare. When the sea warmed up she'd go swimming wearing just two head-scarves, one round her waist and the other round her chest. The beaches or 'strands' were usually secluded, gentle, gravel inclines requiring quite a wade out to deep water while I remained sitting on the tideline armed with a towel. I guess it was an attempt at modesty but the wet scarves only exaggerated the outline of her figure on emerging from the water. When I was rubbing her back, four long thin white scars lying across her lower shoulder-blades were just visible, one slightly crossing the others. At about that time John Huston, the film director, bought St Clerans, a magnificent Georgian pile in Co. Galway, and while in a cupboard playing sardines during a children's party this observation was mentioned to his daughter, Anjelica. She replied immediately, 'Oh, that's babies.' As I accepted her words at face value, the matter would have been forgotten had it not been for the grown-ups occasionally being overheard referring to a 'virgin birth' and a 'sponge baby' when Christabel's hunting antics were the topic of conversation. This gave me something to think about, as the words did not lie well with the religious instruction and catechism being hammered home by a nun in preparation for my first Holy Communion. (The subject faded in significance for some years, but when the argument over the inheritance of Lord Ampthill's title and legitimacy erupted in the press in the 1970s with the gory details of Christabel's 1923 battle in the House of Lords on the grounds of falling pregnant due to the shared use of a bath sponge, various memories of our seashore exploits came flooding back.)

At the village national school 'The Master' tended to focus mainly on the boys in their leaving year when it came to reading skills. The rest of us just fooled our way along, accepting hazel-stick wallops rather than making efforts to progress academically. Rubbing hands on rocks thickened skin and reduced pain levels markedly. For a time my mother experimented with PNEU home-schooling books as it was obvious at what Anglo-Irish social gatherings there were that I was falling behind my age group. The trouble was I had tasted the delights of unrestricted freedom to play on the seashore and forests, so resisted efforts to focus on schoolwork indoors. The distracting sound of gulls or rooks was impossible to ignore as it indicated the state of the tide or time of day to fish.

In the summer of 1958, in a serious effort to correct my lack of reading ability, my mother took me to the Aran Islands on the *Dun Aengus*, an ancient steamboat that had been plying the harbours of Galway Bay and the outer islands off the west coast for the previous 50 years, delivering turf and collecting cattle. I spent the six-hour journey to Kilronan on Inishmore in the engine room, totally mesmerised by the silently whirling crankshaft and watching a huge piston fly up and down with just a suck and a hiss as power was transmitted to the propeller. The tide state was wrong when we arrived at Kilronan pier, so some cattle to be collected were driven into the sea, netted and then deposited on to the deck by a lifting derrick. Mother had rented a cottage for a week and hoped to be able to have me focus without distraction on some reading books she had brought along. On finding that our elderly host, who lived in a cottage right beside us, was an illiterate boat-builder her plan fell apart, with wonderful days spent fishing, learning how to tar canvas and exploring the rock pools. Just two words were learnt on the entire trip, 'Shut' and 'Open', the printed instructions painted clearly in red with arrows on important steam valves in the *Dun Aengus*'s engine room.

On returning from the Aran Islands and in answer to a request for a boat of some sort we went to see a neighbour who lived a few miles along the shoreline. Meeting Wyndham Waithman was a major development: his patient way of instructing on the principles of mechanical engineering and much else was totally captivating, with the willingly absorbed knowledge proving invaluable in years to come. There might have been over half a century between us but a friendship formed that was to last until his death decades later. In the beginning he just took me out in his little sailing boat for practical lessons on the basics of sensing wind direction, tidal flow influences and ways of controlling a vessel under sail through a moving body of water.

Wyndham told me he had left Eton in 1901 after some very unhappy years and his first job on returning home had been as an assistant fireman on the engine pulling the train on a daily return trip from Galway to Clifton, an isolated seaside town lying 50 miles away on the far side of Connemara. Later employment had taken him to Serbia in a military engineering capacity, which was where he was when the Great War broke out and he had witnessed the horrible massacres that had drawn Russia in. At the end of hostilities he had come home to find Ireland in a state of social turmoil and, to escape, had gone for a long sailing trip round the Mediterranean in a Galway hooker called the *Lark*, taking with him a local lad called Paddy Browne. Calling in at Genoa they had visited a scrapyard, stumbling across a cast-iron mountain of obsolete marble-cutting saws. He had bought three, which were shipped home to Galway as there was a defunct marble quarry on the family estate. He'd been advised of enquiries being made by a billiard-table manufacturer for unpolished but accurately cut limestone slabs and this looked like a way of re-activating the enterprise. Then a massive order materialised for black and cream-white marble, exactly what he was cutting. It was required for Stormont Castle, the new building being erected outside Belfast to house the Parliament destined to rule the part of Ireland that had just been partitioned off. He joked about the fact that cut slabs were carted down to Duggan's Quay in Oranmore Bay, within sight of home, shipped round the headland to Galway docks and then, as part of the contract, re-labelled as marble being imported from Italy.

Wyndham had once built a 14-ft boat called the *Gull* which had fallen into disrepair through lack of use, but in answer to my plea it was worked on over a winter and made seaworthy. By the age of ten I was sailing alone all around the inner parts of Galway Bay in pursuit of mackerel. If the wind dropped it was always possible to row either home or to a friendly pier. Sometimes Paddy Browne would come, as he was an enthusiastic fisherman with an uncanny sense for where the shoals might be running. One day, in response to my recounting of experiences in the *Dun Aengus*'s engine room, he told me what the steamer had secretly been doing during the Second World War and what 'the Captain' (Wyndham) had been up to during 'the Emergency years'. At the outbreak of the war a trainload of coal 'the likes of which had never been seen in Ireland' had arrived at Galway and been moved to the docks for onward shipment 'somewhere'. The *Dun Aengus*'s boiler was never cold, as it was continually steaming out to sea laden to its waterline with the Admiralty-grade Welsh coal. Then 'Dev's men' arrived and no more of it came down from the North. Drawing my attention to the row of rotting wooden hulks lying along the shore by his house at the entrance to Lough Atalia, close by the city's docks, he explained how the canoe-sterned ghosts had been sea-going trawlers in their day and had spent most of the Second World War quietly acting as weather ships stationed in a circle reaching far out into the Atlantic. The *Dun Aengus* had been used to ferry supplies of fuel, food, water and replacement crews – all in secret. 'The Captain' ran it all, the training, collecting of information, getting it to Black Sod Point weather-station up at Belmullet in Sligo. The trawlers didn't have great radio range and sometimes had to relay barometer readings to each other. But the information ended up with the Americans, reassuring them that there was enough good weather coming for their planned crossing to France to go ahead in June 1944.

It had taken a lad on a motorbike to cross the border with documents to back up many phone calls from England before Eisenhower and his team believed the reports were sound, as it was slightly difficult to explain where the depth of detail relating to conditions covering a wide arc of ocean originated – the trawlermen who had risked their lives doing it, with two boats foundering in the terrible storm that came in on the heels of the good weather. The old boats were fun to play on, with dark cavernous holds and small pillbox wheelhouses, but there was also a slightly melancholy atmosphere about them which seemed to confirm his story of their past adventures. The dark side was the price Wyndham paid – he lost his family home. When the facts associated with the secret supply of meteorological information benefiting the Allies came to light, Merlin Park had been requisitioned, demolished and a TB hospital built on the site, with not a stone left to mark the existence of the old Georgian mansion.

Fox-hunting was the sole interest of all adults in Co. Galway. Horses, hunting coverts, visiting cads and bounders on hirelings, horse-dealers and good meets with potential for long chases of five miles or more were the mainstay of conversations through most meals and social gatherings. Some of the county's old 'Big Houses' were just ivy-covered, partially collapsed ruins with crumbling boundary walls carving up the landscape. Occasionally the last remnants of an Anglo-Irish family dynasty that was still clinging on in a converted apple house or stable block followed the hunt on bicycles if a horse wasn't affordable. When the hounds 'found' and a fox bolted away across a sea of grey stone obstacles, the knowledge

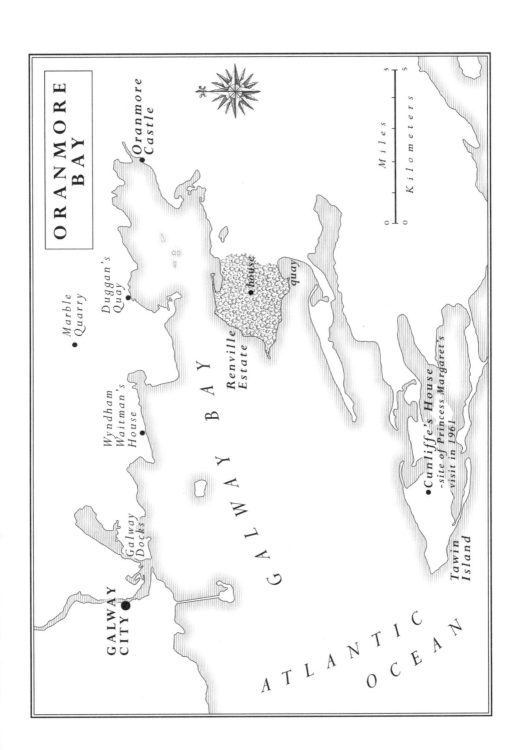

ORANMORE
BAY

Oranmore
Castle

Marble
Quarry

Duggan's
Quay

Renville
Estate

house

quay

Wyndham
Waitman's
House

GALWAY BAY

Cunliffe's House
–site of Princess Margaret's
visit in 1961

Tawin
Island

Galway
Docks

GALWAY
CITY

ATLANTIC
OCEAN

Miles

Kilometers

0   3
0   5

of a coming mad gallop never failed to exhilarate. The first few seconds were the most exciting as one had to negotiate swirling and careering horses all aiming for the same jumps while out of control. The thrill of the chase was escaping the shambles of the start and making it to open country with a bunch of chums. It could be into the teeth of a gale or driving rain, but the fun was always there as one raced for gaps or gave a friend a lead while at full gallop. The hunted fox usually had an uncanny sense of the nearest high double-stone wall and would aim for a small hole in it, cross, run along the foot for a mile or so and then double back. The little russet figure, who I secretly always hoped would get away, could occasionally be spotted fleetingly a few fields ahead of the hounds and, if there was a pause or check in the chase, old hunting hands would throw out suggestions as to where he might be heading. The cry 'He's gone for Knock Doe', 'Dunsandle', 'Castle Ellen' or 'Derry Donnell' would be the trigger words for slightly easier routes or short cuts to be taken. Those who knew the way would call for known thrusters to give leads over the larger walls. A serious obstacle required a sure-footed steed to clatter over the fallen stones of a big gap – at least for the more timid, lacking sufficient courage or a horse capable of jumping a collapsed mass of stones at that speed. There would be a cry of 'Where's Bat' if something looked impossible, and this summoned Dr O'Driscoll to lumber up from the back of the field in a swallow-tailed coat and top hat. His grey mare cantered in a slow rocking motion and had a way of pushing a wall down with its front legs which always proved popular in the frenzy of the moment.

The hunting clergy were quick to seek out Anjelica Huston if she'd been spotted at the meet and cry for a lead, as she was always mounted well. The priests' enthusiasm to follow her studiously in line across the stone-walled fields increased noticeably when she turned 16 and began to appear in a pair of tight-fitting cream breeches. Apparently when being measured for them by a fashionable tailor in a place called Hospital she claimed he had found it necessary to frequently measure her bust. At the back of the field conversations would break out over which priest would be taking whose confession that night. Would it be Father Keyes handing out penance to Father Highland and would they then swap roles and

Father Highland listen to what had been on Father Keyes's mind before both turning on Father McCormack who always took first position behind Anjelica for the run?

The many derelict demesnes littering the west of Ireland with their overgrown jungles of what had once been walled gardens provided endless coverts for the hounds to draw for foxes. During the time they were 'working' to see if there was any quarry to be found, there was usually chat about the history of the places and families that had lived there, bringing a lost world momentarily back to life. One day a visiting priest joined us pony riders to shelter under an enormous evergreen oak opposite the elevated bay window of a giant Georgian 'almost ruin' and spoke of how the crumbling mansion in front of us had been the family home of one Isabel Lambert – the mother of 'Satan' – Sir Edward Carson. Not only that, but as a Dublin law student the man who was later to tear Ireland apart in his demand for a Protestant seat of power had returned to court and would eventually marry a cousin from the same house, Castle Ellen, probably wooing his beloved under the very tree providing shelter for us. Looking across at the dilapidated front steps leading up to the pillared portico, it didn't take much effort to imagine what a lovely place it had probably been in the not too distant past, but the fans of ivy now reaching up to the pediment and the missing roof slates warned that the future didn't look promising.

2
School in the UK

Some time in the summer of 1961 Peter came back from the Bahamas on a visit and commented on my extremely poor reading skills. Even through thick wooden doors the words 'boy', 'school' and 'Eton' could be heard, and I knew I was the subject under discussion. Old Wyndham had told me it was a frightful place and now it sounded as if plans were afoot to send me there, wherever it was. Luckily my grandfather, Shane Leslie, was staying and, as an excuse to disappear, I told him about a ruined 'famine village' that lay out of sight and forgotten in a nearby wood. He was a grown-up I'd found it easy to get on with and we'd gone on many long walks before up at Castle Leslie in Co. Monaghan. Once, while we were exploring the bank of the Ulster canal lying half hidden under trees, reached via a line of stepping-stones straddling a river, the subject of religion and death had come up. Just as he was explaining about the River Styx and the need for coins to pay a boatman, a rotten footbridge was spotted in the shadows ahead. Mistakenly thinking we were beside the actual Styx itself, I'd asked why nobody had thought of building a proper bridge for making the crossing. Now, at Oranmore, he was obviously as bored as I was and showed immediate interest in escaping for a walk across fields and a bit of woodland exploration.

Time had taken quite a toll on the little hamlet of hovels that had once been a social hub of some sort for what were clearly very poor people. Occasional single-storey gables fashioned from carefully chosen field stones still pointed up through ash saplings and out of hazel thickets, but ground ivy spread everywhere, with a layer of thick moss covering most surfaces. Many house walls still stood to shoulder-height and it was possible in the soft light to sit 'inside', so the imagination could run on what life must have been like. There would have been boys and girls my age once living and playing in those small rooms, now inhabited by robins and blackbirds. Since it was located on a slope beside a bog and surrounded by boulder-ridden forest, there was no land worth cultivating anywhere near, and it was hard to work out how anybody could survive for long in such a place, the only conclusion being that desperation alone had driven people to gather stones and put them together to create such dwellings.

The place had a noticeable impact on my grandfather, and he grew silent, resting his hand on my shoulder as we headed home via my school so as to view the great cairn behind the playground. In class 'The Master' often spoke of it as the grave of the 'Aughrim horseman', an Irish warrior who had been mortally wounded at the 1691 battle and died at that spot. In respect for his sacrifice, passers-by began to place stones on the site and so, over the years, a massive cairn had come into being. Shane wandered off, found a small lump of limestone, and, carrying it with effort, added it to the pile. There was something about that day wandering about with my grandfather that was different from others: listening to the stories of Ireland's ancient heroes he'd imprinted a multitude of colourful images in my mind.

A few days later the tail-end of Hurricane Debbie devastated the west of Ireland, washing a female seal in through the west window of the castle's main hall along with much gravel and seaweed, separating it from a pup that remained outside bleating pitifully from the shoreline. While Bill struggled to shovel away the shingle jamming the main door, Shane took it upon himself to try with a yard brush to drive the lunging seal back out of the window by which it had come in – an impossibility because of the drop from the sill to the floor and the fact that seals don't jump. All he did was antagonise the creature to a point where it began to shriek and snap its huge, seriously fanged jaws at the brush-head. Eventually it made contact and that was the end of the brush – and of my grandfather's courageous stand. The seal made a lunge, leaving Shane no alternative but to vault over an upturned sofa and scramble up the chimneystack in his kilt. The fermented fish odours belching from the animal's stomach were truly noxious and it was a relief when Bill finally cried that the door might be open enough for the seal to escape. We all went quiet and let it hear the cries of the pup coming from outside. It's amazing how ungainly seals are out of water but even so, they can still move quickly when the need arises, and this one did.

Shortly after the hurricane, which had left the countryside in tatters, my mother took me to Gloucestershire to stay with a gentle old man called Mr Rolls. We arrived at his house quite late at night and then, to my surprise, my mother just left, departing without ceremony. Panic was allayed by an offer of warm cocoa and then by a softly talking Mrs Rolls taking me upstairs and into a dark room, where she asked me to be quiet as 'the other boys were asleep'. The light from the landing was sufficient to locate a bed. I was given a few minutes, the door closed and all was darkness. Noises of breathing and occasional movement could be heard, but nothing else as I lay there wondering what the morning would bring.

After the initial shock of being left a sense of curiosity began to grow. In a way it felt like the beginning of an adventure. It turned out Mr and Mrs Rolls were a dear, warm-hearted couple and it soon transpired I had much in common with my fellow room-mates. There were six of us all struggling with learning difficulties and Mr Rolls had been tasked with unravelling whatever knots our brains might be in. His associate, Mr Levy-Noble, was a skilled psychoanalyst and we boys covered an amazing amount of ground in a matter of months. One technique was to be seated in a very dark room with a single source of light on a low table. Nothing could be seen other than the printed text in front of one and the glint of Mr Levy-Noble's gold spectacles. Sometimes the sessions in the darkened room were a series of questions, gently and quietly put but nevertheless deep and probing as to feelings, fears and areas of sensitivity. He dwelt somewhat on my freely given description of Lady Ampthill exiting from the sea, but was quick to sense when I was uncomfortable with a question and would back off. We were being crammed as a group. Knowledge was being pumped in, not absorbed, as time was short. A technique learned at the school in Oranmore about how to memorise catechism questions so as to fit answers was applied and proved mighty useful (any mistake had been rewarded with an instant lash). Common Entrance loomed: tests, mock exams, eventually real exams. To mark the day John Glenn went into space the date, 20 February 1962, was written on a bottle and hidden in the garden wall – we felt we had to do something.

Bill escorted me over from Ireland one term and broke the journey in

Cheshire to stay with a friend who took us to visit the Jodrell Bank radio telescope. We were greeted by a naval officer in uniform who turned out to be a Dartmouth College contemporary of his. He explained that as the dish was undergoing servicing we would be able to enter the bowl itself for few moments, but not for long, as radiation being picked up from outer space was continuous and severe whatever the position of the instrument. While we were clambering through a small hatchway at the top of the structure our guide explained that when the telescope was built giant gear wheels taken from a decommissioned battleship's gun turrets had been used to operate the dish movements, and as a gunnery officer he had come with them. To my schoolboy mind this was totally wonderful stuff. After the tour we were entertained by Professor Lovell himself. He showed me a spyhole in a bookcase that made it possible to look down from the ceiling of the cafeteria where all the scientists working at the telescope took their tea breaks. His interest was in chaps who were to be observed silently staring into their cups, just watching the stirred liquid circulate. It was a signal they had been working too hard at probing outer space and needed a holiday. The information was met with silence by the assembled grown-ups, but I could hardly contain myself with amusement.

At Christmas 1961, Mother had received a telegram at the cottage from the Countess of Rosse at Birr that her house party were slightly bored and wanted to see a bit of Ireland 'in the raw'. 'Could she bring them up to see the old castle?' The building had been vacated as work was being done to the floors, but a mini-excursion was organised which it was hoped would be suitable. It started with a tour of the old tower, then a visit to a peasant dwelling at Tawin, an isolated village at the end of a long peninsula sticking out into the middle of Galway Bay – almost an island – followed by drinks in 'the Cottage' and dinner at a local oyster bar.

The party swept up to the castle gates on the seashore and HRH Princess Margaret, escorted by Lord Snowdon, proceeded to climb around cement sacks and wheelbarrows to look at the Norman wattle stucco ceilings, climb up to the battlements and have the strategic importance for the 12th-century fortification at the neck of the bay explained in detail.

They all left for the Cunliffes' at Tawin. I didn't go. Michael, our stable groom, had been told at lunchtime that a lady from England wanted to come and look around Tawin village. He was instructed to bicycle home and warn his parents that my mother might call in, as old Tom Cunliffe was known to be quite a character. Bill recounted later that when my mother, HRH and Lord Snowdon entered the thatched cottage they found two kitchen chairs placed in the centre of a swept flagstone floor and Mr Cunliffe sitting beside the open fire. He greeted them and, looking at HRH, said, 'By the cut of you, you're a lady, will you take a drink?' Mrs Cunliffe's offer of a whiskey punch was accepted. The old man then went on to recount to his visitors how 'back in the times when things were different' De Valera had hidden in the house when on the run from the British and had learned to speak Gaelic in the very room in which they were sitting.

The next stop for the entourage was with us at Bill's cottage. A great escort of Gardai mounted on motorcycles with sidecars had built up during the visit to Tawin and dark had fallen. While the grown-ups were gathered in the drawing room for drinks a serious commotion erupted outside. Due to Michael being sent home early at short notice he had not put the horses back in their stables and they were still loose in the field and woodland round the house. Because of the unfamiliar activity of the Gardai calling to each other and revving motorbike engines, they had become severely spooked. The sound of four large fit animals galloping around unrestrained in the darkness, bucking and kicking in response to the whistles being blown by bewildered Gardai, who had absolutely no idea what they were, built up into a considerable racket. The waxing and waning thunder of stampeding horses on the drive, accompanied by what seemed to be shots but were in fact the motorbike sidecar engines backfiring while being driven round the field in the dark so headlamps could be used as spotlights, proved increasingly distracting for the grown-ups. Finally a very red-faced and breathless officer in helmet and goggles banged on the door and announced, 'the convoy needs to be off'.

All departed for Paddy Burke's bar at Clarinbridge and a feed of oysters fresh from the bay. As soon as the party was in place inside his establishment Paddy, an illegitimate son of a Lord Wallscourt, who as such felt he was of sufficient social standing to take command of the event, announced that Guinness was on the house. Burly backs duly closed ranks tightly around the bar, forming an impenetrable security barrier for the evening. Nobody noticed when the party quietly slipped away.

September 1962 brought another trip to London, ending in being taken to Windsor by both parents to visit a Mr Anderson. It was obviously Eton, the place Wyndham had warned me about, so I was on my guard from the start. The event turned out to be a repeat of the arrival with Mr Rolls, with a sudden parental departure, but in daylight, and this time I had a small room of my own. Almost immediately a sense of foreboding rather than curious excitement descended. The school term had not quite started and I'd yet to be properly outfitted, but it was clear that the man in whose custody I now was didn't like me and didn't really want me staying in his house. There was one other, rather peculiar boy hanging about who began to make fun of my Irish accent, though he had a foreign-sounding one of his own. Frustration building at the situation in general, my temper eventually snapped and we began to wrestle on the poorly lit upstairs landing. It was no contest, as the sense of rising panic over my new incarceration needed release in some way and I was well practised from years fighting my corner in the yard at the Oranmore National. Things might have eventually settled if my opponent hadn't somehow become impaled on a broken banister upright, which had skewered him through a cheek. Mr Anderson caught me by the neck and threw me into an armchair with an order to 'sit!' The contents of my room were packed, a taxi called and I returned to the family apartment in St John's Wood.

That was Eton done and dusted. All I felt was a sense of relief as, from the word go, I hadn't liked the place, with the endless droning aircraft overhead. Within days I was back with Mr Rolls and remained with him until Christmas. During November Bill took me to have a look at Gordonstoun, a school located in the far north of Scotland. Like me, there were some other boys visiting at the same time with their parents. Without warning, we boys were ushered into a big hall containing lots of small wooden tables laden with pens and papers. It was an exam for which I had been given no prior knowledge or academic preparation, with the questions alone completely beyond my understanding. I managed my name and that was about it, and to pass the time while those around me scribbled away I also carved it into the tabletop. Because there had been no advance preparation of it the expedition wasn't taken seriously and, more importantly, I'd already seen a school I liked the look of.

In the summer of 1962 I'd been taken to Milton Abbey in Dorset by my mother and had been shown round by a boy almost my own age who'd assured me it was a pretty good place to be. I'd immediately warmed to it and after the November Gordonstoun débâcle voiced an enthusiastic opinion to Mr Rolls. The result was that I was taken to Waterloo Station the following January after a hasty outfitting and handed over on a platform to a Mr Green.

It was the winter of the great 1962–63 freeze-up. A crowd of other boys was there, some quite tearful. We were about 16 in number and all heading to Milton Abbey for the first time, with the train taking five highly entertaining hours to reach Blandford Forum in Dorset. Mr Green amused us with fun stories of daring-do during his Japanese prisoner-of-war years, and we were well bonded as a group when it came time to venture out into the night to climb into an ancient snow-covered bus waiting outside the station. The extra-ordinarily cold weather was at its peak and the going was hard for the old vehicle, which managed seven of the eight miles to the school but finally ground to a halt at the foot of Milton Abbas hill. From there every boy had to drag his own luggage the last mile along a snowy, ice-covered path, with Mr Green leading the way. Occasionally the crust formed by blizzards collapsed, with the result that a boy or trunk fell into a snow-hole and had to be pulled out. Progress seemed unending, with the white nothingness punctuated only by the occasional tree, which appeared like a spooky brooding giant then silently faded away as we passed. Eventually, a glow could be detected ahead and the snow stopped falling.

Suddenly one of the most beautiful sights I'd ever seen in my life appeared before us. Looking up at the Abbey from down the hill, where the perspective now gave the tower the impression of just soaring up into the night out of a twinkling carpet of pristine snow in the foreground, was breath-taking. We all paused to take in the wondrous spectacle before tackling the final slope past grassy steps, entering the school buildings where the headmaster, Commander Hodgkinson, had something personal to say to each of us. In my case he recounted a story of how, as a young naval cadet before the war, he had played a part in setting up a make-believe opium den in east London which had fooled my mother, who had thought it was the real thing and had screamed in terror to be taken home. The way he entered into playing games at 'the new boys' tea-party' held in his home a week later was a revelation, and soon we discovered he was commonly known as 'Hughie'.

The drama of arrival in the snow at night with the others had been a very companionable experience and made adjustment to the new environment much easier. We new boys stayed with Mr Green at the top of Milton Abbas hill and had to walk down a mile of rough track each morning for breakfast in the main school building. With blizzards creating steep, crusted snowbanks to negotiate, it was hazardous going in wellingtons, short trousers and duffle coats, as the compacted snow sometimes gave way, but we quickly learned to stick together. School scarves doubled up as extraction ropes for the bigger holes, which could be 6 ft or more. The existence was so novel, with every day bringing new surprises as we all learned to concentrate on survival, that homesickness never seriously manifested itself – there just wasn't time.

That first term was exceptional in that the playing fields remained carpeted in snow, with all normal sports being cancelled. Cross-country running along icy forest tracks was the only activity possible. During these there were often massive pile-ups and snow-fights as house teams ambushed each other.

At term end the entire school set off by ferry and train across Europe to cruise around Greece. Milton Abbey's 250 boys departed from the snowbound school to join a mixed bag of 600 boys and girls on a ferry to France, followed by a train to Venice. There we embarked on the SS *Dunera*, an elderly troopship, and steamed to Delphi and its port of Itea. Finding it was also the first time most of my classmates had ever been on holiday or abroad away from their parents was most consoling, and did much to build up my own inner confidence. The ship anchored in the bay, we donned life-jackets, climbed into the lifeboats lowered into the sea and familiarised ourselves with rows of levers that had to be pulled back and forth to operate the propeller via a cam of some sort. Then races for the shore began – in fact races all over the place. Lifeboats carrying girls were targeted for splashing, while other boats went round in circles.

With the following term came an introduction to cricket. It had never dawned on anybody to explain the game to me and, driven by bewildered frustration, I ended up tussling with another boy on the crease. That was the end of cricket, with interest moving to and remaining with the sailing club. The school had a fleet of Enterprises based at Portland and two days a week there was transport to the naval harbour. The bus deposited us at a café in the dockyard called the Greasy Spoon, which was also an active brothel, with some of the working girls serving fish and chips. Uniformed sailors came and went up and down a worn wooden staircase beside the entrance door. Somehow us schoolboys dressed in green shorts didn't really register with the girls as likely punters, though one or two appeared possibly not much older than us. We had the impression of being invisible. Two giant concrete caissons were moored along the harbour breakwater and played havoc with our sailing of small boats in the way they deflected the wind. It turned out they were surplus artificial harbour 'mulberries' left over from the war that had not been towed across the Channel in the wake of the D-Day landings.

The journey to and from school in England and home in Ireland soon became a routine passage via the boat train. At first term had begun with parental escort via Belfast to Liverpool on an eight-hour overnight crossing, but when I reached 12 I had started travelling alone, with the sea passage via Dun Laoghaire in south Dublin and Holyhead in Wales consisting of two almost unseaworthy mailboats ploughing the route. Holidays over, I'd be put on the 4.10 pm boat train in Galway that met a connection in Dublin's Westland Row which, in turn, delivered its full load of passengers direct to the ferry for departure at 9 pm, whatever the weather. As mailboats they had to adhere to a demanding schedule. The bar was duty-free for some reason, and there was no apparent limit to the number of passengers. Often it was standing room only, not just in the lounges but also the corridors and even the stairwells. In bad weather people vomited where they stood and when that was on a staircase it was bad luck on the people below, as the *Munster* and *Leinster* were renowned for their ability to roll to their beam-ends as they trundled and rocked through gale-tormented seas with spray washing the decks. That was the first half of the night's torture. After docking, often in high winds and three hours of nightmare, a draughty five-hour journey to London awaited. By the time the train was boarded I'd normally teamed up with others of my age and they were usually girls who, like myself, had been warned, or had learned the hard way, to steer clear of the train compartments and lavatories. In my case it was a bit of both. There was something in the eyes of a certain type of adult that signalled danger – what I'd learned to understand was a 'weakness' – and for comfort we would bunch together on upturned suitcases in the connecting passages. When I was about eight I'd narrowly escaped the groping clutches of a wheelchair-bound priest, so I knew what to look out for. There was generally a bit of singing as drunks weaved past us staggering to and from the bar, and pressure eased after the 3 am stop at Birmingham. Arrival at Euston was always grim, since the morale of the girls would fade as the train began to slow for the last half-hour of clanking and jolting through the suburbs. Silent tears would flow and rosary beads be fumbled with as bits of paper bearing addresses were sought out. Then there was the horrible half-hour wait until the Underground started, compelling everyone not being met or without a taxi fare to sit on their cases as rather shifty-looking men and women roamed about attempting to engage the unwary in conversation. It was always an unpleasant period that passed very slowly.

Towards the end of the 1963 autumn term the news came through during evening prep that President Kennedy had been shot in Dallas. This was followed at the beginning of next term by the discovery that a classmate, Richard Burca, had been on the cruise ship *Lakonia* when it caught fire and sank just before Christmas while *en route* to Madeira. His 'My Christmas Holiday' essay for the English class at the beginning of term was something extraordinary. My own composition dwelt lamely on the impact of discovering that without warning or consultation my mother had made over the Castle Leslie Estate to her youngest brother and it was now no longer home. The outrageousness of her decision, broken to me at the beginning of the holiday, had introduced a sense of suddenly being without direction, like a small tree that had been abruptly uprooted. There was nothing to be done other than try and keep positive, so the theme of my essay avoided gloom and expressed a sense of freedom from being chained to a farming career.

Cramming for the Common Entrance and Eton exams had yielded results, but they were short-term. Dear Mr Rolls had done his stuff in taking my brain a long way in a short period, but as time at Milton Abbey progressed, yawning gaps in basic knowledge became more and more of a handicap. Maths was a continual nightmare with the only relief being Squadron-Leader Leatherdale's ability to swallow red herrings, with a frequent double lesson being spent giving explanations on how to dodge searchlights in a Lancaster, fly it on just two engines, and the best way to crash-land with no undercarriage. English Language, where one was challenged with probing into imaginative recesses to formulate essays, I found particularly hard going. The only thing I was good at was applying the hard-learned method of memorising catechism to reproduce poems word-perfectly down to the punctuation. I was so good at it Commander Wingate, the English teacher, suspected me of cheating in some way and had me sit in front of the class so all could try and spot the method. In the end it did me no good when it came to sitting for O Level later, and I failed ever to attain a pass in either English or Maths.

My housemaster didn't feature much other than to administer the occasional beating, but 'Hughie' did. One day he summoned a few of us into his headmaster's study for a pep talk. We were instructed to take care in not being obvious but to watch out for the welfare of a junior boy who might be at risk of being bullied. A small boy, Philby, had chosen not to change his name when his father left for Moscow under a bit of a cloud, and it was hoped he would be left alone. We were being trusted to act with discretion and not let him down. The result was the occasional extremely jolly tea party in his house, which formed what might be called a 'debrief'.

3

Teenage Years and the Española Voyage

◯

In reality the trauma of Glaslough suddenly disappearing without warning, after nine years of looking upon it as home, lingered on until the prospect of an exciting replacement emerged. The sense of loss was not to lift until a flicker of light appeared on the horizon in the shape of a County Galway neighbour who was being hit by a new government land law and faced losing a compact estate sticking out into the sea at the neck of Oranmore Bay. Daphne du Maurier's *Rebecca* had recently been read at school and I found it quite ridiculous how closely the Renville property resembled the Manderley of her book. One arrived via a lodge-gate entrance hidden in trees at the top of a hill, with magnificent views of the bay leading out towards the Atlantic Ocean in the distance. Then a mile or so of drive wound down through 400 acres of forests and fields past a lake and finally led up to the front steps of a perfect Georgian house. Crenellations of a small Norman keep peeped above treetops in one direction, while in the other, sunlight bounced off the sea by a sheltered quay. I knew the place well as it was a popular hunting venue for 'lawn meets'. Lord Hemphill began to call, as he needed to unload his property, and it luckily lay inside the government's three-mile legal requirement from my parents' present place of residence. The thought of finally having such a lovely home with all it had to offer by the bay I already knew so well felt like a dream, with only time before it became a reality. The intention was to spend the summer holidays of 1965 giving the shoreline inlets of the peninsula closer study.

Into this scene appeared a British MP, a Mr Ian Lloyd, who made contact stating he was looking for a crew to help sail his yacht along the west coast of Ireland from Killary Harbour up by Leenaun in Co. Mayo down to Tralee in Co. Kerry. It sounded like a jolly break for Bill, and Anita suggested he took me with him. We motored up across Connemara to join Mr Lloyd on *Española*, a splendid old wooden yacht of about 16 tons built in 1902 that had at one time been owned by the King of Spain. As we made our way out in a dinghy to where the vessel lay at anchor, silhouetted in fading light against the surrounding hills, Bill drew my attention to peeling paint on the hull and muttered an aside, 'I think she's seen better days.' (It transpired that wasn't the half of it.)

The plan was to set off the next morning. The first drama of the day was that the anchor was found to be stuck fast. An incoming tide had tightened the chain, jamming the capstan, and as the water continued to rise, with the yacht remaining secured to the bottom, strain increased on the bow. I watched with alarm as small cracks in the deck planking began to open up, before the anchor was eventually released from what must have been mud and we were free to depart. The disturbed decking appeared to settle back into place and we thought no more of it – at the time. On a sunny, windless morning we motored west out of Killary harbour without a care in the world. Mr Lloyd explained that running the elderly side-valve petrol engine at full throttle would cause it to soot up and stop, requiring the spark-plugs to be unscrewed for wire-brushing to remove carbon deposits. So we chugged along at a gentle pace, waiting for a breeze to pick up. The weather forecast gave two days of favourable conditions to reach at least the mouth of the Shannon estuary.

But what had not been factored in was the delayed start, a first day of total calm and an engine running at half-speed. Night came and we continued to motor slowly out into the Atlantic. The next morning brought a fantastic view of the Aran Islands, with the seaward side of the cliff-top Dun Aengus fort visible far over to the east. Clouds appeared later and a sharp breeze got up. Sails were raised and the engine switched off. Bill began to sing to himself and smile as spray washed his face. The wind strength increased and the vessel heeled over in the rising sea. Dark forbidding clouds loomed up from nowhere but this just caused him to sing louder. I was below stowing loose items when there was a snap, followed by pandemonium when the mainsheet broke, causing a large mass of sail and boom to flap violently while a replacement was threaded through blocks. Bill commented to the owner that the boat's hemp ropes were old and rotten as dark stains signifying decay were visible in the cores.

We were away again and making good progress with wind on the beam when there was a particularly strong gust and the mainsail split with a roar. More flailing canvas and the boom began to jump about dangerously. The engine was started and the yacht pointed into the wind while the mess was sorted out. In almost no time the cabin carpet began to float in seawater, with the level rising until the main pump on the engine was engaged. The water didn't show signs of dropping until the revolutions were raised and from experience earlier in the day that meant we had about 15 minutes' running time before the plugs oiled up and required brushing.

Mr Lloyd became completely incapacitated by seasickness as a full gale developed, with the cockpit view downwind – the direction we were being blown in when not under power – revealing a tall wall of white breakers where the tormented sea smashed against rocks at the base of the Cliffs of Moher. A replacement sail of some sort was rigged up but because of the mishap we had lost valuable sea room to make passage round Loop Head, marking the northern the tip of the Shannon estuary, and we were forced to have the old boat face the tempest head-on. Bill came down to me in the cabin as I was again warily watching the rising carpet while dealing with hot plugs and summarised in a firm voice that the situation was serious but there was hope. Though leaking badly at the bow, with no mainsail and no harbour to be reached without driving direct to windward under power, we would make it to safety before nightfall if I continued to keep the engine going, and I was doing well. It was then that he gave me a pat on the shoulder before disappearing back up on deck to make the best of what sail power was available. The unexpected physical contact instantly dispelled a rising sense of fear, which had almost reached panic level. Contact of such a nature between us was unprecedented and indicated that some sort of approval threshold had been crossed, leaving me feeling determined to keep the engine going come what may – something I was pretty confident I could do.

The day happened to be my 16th birthday and most of it was spent sitting beside the old side-valve engine trying to remember everything Wyndham had taught me while removing, brushing and reinserting hot spark-plugs every time it spluttered to a halt. There were four to be handled without being cross-threaded or accidentally dropped into the sloshing bilge-water below. The owner's severe seasickness meant it was impossible to communicate with him to glean advice as to any spares, so I just pressed on, praying quietly and being very careful. Periodic bangs and crashes sounded outside but I never looked out again after sighting the breakers – just watched the floor carpet rise and fall as the engine stopped and ran. Finally, as light was fading, the movement of the yacht changed, signalling that we had rounded Loop Head and now had an incoming tide sweeping us up the Shannon River mouth towards calmer water and safety. Bill selected a place to drop anchor and the rattle of the chain running out sounded like sweet music. I found him grinning from ear to ear as he went about checking the rigging. Murmuring an aside, 'That was a near thing, but don't ever, ever tell your mother,' he then laid into the recovering Mr Lloyd about just how unseaworthy the yacht was and listed all the basic principles of ownership that had been ignored, so putting our lives at risk. It may have been a baptism of fire but on that day my relationship with Bill moved on to a slightly more equal footing, with direct eye contact now usual in conversation.

Shortly after the sailing trip on *Española* Bill went over to England to stay with an old wartime and ocean-racing friend, while I went back to school. It transpired the seeds of a new chapter in his life had been firmly sown by the insane trip, but I didn't know that then. My mother's financial machinations to raise funds for Renville were ongoing and, in the interim, the concept of attempting a non-stop global circumnavigation took hold. Work started on writing a book to finance building a racing yacht, while Lord Hemphill and my mother kept in touch.

During the following autumn term Winston Churchill died, and as Bill was away in Africa I was able to take his place with my mother at the state funeral in St Paul's. We were there because my grandfather and Winston shared an American grandfather, Leonard Jerome, and so were first cousins. We were seated about halfway up the nave, with everyone wearing rows of medals – even my mother sported a group that I'd never seen before. One was French with a small button on it, which raised the occasional comment from highly decorated friends she kept meeting. We were positioned well to observe the world's heads of state as they filed slowly up the aisle, but the one that stood out was Archbishop Makarios with his black attire and enormous stove-pipe hat, which raised his silhouette to nearly seven feet. Little did I know it then but I was destined to cross paths in a military hospital years later with the young Grenadier officer leading the pallbearers down the aisle. From St Paul's we made our way to the Savoy and were able to watch the flag-draped coffin on the barge make its way along the Thames, receiving a salute from the cranes that lined the far shore dipping their booms in unison as it passed by. Anthony Mather, the bearer party commander, told me in 1976 when we were in adjoining rooms at Woolwich military hospital that there was one terrible moment at the foot of the cathedral steps when the coffin began to fall forward and he had to put his hand up to keep it steady. One guardsman cracked a collarbone because of the weight.

When I returned to Oranmore for Easter, before the summer's O-Level exam ordeal began, there was an interesting parade in the village to celebrate the 50th anniversary of the Rising in 1916. After Mass everyone gathered to watch a group of veterans march past the IRA memorial, the life-size statue of a soldier mounted on a high plinth drawing a pistol. Standing at the side of the Galway–Dublin–Limerick road junction, it acknowledged the leadership shown by the local publican's uncle in Ireland's War of Independence from Britain – the statue always had flowers and an occasional wreath at its foot. I was taken aback when one of the leading figures momentarily caught my eye and smiled, raising a finger to his peaked cap as he marched by wearing leggings taken from a British officer he'd once ambushed and shot. It was going to be years before I found out what lay behind his action on such a day, but it turned out there was a lot more to it than having been at school with the man's grandson.

Having not made it into the sixth form at Milton Abbey, I went to a London crammer in January 1967 with the aim of obtaining passes in the required A Levels for Bristol University, where a Marine Biology course would be relevant to a future life by the sea at Renville. Unfortunately, not having full family support over the idea of this step into further education, I made all the arrangements myself and mistakenly enrolled in not the recommended and respected London-based crammer, Davis Lang and Dick, but one called 'Davis's', a language school for foreigners based in Victoria, with a small facility for other subjects served by very mediocre teaching staff. Knowing no better, I remained at the institution and set up residence in my mother's flat in Cleveland Square, within walking distance of the Portobello Road where, on passing my driving test, I bought an ancient 1934 Morris 8 for transport. The move eased my path socially as it attracted new friends when it came to party-going, but that in turn bit hard into the self-discipline required to make full use of what little the crammer tutors had to offer.

Easter 1967 was spent in Galway and a family called Rattray arrived to rent Lough Cutra Castle for the holiday period. Patrick became a good friend and later left an easy-to-follow wake on the London social scene. During the summer term Diana Daly, the stern godmother from Galway who had saved my life as a baby when the ceiling fell down, and now lived at Syon Lodge near Kew, invited me for lunch. It turned out to be hard going as it was a fairly formal occasion, but luckily a corner of her wonderful garden provided a safe if temporary refuge from the gathering of unknown people. After a while an American girl about my age appeared, introduced herself as 'Sasha' and sat down. There was something about her body language that put me at ease as we began to talk. Discussion on how to deal with personal fears and awkward social predicaments was entered into almost immediately. It was like finding a kindred spirit that I could allow myself to open up to about inner feelings and emotions. We left together, remaining in deep conversation for the remainder of the day, finally parting at a coffee shop in Marble Arch. There she'd asked for my address and given me her surname, 'Bruce'.

A couple of weeks later an invitation arrived from Mrs David Bruce, the American Ambassadress, to attend a reception at the US Residence in Regent's Park. There I recognised the Ambassador as a friend of my mother's, having once seen them chatting earnestly at a function, but Sasha didn't appear. The room was large and filled with people, so it took time to really search through the crowd, during which time I learned that the Ambassador had played a key part in constructing the CIA as an American external intelligence force after the Second World War. Then I ran into the Ambassador himself and with this knowledge fresh in my head was rendered almost speechless. Mr Bruce seemed to know I'd met his daughter but didn't enlarge on her apparent absence. Instead he just asked after my mother, confirming that they were old friends. When our rather one-sided conversation was eventually interrupted I left, as with no friendly Sasha to talk to there didn't seem much point in remaining. A little spark of hope quietly died. Seven years later I heard that she'd been shot dead in a park, but even with the time lapse it was a blow that left a surprisingly deep feeling of loss and concern that I'd never meet anyone like her again.

During the non-hunting months of the year – April to September – my mother always moved to London to work at her books. Members of her wartime generation were the main visitors to the Cleveland Square flat, usually coming to reminisce on life in Cairo and the Middle East. Her editor at Hutchinson's, Harold Harris, loved re-telling how he had 'bagged von Ribbentrop' with the story of a clever trick played on the Nazis at the end of the war in Berlin. The antics of a bent Egyptian general called Azziz el Masri, who had been a great Cairo party-thrower and admirer of my mother and her girlfriends, was another visitor's favourite topic. Jolly and ace joke-teller though Nicholas Elliott was, it was pretty clear even to me that he had been deeply steeped in intelligence work during the war. I gave him the nickname of 'Lightbulb', not thinking that in the not-too-distant future I would be strongly suspecting him of orchestrating certain aspects of my career path from the shadows.

The summer holidays of 1967 were spent at Oranmore and ended up being the last days of the *Gull*. With a heavy heart I sold the old boat in which I'd spent so many happy hours alone over the years, but it needed the love and attention I subconsciously knew I was not going to have the time to give. As it left the quay by road on the trailer Wyndham had once made, I felt a deep pang of sadness. The little craft had never let me down when we'd hopped off rocks or been hit by unexpected downturns in the weather, as we had always somehow made it home. The sight of the stern I'd lovingly painted many times disappearing round a bend in the drive hurt somewhat and it was clear the moment marked the end of an era.

The autumn cub-hunting presented a temptation to stay on in Ireland, but I headed back to London as I still had hopes of the Bristol course, which was vital if the plan to farm seaweed at Renville was to succeed.

Unfortunately, distractions were beginning to multiply. As the London social scene of 1968 cranked into gear Patrick Rattray started to pass me surplus invitations to débutantes' cocktail parties followed by coming-out dances which he could not attend, as he sometimes had four invites for the same night and at best was only going to manage two. So, periodically, I became 'Patrick Rattray' and with the stiff invitation in hand had little trouble entering most venues. The London Season had kicked off with tea parties where debs gathered to compare notes on dates for coming-out balls and we went to one in Pont Street – 'a good spot to learn when it's the right moment to chat someone up'. I found we were the only two guys in a room full of amazing-looking girls who were supposedly putting dance dates in their diaries. Years later one of the gathering was to bounce back into my life in an exceedingly big way, but at the time they, as a group, resembled a celestial branch of the human race that was totally beyond reach.

One tricky moment occurred which fortunately had a lucky ending when, masquerading as Patrick at a ball being thrown at the Riverside Club on the Embankment, I'd noticed a girl appearing a little sad, often standing on her own, and ended up dancing a good deal with her. We were getting on well until she asked, 'Have you met my parents?' and led me across the room to two adults whose questioning gaze I'd become aware of. When she introduced me as Patrick the lady fixed me with a steely stare and said firmly, 'Oh no you're not – I know Patrick!' Then Mr Quintin Hogg (it was his daughter's coming-out party) gently took me by the arm and led me away towards a window overlooking the river. He was very polite and thanked me for being nice to his daughter but requested I leave quietly without delay. He asked what my real name was and, on confirming that, yes, my mother was indeed Anita Leslie, the writer, he marched me back to his wife and said, 'Why isn't this friend of Louise's on the list?' Though I probably could now have stayed, the atmosphere had changed and I left. It was my last 'Paddy Rattray' outing, as from then on I was determined to be myself. I'd made a number of friends of my own, confidence had built up and invites to house parties had begun to arrive.

The pace of social events increased as the summer wore on, impacting ever more heavily on academic efforts, but real disaster struck when Gay Buick discovered the entrance to the warren of tunnels under Covent Garden known as 'the Middle Earth' and took me there. The knowledge of the subterranean venue had come via an overheard conversation in her sister's Beauchamp Place shirt shop, 'Deborah and Clare', which was state-of-the-art coolness itself, so the venue had to be explored one evening. The flight of steps down from the pavement by a church provided transportation into another world where time seemed to just melt away into a sea of nothingness but song, music, chanting and general unrestrained hippiedom.

Emerging into the cool morning air of the next dawn we found ourselves madly hungry, and luckily stumbled across a fallen box of ripe avocados beside a church pillar. Most were squashed but some retrievable. While we sat feasting, two market porters could be heard discussing Enoch Powell's 'Rivers of Blood' speech of a few months earlier. Steeped in studies, I'd not bothered to pay much attention at the time, but hearing the issues he'd raised concerning immigration being repeated and argued over with many added expletives made us both realise that raw nerves at the heart of society had definitely been touched. The time came to sit for exams, but with all the unfolding distractions I was unprepared and nothing useful was achieved academically – not even the elusive, fundamental English Language and Maths O Levels, leaving dreams of becoming a Marine Biologist and following in the footsteps of Jacques Cousteau finally to disappear for good.

In August Bill set off in a newly built yacht, *Galway Blazer 2*, as a competitor in the *Sunday Times* Golden Globe non-stop race circumnavigating the world. He'd not wanted to be distracted by family while preparing for the adventure, so I had not seen him off from Plymouth and had returned to Galway to ponder what to do next. The Renville purchase was still in the air and in the wake of disappointing exam results no particular career direction materialised other than schooling horses for the coming hunting season. The one thing I could do well was ride. With Bill absent at sea and four fit animals in the stables it was possible to spend three to four days a week tearing across the countryside after hounds. It might have been to distract herself from Bill's absence at sea but my mother began to invite horse buyers from England to stay and acted as a broker with local dealers. A role for me began to develop whereby I rode the hunters to show how well they could perform.

Round this activity a new social life of sorts began to build, and feelings of loneliness subsided. One day a neighbour who had been studying in Paris during the riots of a few months previously was in the middle of giving a lurid account of the street violence he had witnessed when an out-of-control horse careered into our somewhat compact gathering. Lady Ampthill, my old camping friend, was on the periphery and was knocked out of her side-saddle, landing head-first on to a large flat boulder. Her veil and top hat had come off during the fall, leaving her skull no protection whatever. Sharp fragments of broken bone could be seen poking through hair, but surprisingly little blood. We gathered round and formed a carrying party to get her to the road, which was some fields away and involved negotiating a high gap in an old demesne wall. A passing car was waved down to take her to hospital. We then returned to our horses and continued the day's sport. Months later she was out again, still riding side-saddle but head encased in a crash helmet.

October brought news that Bill had failed to make a routine call to Tristan da Cuña and his last location had positioned him in the path of a severe storm. As days of silence dragged into weeks, with letters of condolence beginning to arrive, my mother started to look to me for comfort. Then, to compound matters, a girl I'd been fond of in England came on a visit, but the cultural gap between her world, which I'd left, and the world I now felt at home in proved impossible to bridge. Somehow I didn't worry about Bill and had faith in him surviving, so when information came that *Galway Blazer* had been spotted 1,000 miles out from South Africa I wasn't surprised. He had lost the mast carrying his radio aerial in the storm, but had been able to limp along with a jury rig.

Shortly after he reached Cape Town I flew down to help with repairs. Bill was found to be in good heart, disappointed at being out of the race but still determined to complete the circumnavigation in his own time. Plans to repair the yacht for another attempt the coming year were under way and I was given the job of helping to prepare *Blazer* for a lift home on the deck of HMS *Eagle*, an aircraft carrier shortly to be passing. He looked up a chum from his pre-war China Station days and we went to stay with Commander Pankhurst, who had a spare garden house at his property in Somerset West, a Cape Town suburb serviced by trains designed to comply with apartheid regulations.

It was difficult adjusting to the way the rolling stock was divided up into carriages clearly labelled 'Nett Blankes' ('Whites only') with soft seats, coupled to very different ones for Blacks, fitted out only with basic wooden slatted benches.

Unfortunately Mrs Pankhurst, a one-time American B-movie starlet now middle-aged and hitting the bottle, took a serious shine to Bill and began to croon under the window at night as we attempted to sleep. Bill and I bonded closely as we pulled pillows over our heads to drown out the sound and began to talk almost like brothers as he described how he had no memory of his own father, who had gone off to war in 1914 when he was four and was later killed. He had been left to be brought up in a post-war world of women and sent off to a Royal Navy feeder school aged 13. It had been his life until he met my mother.

Eventually we relocated to Muizenberg at the invitation of a Cape journalist and yachting enthusiast, who also provided a car for transport to the boatyard. This meant I could make the occasional trip alone back to Somerset West in the evening to take out one of the Pankhurst daughters, who grabbed any chance to escape from home. The journey to and from Muizenberg involved a bit of a loop and late one night, not understanding various signs in Afrikaans, I decided to try a shortcut across a flat plain where the road appeared to go in the direction I wanted. About halfway across a loud ticking heralded that the Mini was running out of petrol, and then the car rolled to a stop beside the outlying buildings of what appeared to be a sort of shanty town. Moments later a pick-up pulled up behind me and two armed policemen appeared beside the car door. After lots of unpleasant yelling I was asked where I was going and told I was totally off limits in a black township called Cape Flats, but then a radio sprang to life, causing the two officers to hop back into their truck and race off – but not before something looking like a machine-gun on a tripod under canvas was spotted mounted on the back. There was nothing to do other than wait and see what dawn brought, during which time a black man on a bicycle pedalled past. I watched him go about half a mile up the road, turn round, come back and dismount. He wasted no time in telling me I should not be there and would be in big trouble if caught. On asking where I might find some petrol he said nothing and bicycled off, only to return about half an hour later with a bottle of fuel. He refused any offer of payment – he just asked me to go quickly, using some strange name I couldn't catch when referring to the policemen. The Mini pump picked up the small infusion, enabling the outskirts of Muizenberg to be reached. Walking into the town I spotted what looked like a police station and it seemed a logical place to ask for directions to the nearest petrol station. It turned out to be rather a mistake as, on entering, the group of uniformed personnel all jumped and began to shout in Afrikaans before eventually breaking into English. One said that people don't walk into police stations – they get dragged in – before telling me to fuck off. I eventually made it back to Muizenberg, but wasn't allowed to borrow the car again. The drama, with such a muddle of human relations, left me somewhat confused and suddenly sick of South Africa's complicated social infrastructure. The work on the yacht was finally completed and I flew home, leaving Bill to travel back as a guest of the Royal Navy. The way our relationship had developed during the couple of weeks was heartening but we never discussed the Renville estate, almost as if it was bad karma to do so.

Returning to Galway, I found Oonagh-Mary, my childhood friend, struggling to handle a yard full of horses on top of handling a big Georgian house while Lady Molly, her nightmare mother, was absent on a long holiday in Greece. I began to help her a little but spent most evenings working on the frame of a new boat in Wyndham's workshop. An added bonus was that he had a granddaughter residing on a long-term basis. Dawn and I started to go to the cinema in Galway while Oonagh-Mary was busy generating income by taking in paying guests.

One day my mother, who was unaware of the nocturnal goings-on, announced she was giving a dinner party the following Thursday and asked me to bring Oonagh-Mary. She replied to the invitation that it would be a tremendous help if, instead, I'd take a guest she had staying who was very bored because her musician boyfriend was away. The arrangement was that she and her guest would meet me at an oyster bar midway between us and I'd bring her back to Birminghame House afterwards. The Thursday evening duly came. I went to Paddy Burke's Bar and was introduced to Marianne, a blonde with hair in a make-shift beehive, white coat, white lipstick, heavily black-mascara'd eyes, and tottering in white boots. (I missed the surname 'Faithfull' if it was ever mentioned.) During the 15-minute journey home Oonagh-Mary's briefing that my family were authorities on flying saucers was the sole topic of conversation. Marianne lit up a joint as we moved towards the front door and tripped badly on a sill as we entered the room where my mother's guests were assembled. Having to grab her resulted in us entering in what appeared to be a clinch. I caught sight of my sister sitting on the stairs agog, with tears of amusement running down her cheeks, watching me make a complete fool of myself. Introductions were a nightmare with everyone either a Colonel, Major or Commander, expecting to greet Oonagh-Mary whom they all knew and liked, but instead having to search for common ground with my reefer-waving squeeze, who appeared somewhat unsteady on her feet. Eventually one of the guests, Mrs Trench, asked Marianne directly, 'What exactly are you doing with Tarka?' I don't know where her reply 'We're thinking of going to live on the moon' came from, but I had to terminate the nightmare situation and explained she was staying with Oonagh-Mary. Marianne's and my eyes met and she gave me a 'get me out of here' look, but while she was doing so Mrs Trench went to great lengths to interrupt my mother, who was deep in conversation down the table about some dire horse drama. When she finally had her attention she said, 'Anita, Marianne is Baroness von Sacher-Masoch's daughter,' at which Mother turned and said, 'Oh, my Deeeear, but Hello!' Shortly after that we left and she slept most of the journey back to Birminghame House. Slowly, on the way home, the penny dropped that my guest of the evening might have been the Marianne who sang 'As Tears go By', but what was sure was that she and I were on very different planets.

Though the evening was not particularly dramatic in itself, there were consequences. Two weeks later I was woken one morning by godfather Peter brandishing my passport containing a freshly stamped US visa and an airline ticket for New York dated for a few days' time. He explained that arrangements had been made for me to go to America where there was something important to be done before returning to a job in Baring's Bank in London, which had been fixed up by an old naval friend of Bill's. Surprisingly, the news came as a relief, as the hunting season was over and, my university ambitions having died, the dreaded question of what to do next was beginning to loom with increasing intensity. The legal negotiations leading to capital becoming available to purchase Renville were grinding on but there was still no firm end in sight.

4
America

I was supplied with a list of elderly relatives to be visited in New England and details of a function to be attended at Fulton, Missouri, where I'd been given the task of representing the family at a church dedication service in memory of Winston Churchill's famous Iron Curtain speech in 1947. New York was terrifying. The subway map represented a giant pile of psychedelic spaghetti and was never entered in the week I was in the city. The Haights, an elderly couple who were my first port of call in America, resided in a big house on Fifth Avenue overlooking Central Park. It was a dark gloomy building with a strong Victorian feel and was staffed by a healthy Chinese community who lived in the rear quarters. Harry, my hosts' son, who had been badly wounded in the head during the Korean War, kept a boat on the Hudson, equipped with a large bell which he rang enthusiastically when chugging about on the water. The family business had something to do with proprietorship of the *National Geographic* magazine and both son and father departed early every morning for offices in the Empire State Building, leaving me to make what I could of the city on my own. After a weekend with the family at their home in upper New York State sitting in respectful silence as they listened to Walter Cronkite's nightly news broadcasts, I caught my first Greyhound bus and became instantly addicted to the mode of transport.

The first journey took me to St Johnsbury in Vermont, the birthplace of my great-grandfather, Henry Clay Ide. Starting out as the son of a railway level-crossing keeper he had managed to work his way up through law school and, after first being appointed Chief Justice in Samoa, had become Governor General of the Philippines, where he'd built the Malacañang Palace in Manila as his residence. He finally retired, having been US Ambassador to the court of Spain. His wife died early, leaving three daughters, and my grandmother, the eldest, stepped into the supporting role of Ambassadress in her late teens and had been a close friend of President Roosevelt's daughter, Eleanor. There were still quite a few elderly Ides in that corner of New England, who all insisted on giving me cemetery tours where exploits of other long-dead cousins were recounted.

I eventually escaped and, catching a Greyhound bus, headed for Cincinnati where some guys of roughly my age encountered on the bus offered accommodation. It turned out to be in a freight car on a siding close by a housing estate, with electricity provided by wires from the home of a friendly First Nation Iroquois girl called Waka. One chap had received news that he had been drafted for a military stint in Vietnam and was about to face a medical exam. Discussion never drifted far from how to make a heartbeat go bananas at the right moment in a way that could not be detected by army selection doctors. Waka was very popular because of the washing facilities and air-conditioning on offer when her parents were at work, but access to the house included having to listen to horrific monologues on the current plight of Native Americans in their own land. We became friends as the days passed and I attempted to balance her tales of woe with a description of that of Ireland as interpreted by my old schoolmaster, but she was too full of her own spirited anger to really listen. The shoulder of the naked lightbulb dangling from the freight-car roof bore a dark coating of grime and was generally viewed as symbolising President Johnson's current campaign to help 'the Poor'. One day part of the river caught fire because of heavy pollution levels and while watching various fire engines career from bridge to bridge an old man on a bench told me with pride that the city was Number 5 on the Russian bombing list thanks to the big electrical works. The Cincinnati visit was an abrupt introduction to grass-roots Americans my age and quite an eye-opener after the somewhat closeted days in New York.

Next I caught a Greyhound to Ann Arbor in Michigan to look up Hazel Smith, an old girlfriend of my grandfather Shane. Her son ran a nuclear reactor and took me to watch rods being changed at the bottom of a blue pool. Because he was in a sensitive post his house was fitted with a tap phone rather than one with a dial, and was the first I'd ever seen. His ten-year-old son gave a complicated explanation of how its mechanism operated while Hazel seemed to be still besotted by my grandfather and never stopped reminiscing in explicit detail over episodes in their love life, even going so far as to describe how they'd once had intercourse behind a church altar 'amongst the broomsticks'. She expressed a theory that he was driven by frustration because Marjorie, his wife, was very 'advanced', having been schooled in the arts of the harem in Peking when accompanying F.D.R.'s daughter Eleanor Roosevelt to an audience with the Empress Dowager in 1906. Hazel was emphatic that Marjorie had passed on the 'instructions' she'd been given by the Chinese courtesans to her long-standing girlfriend Wallis Simpson. 'The two of them used to be bridge partners on the trans-Atlantic liners between the wars where, as fellow Americans, they were in the habit of discussing the complexities of marrying into European aristocracy.' One thing they did know, Hazel stated, was that the 'Singapore Grip' gave an edge over local competition. I tried not to visualise what 'edge' Hazel had of her own and had been wielding over my grandfather but the memories seemed to be keeping her going in old age.

It was time to get to St Louis for the Fulton dedication and I was escorted to a fine suite on the seventh floor of the designated hotel. The first evening was fairly quiet and focused on briefings for the next day. About 200 dignitaries mustered after breakfast for transportation by bus to a museum exhibition of works by Sir Christopher Wren. It was the warm-up before being taken to the site at Fulton where Winston had made his famous 'Sinews of Peace' oration.

After various speeches and a tour of the Wren exhibition, a church service was held in a building salvaged from a bomb site in the City of London. The 600 tons of stone originally comprising the City church of St Mary, Aldermanbury, that had fallen foul of the Blitz bombing had been rebuilt in the Missouri countryside to commemorate Churchill's historic 1947 'Iron Curtain' warning. The sounds of a Second World War Spitfire and Messerschmitt acting out a mock dogfight overhead could be heard during the singing of 'John Brown's Body' and 'Land of Hope and Glory'. Even the crypt had been taken from London, rebuilt beneath the structure, and was now being used as the venue for post-service drinks.

The warm afternoon made the trays of refreshments attractive, but it was a little difficult to differentiate between strong spirits and lemonade, which proved to be an undoing for some before the return to St Louis and the evening banquet. Lord Mountbatten was the guest of honour and, like others, gave an address dwelling on the current status of the Cold War – the threat to which Winston had drawn the Western world's attention decades before. It had been a long day and by coincidence I chose the same moment to retire as Lord Mountbatten, entering the same lift as himself and a bunch of American escorts. It began to ascend and then just stopped. There was a muffled 'wuzz-click' sound from a side panel followed by a slight sense of descent followed by a further 'wuzz-click'. This repeated noisy movement jolting downwards was not reassuring for the Americans on board, who began to jabber, struggle, sweat, loosen ties and shout while competing for access to the telephone. All sense of decorum evaporated in an instant, with the pandemonium continuing until we reached ground level, at which they piled out into the lobby in complete disarray. I joined Lord Mountbatten and the vicar, from whose London parish the church had been taken, in entering another lift. The VIP escort had disappeared and we were just three. He took command of the button-board and I gave my floor number. In reply to a questioning glance at the beaming vicar, who was clearly as tight as a tick and oblivious to everything that had just happened, I said, 'It's all right, Sir, he's one of us, same floor.' Floor 7 came up and I wheeled the now hymn-humming clergyman out and to his room, acknowledging a parting 'good luck' from the lift as the doors closed. If I'd been able to recall the name of his wartime command, HMS *Kelly*, a joke would have been cracked but my brain just wasn't fast enough.

The following day it was back to the Greyhound station to catch a bus to Dallas, Texas. At Joplin, Missouri, a quite fit young man boarded and made his way to the rear. He'd been seen off by a somewhat tear-stained girl but by immediately hunkering down he'd missed her rather pathetic little wave as we pulled out on to the highway. About an hour later two police cars stopped the bus. Lots of shouting led to the driver making his way down the passageway with pistol drawn. The guy was removed through the rear exit at gunpoint from many angles. The driver then calmly resumed his seat, re-holstered his pistol and we continued as if nothing had happened. Thinking the scene over as the bus rumbled along it became clear that life in America could be volatile, with the possibility of situations changing in a flash. A momentary thought of breaking the trip at Oklahoma died instantly at the sight of a fairly hefty brawl in full swing in the station foyer, with life seeming to have been transformed into a strange movie where the bus had become a space capsule. America glided by outside the window and there was no knowing what madness the next stop would bring.

Arriving in Dallas I took a cab to 8601 Turtle Creek Boulevard, the address I'd been given for another friend of my grandfather's, Mrs Owsley – I had telephoned from St Louis. It was quite a ride and I was eventually deposited at the foot of a longish lawn. I paid off the cab, picked up my bag and walked up to the house, a low wooden structure with a dishevelled veranda. A dog ran out at me until its retaining rope tightened, yanking it over on to its back. It was followed by a tall, youngish lady in jeans and knotted shirt who greeted me with a 'Well hello, who are you?' and introducing herself as 'Yogi Batty'. It was clearly the wrong house. I looked at my note of Mrs Owsley's address and definitely had written down 8601, so asked if I could use her phone. I was invited in and followed her round stacks of newspapers and magazines, all piled to above head height. A bikini-clad daughter appeared and handed me the phone. Speaking to Mrs Owsley I realised I'd got the house number wrong and should gone to 6801. The news had an electric effect on Yogi, who instantly offered to drive me there. We climbed into an old white convertible with a dented front wing and set off along the winding boulevard for what seemed a good mile or so, with the sulking daughter in the back now sporting sunglasses as the sole addition to her wardrobe. The scenery changed, moving upwards from lawns to gravelled drives to drives with gateways. We turned in at 6801, with Yogi and her daughter now cooing with excitement. Pulling up to the house, both jumped out and made a point of introducing themselves when the fairly elderly but still spry Mrs Owsley appeared at the top of a flight of steps. My bag was lifted out of the car by a black servant; Yogi was thanked and eventually left. An explanation of the encounter was asked for and given. 'Well,' she said, 'I guess I can't stop you seeing ALL of America!' She then informed me that the Apollo 10 moon-shot was about to launch and she wanted to watch it on TV. During the entire count-down she sat with a phone line open to her son as he had a senior job in security at NASA HQ in Houston, so the occasion was experienced live on two fronts.

The next day she took me with her to lunch in the Texas countryside at a friend's place called the Black Ranch. It was just me and four elderly ladies. Unfolding developments in Vietnam and President Johnson's 'Poor Policy' dominated the conversation, with them not thinking highly of either subject. I was tempted to describe my experiences in Cincinnati, but sensed their minds were firmly set and it was better to remain silent. The only real deviation was when Mrs Black mentioned, almost as an aside, that she'd had some unwanted visitors on her property a few days before. 'They were a group of young' who had dared to ask if they could use her pool but had been warned to leave immediately or risk being shot. Mrs Owsley asked if she would have really gone ahead and, nodding to her handbag, the old girl replied, 'Yes, but only in the knees'. At this I felt much relieved that I'd kept quiet about having recently comforted a draft-dodger.

The next Greyhound trip was a long journey to El Paso. On arriving in the late afternoon I booked into a motel, had a short sleep and then it was evening, with the need for a walk. I found the town pretty dull until my attention was caught by the sight of bright lights beyond an iron bridge over a dry river-bed and made my way across, passing through a turnstile. Round a corner the contrasting sight of a mass of bars and striptease joints came as a bit of a surprise. It was quite a jump from the gentle world of Mrs Owsley I'd been cocooned in, and after about an hour of wandering and just $15 in my pocket I headed back to the bridge, to find it shut tight with a notice in Spanish and English stating it was closed between 9 pm and 6 am. Only then did I realise I must have crossed the border into Mexico, leaving my passport in the motel room back in the US. Wandering about a bit more, I appeared to attract the attention of a couple of policemen, so I stepped into a bar with a door fee of $10 that turned out to be some sort of club, with scantily dressed dancers on tables. To avoid continual pressure from hustlers I soon left and headed back to the river bed. My idea was to find a safe place to hole up until the morning and then try and explain my situation to a bridge official.

The temperature began to drop quite swiftly, but by luck I'd donned my duffle coat, legacy of Milton Abbey, and it proved invaluable in the circumstances. Finding a good spot under a dense bush overlooking the river channel it was possible to bunch up inside the coat with arms withdrawn from sleeves and knees tight against chest. A few hours passed and for a while I dozed but then noticed two Alsatian dogs approaching. They were on a long lead held by a patrolman who was walking up the centre of the river bed. He was below me and I prayed almost audibly that my scent was rising above the level of the dogs. Luckily I'd not ventured down on to the bed itself and therefore left no trail to be picked up. As it was I was totally helpless should the dogs find me in my trussed state. The patrolman wandered on. Then in his wake I saw a little group of three figures hopping from bush to bush down the bank, scuttling across the river bed and up the other side. This was followed by another group of what looked like four. Then two more. They all seemed to be heading for the same place on the other side. The last couple had passed quite close to me. Worrying that the next dog patrol might pick up their scent trail but hunt the wrong way, I set about wriggling free and following, only to find my legs had gone to sleep from compression, making descent to the shingle bed agonisingly difficult. The centre was reached at a crawl but the blood supply gradually kicked in and I managed a slow if wobbly run to the bank where the others had disappeared. It was a steep climb, ending in a seemingly impenetrable chain-link fence. Feeling the ground in the darkness a worn trail could be detected which led under a thick bush to a spot where the ground wire was loose. I emerged on the other side into what appeared to be a closed gas-station parking area. It was vaguely familiar from my walk before crossing the bridge and gave me a bearing for the motel. On my room doorstep I found a carton of milk and a newspaper. Dawn was breaking but I thought nothing of it, showered and was almost asleep when there was a loud knock, which was repeated with a shout. Opening the door revealed the motel manager and a uniformed policeman who immediately demanded identification. My British passport seemed to confuse him and, after a moment's thought, I remembered I had a recent bank statement given to me by the Citizens' Savings Bank in St Johnsbury only weeks before. This pacified the officer somewhat, but an order was still given 'to be out of town' by 4 pm.

Santa Barbara was the next stop. Arrival at the Pacific Ocean was grim, as a massive oil slick had washed up on the beach and the on-shore breeze was rank with the odour. I'd stopped there to look up Patricia Ryan and her brother Michael, who had emigrated from Galway some years before, relocating their dancing school operation to premises about half a mile inland. It was a step back in time for me in that they'd not changed in any way from how I'd known them when I was aged six, and yet they seemed to have slotted completely into the American way of life. Patricia particularly, with her long mane of wavy blonde hair, looked like a caricature of 50s America. Being low in funds I'd picked a cheap hotel, reflected in the fact that the clothes of a previous occupant who I was assured would not be returning were still hanging on the hooks, a corner of the ceiling was missing and some plaster had recently fallen off the wall. A jolly evening was spent with the Ryans, whose friendship and down-to-earth company did much to cheer me after the Dallas and El Paso experiences.

Journeying on to San Francisco I looked up Bill Vincent, another Irish-American family friend. He was held in great esteem by the Irish Department of Foreign Affairs since his father had given the family home, Muckross in Co. Cork, to the Irish nation just as the emerging Republic was trying to develop a Diplomatic Corps which could operate independently of the British Foreign Office. The house had been stuffed with fine furniture, which was used to help fit out the first Irish embassies, and part of Bill's legacy was that he was always invited as a standing member of the Irish diplomatic contingent to any party going on in San Francisco. As a house guest he took me to whatever venues he attended, but low funds and the pressing need to leave the USA before my visa expired meant I couldn't stay for long. The situation stabilised when he offered to buy me an airline ticket to Australia, as I could find work there to pay him back and it would be an opportunity to see more of the world.

While plans for this new adventure were being laid he took me to an official function and introduced me without warning to a prominent Irish-American matriarch, emphasising the fact that I had a family connection to a long-dead Washington Congressman called Bourke Cockran. The subsequent grilling was executed without mercy until I confessed all I knew was that Bourke was a great-uncle of some sort, as he had married my Vermont grandmother's sister, I was partly named after him and the family home back in Ireland continued to exist purely because of the trust fund his widow had used his fortune to set up. Other than that, I was fairly light on facts. The old lady seemed shocked, suggesting I did some homework, starting with reading Churchill's greatest speeches and advising that I'd find Bourke mentioned by name in every one. The reason was because he'd been able to teach the young Winston how to overcome the vocal impediment that had initially prevented him from entering the political arena on leaving school. Bill eventually came to my rescue from the old dragon by interrupting to say he had a book on Bourke's life he'd shortly be giving me to read as I crossed the Pacific. I was then asked to escort a girl back to the Nicaraguan Mission a few blocks away. It being a fine night and not a great distance, Sara Pineda, a tall dark beauty, suggested we walk as she wanted to clear her head after the hubbub of the party. We had not gone far when a tramcar came up a steep hill, levelled out on a cross-road junction and then climbed on up the next gradient. To me the underground cable mechanism layout pulling the tramcars around the city proved totally fascinating, and I embarked on trying to sum up how I thought it all worked. Next moment there was an almighty bang, followed by a receding crackle. Sara screamed and threw her arms round my neck as we collapsed on to a bench with ears ringing. All was now still, with no smoking crater, wrecked vehicle or destroyed building, and next day I found out we had experienced a sonic boom as the sound barrier was broken. The up side was that, though acutely painful at the time, it had been a bonding experience which blossomed into a romance, with my new Central American friend proving a great guide to the city.

She showed me giant gold ingots exhibited in a bank, the initial discovery of which had triggered the notorious Gold Rush stampede west across the Rocky Mountains, and even arranged for us to stay over on a houseboat in the artists' community at Sausalito under the Golden Gate Bridge.

It was time to leave and, armed with details of an irresistible contact in Hawaii, I flew to Honolulu and looked up Matthew FitzGerald. He'd been born in Dublin, reared in Hungary, lived in Waikiki harbour on a barge, was married to a Japanese and taught French. We exchanged notes on the old country, on which he needed considerable updating. Meeting him was a revelation in the way it portrayed aspects of the Irish Diaspora and how it was clung to when even only the most tenuous of threads existed. My host's strongly expressed view was that to possess linkage of any kind to 'the old country' was one of the greatest asscts to have as it meant there were doors open in every city on the planet.

5
Samoa to Australia

The air ticket allowed me to stop at Pago Pago in American Samoa. The intention was to see where my grandmother Marjorie had grown up when her father was Chief Justice, but unfortunately I landed on the wrong island. The Ides had lived on nearby Apia along with the writer Robert Louis Stevenson, who had been quite a family friend, and I'd once read her detailed description of the day he died, recorded in her own book of memories *Girlhood in the Pacific*. The family friendship was so close that he had taken pity on Marjorie's younger sister, Anne, who had a birthday on Christmas Day, and used his connection with President Taft to have it exchanged with his own. Anne being an American citizen, President Taft had to put a bill through Congress, but it had been done, officially processed and recorded. The knowledge made me feel there was a linkage to Samoa worth exploring – a valid reason to visit.

Walking from the airport looking for a boat to take me to the correct island, I encountered a guy with an amazingly bent face who began to just silently follow behind as I made for a group of distant factory buildings. With zero traffic and no obvious harbour to be seen we fell into conversation. Things turned out well in that he spoke English, had a boat, not a big one, just a dug-out with an outrigger, but more promisingly made an offer of accommodation. Pago Pago appeared to be a complete dump, just a high jungle-covered mountainous landmass sticking out of the sea like a giant tooth, and it was clear where Stevenson had found his inspiration for *Treasure Island*. Rain forest, distant, permanently roaring reef, cascading waterfalls, it was all there. 'Bent Face' took me down the shore and we boarded the dug-out, which was then poled around a few headlands. The water was calm and clear, with much to see as we glided along. Gradually the shore rose to become a cliff face and climbed into a canopy of overhanging plants and creepers punctuated by the occasional waterfall, not broken until we rounded a bluff into a small bay with a shingle beach and some huts dotted about. The backdrop was still the dark menacing cliff, which rose high into mists, but now a small sloping plain lay between it and the water's edge with the only way in and out appearing to be the way we had come.

A crowd of children gathered as we made landfall, followed by a friendly old man who emerged from one of the grass huts and introduced himself as Pa-le Ul-Fale, the village chief. A coconut neatly pierced with holes to drink from was offered and then, while I was still standing on the beach trying to take in what was happening, the sun went down and darkness fell, all in a matter of a few minutes. Little oil lights appeared and 'Bent Face' led me to a hut and introduced me to two smiling sarong-clad girls, one large, one small. Dumping my bag, I made my way to the site of a fire where everybody seemed to be milling about. More coconut milk was offered and accepted. Thinking about what hazards the local drinking water might contain, I guessed it sensible to stick with the coconuts. Sitting by the fire Pa-le explained that he was the village chief and was responsible for my welfare. Going on to say I must have 'wives' to look after me, he beckoned to the two girls I'd met earlier to come forward and stated that 'these were they'. Violena, the larger girl, who sported filed front teeth when she laughed, became a good friend over the next days. She showed me the one safe place to swim in the sea, some amazing waterfalls, the thunder of which made speech impossible, and mad flower-covered escarpments reached by trails lying beneath a dense tropical canopy. It was serious rain-forest and we were absolutely in it. About every two hours there would be a torrential downpour, followed by a spell of hot sunlight and steaming jungle. Sadly, it was clear I wasn't going to last there long. The girls did their best to guard me from the dragonfly-sized mosquitoes, but the inevitable bites suppurated and began to weep rather than heal. On the day of departure my host told me the previous visitors of a couple of years before had placed a small plaque on the beach to record the demise of a French ship's crew wrecked on the reef in the 18th century. Some survivors had made it to the shore, only to be subsequently corralled and eaten. He smiled and assured me I had been at no risk of enjoying the same fate. 'Bent Face' took me back to the airport road in his little boat and eventually I caught a flight to Auckland, New Zealand. The insect bites began to heal even as I sat in the aircraft reflecting on the magical interlude that had been experienced. Within a couple of days in rainy, cold Auckland the sores had pretty well healed.

My plan on reaching Wellington was to fly on to Sydney the next day, so I booked into a small clapboard hotel. Within an hour a Maori girl came into my room and asked if I wanted to go to the cinema and see *Gone with the Wind*. She quite insistent, even offering to pay for my ticket. I eventually agreed, as I had not in fact seen the film myself. She proved to be packed with emotion, crying her eyes out and wailing so unrestrainedly into my shoulder that concentration was rendered almost impossible. At the end we parted calmly in the foyer and I wandered back to my lodging, somewhat bewildered by the cultural complexity of the encounter.

Arriving in Sydney, I looked up my Galway friend Tony Huston, who had given me an address where he might be at should I ever reach the continent, and I found him in a garden firing at tin cans with a rifle. Unfortunately accommodation was tight and my bed was a dentist's chair. He and a friend were working on a plan to drive back to London on motorbikes and were in the process of applying for the necessary visas for the transit countries. He suggested I came on the expedition, so I joined in on visiting the relevant consulates to have passports stamped with the required permits. Getting a job to replenish funds did not turn out to be that easy and after looking up and staying a while with Dawn, my old Galway girlfriend, who was also in Sydney, I departed for Queensland and another godmother, Betsan Coates, one of my mother's oldest friends. She owned an up-market hotel at Alexandra Headland, Maroochydore, called the Boolarong Park Inn, and proved another absolute life-saver. I told her I wanted to find work quickly and earn enough money to be able to join the biking expedition, but she quickly talked me out of the idea, explaining that there was a vast amount to see in Australia and that to race off having just arrived would be a mistake. So the bikers left without me, but luckily my passport remained stuffed with visitor visas for countries I'd only vaguely heard of.

A trip was made by boat to see the Great Barrier Reef and then, having watched Neil Armstrong walk on the moon on TV (July 1969), I headed for Canberra, followed by Melbourne where a fellow traveller offered accommodation in the back of a shoe repair shop. I awoke in the early hours and, as the light strengthened, began to realise I was in a workshop that made shoes for people with deformed feet. Wonderfully shaped and very worn tools were neatly hooked on wall racks above an assortment of the strangest footwear ever seen. Below the bench was a line of wooden lathes shaped in the form of the human foot but with varying distortions. A sense of intrusion into the world of a serious craftsman, coupled with one of gratitude for being blessed with a set of sound limbs, made me rise and leave before my presence was discovered. I had a brief early-morning exploration of Melbourne on foot before I headed to the railway station and north to Adelaide.

On the journey someone suggested I look for a job at Port Augusta. The town lay at the bottom of the South Australian plain with all traffic passing through it, road or rail, heading east–west or north–south. It was described by one chap as 'the arse-hole of the Continent'. Port Augusta proved to be a dump and fitted the description. The idea of hitching a lift to Alice Springs suddenly seemed like a novel plan. Walking to the edge of town I hailed a pick-up heading north for Woomera, which took me a few hours into the rocky outback and a point where a rusty tar barrel marked a fork in the baked dirt track. The guys left me there at around 11 am as they were turning east to the rocket range. Other than the barrel there was not a single man-made object in sight and the gravelly landscape reached flat to the horizon in every direction.

A few hours went by. Dust from a truck of some sort raised my hopes for a while but it passed by a mile or so away and then I came to realise there was no organised or set roadway which would guarantee my being seen by a driver. The only other excitement of the day was when an emu appeared and poked about for a while before casually wandering off. In my bag I had a bottle of beer and a tin of meat but thought I should ration them for the present. A breeze got up and a sense began to grow that the skin on my face was tightening into dried plates. The tar barrel was a boon, as it provided a wind-break and something to sit against, with the duffle-coat hood acting as an added shield. The sun began to sink and the temperature to drop. Darkness fell and with it the wind, giving way to a singing silence as unfamiliar star constellations appeared. Wonderful though the spectacle was, it was undermined by the cold and a sense of fear. Eventually headlights appeared in the distance, approaching from the direction of Lake Eyre. My spirits soared, only to plummet when it became clear that the vehicle was going to pass about half a mile away and would not see me waving if I didn't move quickly. Occasionally the angle of the beams changed and it was obviously going to be a close-run thing, but finally the note of the engine dropped and I knew I'd been seen. My saviours were two scientists who had been out digging for shrimps in states of suspended animation buried deep in the lake bed. Gratitude towards the two men knew no bounds, but it was impossible to keep awake in the heat of the cab for the drive back to Port Augusta.

I was woken from a deep sleep by the driver, who explained he was staying at an institute and had to leave me where we now were, on the outskirts of town. He suggested that a fairly basic-looking but illuminated boarding house across the road was a good bet, as it was quite late. I thanked him profusely, picked up my bag and made my way to the entrance. A tall woman in a black leather skirt greeted me and gave the impression I was expected – she immediately reached for a room key and asked if I'd eaten. After a steak and chips I collapsed on to a hardish bunk and basically passed out, too tired to worry about the rather odd reception. There was another bed and at some time in the night it too was occupied.

As dawn broke I was woken by a lot of shouting and the sound of doors being kicked. In time mine was banged on and the woman's rasping voice ordered me and my new room-mate to get up immediately. I opened the door to face the black leather skirt, who now had an Alsatian on a chain and proceeded to state in expletive-laden language that 'the Ghan' was about to leave. 'No fucking buts' was yelled repeatedly, giving no opportunity to protest, and the only thing to do was lamely to follow an assortment of men who were shuffling towards the stairs. Until what was going on could be properly understood, moving with the flow seemed the best option. Outside there was a flatbed truck which took us all to the rear of a large railway station. I was still half asleep as an enormous black man appeared and automatically took charge, introducing himself as 'the Ganger'. He walked us over rail tracks to an area of the marshalling yard where we were presented with the sight of a set of four narrow-gauge wooden carriages straight out of the American Wild West. Each had a little iron balcony at the end and at the head was a small diesel loco. An instruction was given by the dark-skinned giant to climb on board and while we were doing so a noisy altercation erupted between him and the recruiting lady, who turned up in a pick-up, the row only terminating when the train slowly began to move. From overhearing the argument I deduced she had rounded up a group of 'fettlers' for him to take out for track repairs and wanted a back-hander of some sort. That explained why she had been glad to see me the night before and been so hospitable.

I expected the train to pick up speed but it just rocked along at about 15 mph. From the rear of the train civilisation, or what Port Augusta represented, slowly disappeared as we rattled north, the idea of jumping off not occurring until far too late. Another day in the sun stuck somewhere out in the wilderness didn't appeal and I'd picked up that eventually we would end up in Alice Springs, so I decided to sit things out – at least I was seeing Australia's outback. At one point the track wound up into some mountains and the loco stopped for a tea break. I walked over to the edge of a cutting and noticed oyster shells embedded in the gravelly bank. (I learned later we were in a pass cut through the Flinders Range.) Fuelling points and rest stops at Oodnadatta and Marree were passed, but the centres were largely without shops and populated mainly by fairly destitute Aborigines. (Any Europeans encountered were generally of a grim type, rough and belligerent.) Eventually, after a branch line to 'somewhere', we set to work at the task for which we'd been recruited – or 'shanghaied'.

One wagon contained bundles of iron bars which had to be driven through old holes in the sleepers to reinforce the track. They were much longer than the originals used when the rails had been laid, along what had been known as the Oodnadatta Camel Trail connecting Port Augusta to Alice Springs. Gradually I learned that camels and their Afghan drivers had been imported to open up the territory in the 19th century, before the

900-mile rail link running from water-hole to water-hole for the steam engines had been built. The line was teetering on its last legs – termites and erosion had taken a heavy toll. The only thing to drink was beer, which was stored in one carriage and rationed out by 'the Ganger' in his role of foreman and who, I came to learn, was a Thursday Islander. He kept order through pure brute force and was so strong he could lift me off the ground by my duffle coat with one hand. Night-time brought a huge drop in temperature and a general retreat to sleeping bags in a rail-car. What might possibly be termed conversations took place during the cooling hour after sunset. It seemed nobody had been near a city in well over ten years, but all had expansive views as to how man might one day explore the heavens – 'electro-magnetic propulsion' of some sort being the general theme. Trying to convince the Ganger that man had actually escaped the earth's gravitational clutches was met with total disbelief and being half-choked by him until I agreed to desist talking rubbish. He wasn't having any of it and I learned to keep my distance after the encounter. Everyone had a mate of sorts and I teamed up with a middle-aged chap with long front teeth called Toothie who had spent most of his life in the outback prospecting for opals. Like all the others he had a dream of a glorious windfall which would lead to a luxurious retirement.

There was the occasional siding the wagons pulled into so as to let a train shuffle past every second day, but otherwise there was no contact with the outside world. I wasn't too worried as the pile of stakes was declining and talk of 'Alice' was growing. All thought just focused on getting through the day in my role as a 'tonger' in a state of mental numbness while holding bars to be driven. In the middle of absolutely nowhere an aborigine with red-blond hair was spotted standing on a rock with a staff, just watching us. Moments later he was gone. Looking around at the arid, rocky landscape, all that could be seen was the prospect of death in every direction. Somehow he had a way of survival, but the details were lost on me as the iron rails at my feet represented the only hope of further existence. The encounter was humbling as it left an impression of having been briefly in the presence of a fellow human being who was totally at home in what was a frighteningly dangerous environment.

Finally all the bars were used up and it was time to head into town. The Ganger had a list of our names and record of days worked. We would be paid at the station. Unfortunately a vicious fight involving Toothie broke out in one carriage as the train came to a halt. The altercation spilled out on to the ground under the station's wooden awning and the last I saw of my friend was his motionless body lying in the dust as the police arrived. Everyone present was carted off to a secure holding compound and then just left for a couple of days.

Being the youngest by about 20 years I was singled out as a target for mistreatment by the lead figure in the train fight, as he knew I had been on the fringe of the brawl and witnessed what had happened. One of his wrists concealed an L-shaped length of iron bar under a bandage which he used as a club to crack me repeatedly across one temple – not particularly hard, but always in the same place, inflicting maximum pain for minimum damage in order to keep me away from the only tap in the yard. It was all very simple and his rule over all the internees was absolute. The single warder paid no attention to what went on whenever a trolley of sustenance of some sort was wheeled in and I never got to know what was on it, as I was always being sat on with any attempt at struggle being rewarded with a thump in the kidneys. The spectre of dehydration began to manifest itself quite severely as a blinding headache developed, accompanied by stomach cramps and a sense of nausea. I lost track of time until I dimly sensed being dragged out of the place by somebody and put in a chair. One eye was now so bruised it remained closed and was what may have attracted attention. A damp cloth was put on my head and another into my mouth, extracted, re-dampened and re-inserted, with the exercise going on for some time. My tongue was fairly swollen but suddenly, from nowhere, came saliva and the ability to speak. I could hear myself imitating Bill's clipped, crystal-clear English naval voice of command instructing the policeman to 'call Mrs Coates immediately at the Boolarong hotel' in Queensland and say my name – 'Tarka'. The officer paused for a moment but then went slowly to his desk and made a call. Having asked me for confirmation of the hotel address he dialled another number and I guessed he was speaking to Betsan, as he began to say 'yes ma'am' quite a lot.

The wet cloths were doing their work and I began to vaguely pick up on what was going on around me. A nurse arrived with a bag of medical equipment and asked questions while examining my eye and temple bruising. However, the ability to speak had faded and I could only mumble incoherent answers because of my swollen cheeks and tongue. She queried how long I had been in custody and through a fog I heard the policeman say, 'Dunno, about two days I think. Came in on the Ghan – was here when I came on. All I know is he has a name that's given the Skipper the shits.' I hadn't the strength to resist having a suppository administered as I felt the treatment unnecessary, though it appeared to speed up recovery. Betsan had arranged for some funds to be forwarded and I moved from the police station to a hotel to rest up before making a detailed statement and heading back to Queensland. On asking after Toothie the policeman just looked me in the face and bluntly replied, 'He didn't make it'. Not knowing we had been quite close friends out in the desert he was a little confused by my reaction, but though still weak with what was probably delayed shock of some sort and an eye only just beginning to open, my immediate response was to attempt to retch. Without much to bring up the ordeal was painful and didn't deal with a sense of survival guilt. To have intervened in the fight would have been pointless, bordering on suicidal, as I was no match for Toothie's assailant, but the feeling that perhaps I could have somehow done something remained. All too late now – the only hope was to leave town and rely on memory of the 'Alice experience' fading with time.

The bus journey back to Queensland was a series of leapfrogs from Alice to the Tennant Creek road junction, stopping briefly at the galvanised tin city of Mount Isa, then on to Townsville and down the coast to Maroochydore. It was followed by a good rest and much teasing over the fact that my voice had altered considerably in the weeks I'd been away. On reflection I guessed some sort of change to the vocal cords had happened when ordering the policeman in Alice Springs to get on the telephone. The trauma seemed to have reset throat muscles so sounds came out differently – sharper and without any trace of a soft Irish brogue.

After a couple of weeks' rest it was time to head for Darwin and on to Singapore. A freak rainstorm caused two enormous road trains to bog down in the dust which had turned to mud, totally blocking the unmetalled highway at Mount Isa, and so I had to hang around the town for a day. The main bar had an outside jukebox on a veranda that played Credence Clearwater Revival's 'A Bad Moon Rising' continuously. At first I thought the machine was stuck but it was just that the Aborigines loved dancing to the melody and kept hitting the same button, until it became a form of torture.

Darwin was found to be an even more serious dump: nothing but flies, drunks, sporadically generated electricity, mosquitoes and high humidity, while the sea was an unpleasant no-go area thanks to crocodiles and massive stinging jellyfish. When I enquired in a bar about ferries to Singapore the whole place erupted in laughter. Somehow I'd managed to get all the way to the north of Australia without anybody advising me of the existence of Indonesia as a serious country of 100 million people in the way. Mentally I'd muddled it up with Polynesia, and not given much thought to the need for the visa stamped in my passport but luckily still valid. The flies became an absolute torment, with at least six permanently in your eyes when eating meat in termite-riddled shacks. There was no other food on offer and air-conditioning didn't exist. A lucky break came when returning to my lodging late at night after a fruitless expedition to find a church of any sort, as I met an Australian guy my age who had also been locked out. Through the fly-screen and dim generator light we could see the unconscious forms of two office staff slumped in easy chairs surrounded by a floor littered with beer cans. One blade was missing from the ceiling fan, so it was revolving in a mad way and lent a ridiculous touch to the scene. Eventually one of the other occupants was roused and let us in, but not before I learned that my new friend, who was trying to reach an island called Bali, had found a way round the problem of the ferry to Singapore.

6
Indonesia to Cambodia

The next day tickets were bought for a four-seater plane flying to Dili in Portuguese Timor. Landing on a grass strip, we made our way to the only modern structure in sight – a boarding house run by an unfriendly Chinaman who stated that there was no road to the Indonesian part of the island. Our only option was a small plane flying across the border to Kupang the next morning, so we paid an extortionate fee for a small room. The afternoon was spent exploring the locality but Dili town, the capital, we never saw, just some old Portuguese cannon pointing out to sea from the crumbling ramparts of a shoreline fortification buried under flowering creepers.

The little plane appeared at midday, smaller if anything than the one that had brought us from Darwin, and took about 40 minutes to make the journey over mountains into Indonesia. Coming in to land on a grass strip seemingly in the middle of nowhere, it rolled to a halt beside a Second World War vintage Dakota DC3, with an American pilot who invited us to board straight away as he was about to head for Bali. A lorryload of armed soldiers arrived and once they were all in we were off.

The soldiers behaved like schoolboys, jabbering loudly among themselves, obviously full of excitement about the flight, with nobody giving us a second glance. A peep out of the window and the sight of puffs of white smoke from the exhaust of a misfiring engine had been enough to make me sink back quietly into my seat, close my eyes and pray. Finally the descent began, and braving a second glance out we saw we were almost skimming wave-tops. There was a cry 'Bali Beach, Bali Beach' and the soldiers all piled to one side to look out, causing the wing to dip thanks to the shift in weight. Then, instead of a crash into the sea there was a heavy thump signifying that we were on the ground, rolling past bulldozers and road-building machinery. The Dakota taxied to a corner of a grass airfield by some palm trees lining a beach, and everyone disembarked once the American had kicked the door open.

We set off on foot along a nearby sandy track shaded by tall palms that served as a road for the occasional truck and led into Denpasar, the capital of Bali, only to be confronted by the spectacle of Kuta beach curving away to infinity with a setting sun on the horizon. There was nobody to be seen other than a few fishermen and a small group of locals, conducting a ceremony of some sort at the water's edge – not a European anywhere. The Adi Yasa guest house was run by three sisters who cooked delicious meals in beaten-out car hubcaps. One, a heavily pock-marked girl called Mah-de, became a friend, as she spoke good English, and happily shared her views on the Indonesian political situation, which was still in a state of transition. She had liked the former dictator, Sukarno, and was a little concerned over the new regime's attitude towards former Communists. There were few Europeans in the town and over the following days I spent quite a lot of time talking with her about the depth of Hindu culture that seemed to permeate all walks of life on the island. Having known absolutely nothing about Bali until I actually arrived I was keen to learn and she proved a wonderful guide. Finally, after a week of exploring outlying villages and temples, it was time to catch a bus for Jakarta at the far end of Java. When we parted she pressed a carved cream-coloured stone on me for $25, saying it would be worth a lot more in Singapore. I had planned to fly home from the city state as I was low on money, with just enough funds to get there. Thanks to her friendship and staying almost for free, I did the deal as I thought it would still be a nice memento of our time together, even if proving to be worthless.

The bus took a day to reach Surabaya, a coastal town and halfway point along Java. Dense crowds were encountered the entire way, with all aspects of life from roadside foundries to slaughterhouses to be seen. On reaching Jakarta, a gloomy smog-laden sky and streets swamped with military police immediately indicated that it was no place to hang around, and I headed to the airport before something went wrong. There, a ticket to Singapore was purchased, security was negotiated and I was suddenly but safely on the way out of Indonesia. The filthy air and omnipresent grim political situation had been one long dark shadow hanging over not only the city but Java itself – something angry and unseen but threatening. Danger was sensed everywhere other than on Bali, and it was a relief to have escaped unscathed.

Sam Leong Road in Singapore had been recommended as an economical place to find somewhere to stay while still roughly at the centre of things, and it proved to be exactly that. Every six hours the roadway went through a total change of identity. From early morning to midday it was a market, with everything from food and clothing to dodgy antiques and machinery parts on sale. Midday to 6 pm was the time for street actors and theatre. Then pop-up restaurants with kerbside cooking facilities materialised, with shops and cigarette kiosks turning into bars. At midnight the scene changed yet again as prostitutes and transvestites literally filled the road until dawn. Taking a small room high up over a music shop led to my buying a Sony tape player plus cassettes and meant I quickly made friends.

Mah-de's stone made $500, which was a surprisingly lucky windfall. I'd arrived in Singapore with just enough money to buy an air ticket home, the fallback position, but now a look at India on the way became a possibility. One evening, while returning from the cinema feeling very happy with life, having watched *Cool Hand Luke* with Chinese sub-titles flickering vertically at the screen's side, the monsoon arrived with a sudden crump and torrential downpour. The dry garbage in the storm culverts beside the pavements floated on the surface of the rising water, and while observing the spectacle with amusement from the shelter of a doorway I spotted a pair of white arms thrashing about in the suspended trash. The logical thing to do was to reach out and help whoever it was to find a firm footing. A hand was grabbed and found to be belonging to a European girl in a state of utter hysterics. As she sobbed before me in the rain I noticed she had no bag or anything, just the flimsy wet dress she stood in, sandals and spectacles. Eventually she calmed down enough to take in that I was speaking to her in English and, surprisingly, was able to reply. It transpired that my new acquaintance was Swedish and in dire straits, as all her belongings and money, absolutely everything including passport, had been stolen by someone of whom she was terrified. The best thing to do in the circumstances now that we had begun to converse appeared to be to get her into a shower and her dress cleaned, so I led her back to my room. While she washed I rinsed her clothing and gave her a towel and sarong to wear while it dried. It was clear a decision had to be made in the very near future about what happened next: either she needed to be returned to the street as soon as her clothes were dry or I should agree to be of further help, which meant becoming involved. The circumstances of our meeting revealed her as an intelligent human being genuinely in need of emergency aid, and the unexpected financial boost of the stone sale made it seem churlish to just tip her out into the night, so I made up my mind to be of assistance.

The shower had had a calming effect. Sitting on the bed, she told me her name, Maria Bergen, and roughly filled in the details of her situation. The year before she had met a Frenchman when on holiday in Singapore and, on returning to Sweden, had been bombarded with letters begging her to come out again. Stupidly she had done so, as almost immediately he began to demand that they marry. It was because he was stateless and she was his path to Swedish citizenship. He had grown up in French Indo-China but when colonial rule had come to an end he, like many other ex-French colonists, had been abandoned, with no right of residence in France. He had raided her room and was holding her belongings as a ransom. She had been told someone back in Sweden needed to vouch for her before the embassy could help with a passport and money. Answering that demand was going to be difficult as she lived alone, had no siblings and only an estranged father whom she blamed for her mother's death. Her big fear was that the Frenchman might become dangerously violent if he did not get his way. He carried a knife and earned a living running cockfights on the Songkhla ferries which plied the east coast of the Thai/ Malay peninsula.

I played her a newly purchased Joan Baez tape while thinking about what to do. It seemed all that was needed was some way of buying time until she made contact with her father, and the way forward was to assist in achieving that goal. The immediate need was to get out of Singapore and seek help from elsewhere. The trouble was that at the other end of the causeway to the mainland lay a different country, Malaysia, and entering it at the Johor Bahru frontier would require a plausible identity. Chewing things over in the downstairs café with Barney, a fairly wacky Australian hippie I'd become friends with, the idea of knocking up something for insertion in my British passport was mooted. Barney's other bit of advice was to head for Goa on the Indian west coast, 'where it was all happening'.

I dug out a T-shirt and sarong for Maria to wear, and we went for a bite to eat and get a photo. The passport was fixed up that night with a mugshot of her in the window labelled 'spouse' of the holder and, on buying two train tickets in the morning for Kuala Lumpur, we set off for the Malaysian frontier checkpoint. A talkative American had joined us, which probably helped as the passport was stamped without a second glance. Kuala Lumpur railway station was so stunning that I could not stop walking round it from the outside. Maria contacted the Swedish embassy but was turned away again for the same reason as at Singapore – it was under heavy siege from destitute hippies looking for free passage home. She had an office phone number for her father but had no luck, as he appeared to be away on a business trip. Our trouble was that we had no contact number, as we were on the move and I knew nobody in that part of the world who could take a message.

We caught a train to Penang and headed for a place by a beach that was cheap. A cinema featured Michael Caine in *The Battle of Britain*, and as with *Cool Hand Luke* there was the distraction of Chinese subtitles running up and down the margin. The translators had obviously had great trouble understanding RAF wartime slang as some short comments required rows of characters – particularly those uttered by Trevor Howard. Walking back from the cinema, Maria suddenly froze and pointed. Sideways-on across the road by an apple stall stood a fair-haired man. Apparently it was the dreaded Frenchman. Fortunately we had come out of the cinema using a side door or he would have seen us, and goodness knows what might have happened, but the only thing to do now was to bolt for Thailand. We collected my bag in the dark and headed for Butterworth Station, intending to catch the next train to anywhere. There was nothing moving until the early morning when a train already on the platform was leaving for Bangkok. We climbed aboard and found a shadowy corner to hide in. Using the early morning activity on the station platform as cover, I crept out and bought tickets for the journey, expecting the Frenchman to appear at any second. Fortunately he didn't.

The sound of a loud whistle announced departure, followed by the carriages beginning to roll gently forward, with the deep, just audible chuff-chuff of a steam locomotive under load. My excitement was totally lost on Maria, who I then realised was absolutely exhausted by the night's drama. Gathering speed, the train rattled out into the suburbs and then off into the Malay jungle, heading north. We sat back, relaxing in the belief that our troubles were over, as the jungle whizzed by.

A few hours passed and then, with a ferocious squealing of steel on steel, the train shuddered to an abrupt halt. We were in deep jungle with the forest canopy almost meeting overhead. An English-speaking fellow passenger got out and disappeared up the track to see what the trouble was – there was much running about and shouting outside. He came back and told us a bridge we were about to cross had been blown up. I felt compelled to go and have a look, as it would also mean being able to check out the steam engine. Walking up the track it was possible to stand as close to the piston assembly as the radiating heat would permit, to admire the giant driving wheels. From my position on the ground it appeared a truly vast machine, with the pressure-release valve going 'hiss-clank, hiss-clank' as if poised for action like a crouching tiger flicking a metallic tail while preparing to lunge. An improvised wooden barricade could be seen placed across the rails further up the line just before the beginnings of a metal bridge with slogans of some sort daubed in white paint and remains of shattered sleepers lying around a small crater in the track chippings. The whistle blew a few times and I ran back to the carriage as all began to move in reverse down the line. Climbing up I found that a bunch of armed Chinese-looking men mainly in green shirts had joined us out of the bush, with one carrying a light machine-gun. Then the train briefly stopped again and they wasted no time in melting away into the trees.

After a further reverse shunt we halted at a small station, allowing everyone remaining to disembark at a the edge of a place called Pedang Besar before the train finally disappeared down the line. The stop appeared to be a Malay border check-point, as there was a small police post where the passport was inspected and stamped. We were now a group of about 100 people, including some Buddhist monks in saffron robes. Everyone had papers of some sort. Time went by and eventually an assortment of vehicles appeared, consisting of a bus and some lorries. Maria and I climbed aboard the bus and the convoy moved off. An hour or so later it ground to a halt at another roadblock. We had reached the Thai border.

It was a relief to be leaving Malaysia behind, as with luck it meant increasing the distance from the Frenchman, and everyone appeared in good spirits other than the sunglasses-wearing Thai security police. After the checkpoint, passport inspection and stamping, it was a hefty walk to the next village, Haadyai, which had a train stop. Some carriages shunted out of the jungle and halted, but it was a very different vehicle from the one we had been on, no lovely steam engine, just a boring diesel with all windows and doors boarded up along one side and a lot of sullen soldiers milling about. The journey to Bangkok was long and uneventful, punctuated only by halts to let trains laden with armoured vehicles heading south clank slowly past. At one point a fellow passenger noticed the camera in my bag and told me in broken English I'd face immediate arrest by the military police if it was discovered. He urged me to dispose of it immediately, explaining that South Thailand was under martial law and such items were absolutely forbidden. The conversation ended abruptly when uniformed soldiers entered the compartment and sat down, making such an act impossible. Morale began to sink at the first impressions Thailand was offering, but things were not destined to improve over the coming days.

No good news awaited at the Bangkok *poste restante* so, deeply depressed, we found a cheap wooden boarding house and booked in. The grey sky and generally gloomy street atmosphere generated by the omnipresent awareness of the nearby Vietnam War didn't help, and in addition we discovered colour film for the camera was unavailable. We looked at some temples and Buddhas, finding ourselves usually the only visitors, while what bars and cafés were open were mainly occupied by stunningly low-calibre, mainly drunk American GIs on R and R. US military police in white helmets and spats, and sporting truncheons, cruised around in open jeeps, picking up those too drunk to walk. It felt like being incarcerated in a sort of madhouse. Maria sent a frantic telegram to Sweden and we decided to stay where we were for a time in the hope that it would generate a result to help guide what we did next – there was no plan as such.

Days went by and, with our relationship coming under strain at being cooped up in the little boarding house, I went for a walk alone to have look at the zoo, which was found to be almost deserted. While admiring an enormous owl in a circular cage a group of three Thais in military fatigues caught my attention, two men and a woman, all taller than average. Noticing me they came over and one asked where I came from. My reply of 'Ireland' caused an initial, slightly hostile atmosphere to turn to one of curiosity.

'Not American?'

'No.'

'Have you ever been to Moscow?' Quite why I acted as I did was probably due to the boredom of my situation as much as anything, but I replied, 'No, but I had a sculptress cousin who once stayed in the Kremlin for a while shortly after the Revolution' – guessing that the subject matter might trigger interest. It did, and I filled out the story of Clare Sheridan's trip to Moscow back in 1920, asking if any of them had been to Russia themselves, and adding the suggestion that if they did go they should look out for her bust of Lenin. This led to an invitation to join an expedition to Vientiane in Laos. As the concept looked like a welcome break from Maria's seemingly endless troubles, it was taken up and the next day we set off in two trucks.

Cambodia was ducked into to avoid North Thailand's military zone, with the border crossing being a complete non-event. The trip came to an end when we came across a bombed-out bus blocking a river crossing at the end of a day's driving. There a view of hell was glimpsed through momentary eye contact with a blood-soaked woman whose facial expression was one of abject despair as she cradled the twitching body of a dying child. The Thais decided the trip was over and left me at a bus stop, having turned round and recrossed the Thai frontier. During our time together I'd spoken about my problems and was given contact details of someone who might help cross Burma to India by air. Everyone had been highly amused at my total lack of understanding over the geographic obstacle the closed country presented.

On returning to Maria it was to find she still had no news from Sweden. Before looking up the address I'd been given for flights we called in on Pan Am and asked for two tickets to Calcutta, but found it was as the Thais had warned: a clear passport identity was an absolute requirement for the major airlines. Later that day we sought out the office of the guy the Thais had recommended, and he made arrangements for a flight via Rangoon. Maria travelling on my passport didn't seem to be a problem other than generating a warning not to draw attention to ourselves when in Burma as, if we missed the connecting flight, we'd be totally stuck there. With still no news from Maria's father we headed for the airfield located across the runway from the main airport building. Passing through a low-key security gate, my passport was stamped without issue and we boarded a brown-liveried twin propeller aircraft. Flight time to Rangoon was short and we landed at a small airstrip. All on board were Indian and, like us, in transit. While in Rangoon we sat about for a couple of hours in a pleasant temple-like structure. Armed soldiers wandered about and we sat in the shadows, trying to remain as inconspicuous as possible, but, like the night in Butterworth railway station, the passing minutes seemed like hours and the interlude an eternity, with adrenalin rendering any attempt at reflective contemplation quite impossible.

7
India and Mother, Then Istanbul

〔✍〕

The connecting flight was longer and circled Calcutta for some time before landing at Dum-Dum airport, providing splendid aerial views of the old fort outside the sprawling city. It might have been the tweed jacket and white cotton trousers I habitually wore but the Sikh official manning the airport security desk just smiled at us as he stamped my passport, scribbled something indecipherable in it and said, 'Welcome to India'.

A fellow passenger had strongly advised us to head to Darjeeling for Christmas and so we boarded the Assam Express train to take us north. A steam locomotive belching smoke took us to the bank of a river. There the entire trainload of passengers dismounted and walked to a long thin pontoon stretching out into the water. Minutes later, out of a misty haze, an ancient lopsided paddle-steamer appeared ahead of two others following like ducks, and the entire trainload of people proceeded to climb aboard the vessels. I was trying to squeeze my way to an open area amidships, where a huge crankshaft had been spotted silently revolving as the craft moved away from the pier, when there was a tugging at my sleeve. A small boy was saying 'chai, chai' and gesticulating upwards towards the bridge with a finger. He led me to a stairway at the top of which stood a smiling Sikh in immaculate white uniform. He offered me a cup of tea and in splendid clipped English asked where I was going. I told him and then asked, 'Why wasn't there a bridge for the train to cross?' He replied that it was always very foggy in this area and when the line was being built across the Ganges, which was very wide at that point, there was a mapping mistake. He moved his hands towards each other in the air but passing about 12 inches apart to emphasise the case. I felt there must have been another reason for the lack of a bridge but it was his take on it. The procession of paddle-steamers chugged away for about half an hour, weaving around a series of sand bars, until another pier on the other bank came into sight and behind it the dark line of carriages headed by another smoking steam loco. We boarded and headed north until the Himalayas suddenly appeared like an enormous wall at the edge of the plain we had been crossing.

The stop for the connection to Darjeeling came without warning. I'd not been expecting a train to be taking us up to the hill station, but an ancient narrow-gauge assembly of wooden carriages and yet another steam locomotive in polished blue livery sat waiting for its passengers to dismount from the Assam Express. It took the rest of the day for it to wind backwards and forwards up to the hill station, with the beauty of the ever-changing mountain views putting the mind into a dream-like trance. Sherpas with enormous loads were everywhere and a noticeable steady drop in temperature was the only contact with reality. It was evening when we finally arrived and, on exiting at the terminus, a friendly man appeared out of nowhere and invited us back to his home. It was Christmas Eve. We were rented a room and told there would be a meal shortly. His wife, a portly lady with beaming smile, produced huge bowls of vegetable stew. Unlike him she didn't speak English other than to say she was Christian and her husband Buddhist. The next few days were spent exploring the tea plantations and Raj-era buildings. A pony was organised to take me up to Tiger Hill for the sunrise on New Year's morning as, from there, it could be seen hitting Mount Everest in the distance before anywhere else. And so it was from that spot that the first dawn light of the 1970s was witnessed – a distant spike of gold suddenly sticking up out of a sea of white. On the ride back down I thought briefly about home and wondered what the coming decade held in store, but it all seemed far away and rather irrelevant.

We returned to Calcutta for a couple of days and had a look around St Paul's Cathedral, where a plinth marked the graves of Irishmen who had died fighting on the Indian side during the Mutiny. Nearby a line of deep trenches snaked off across a large park that had been dug as air-raid shelters in 1956 after China invaded Tibet. There had momentarily been great alarm triggered by a belief that India was next to be overrun and the population needed to be protected from air raids. The quickest fix was to dig shelters in the parks – hence the trenches. Unfortunately, a gap of two weeks between completion of the earthworks and the installation of warning sirens to mobilise the population provided an opportunity for the freshly dug pits to become popular as open-air latrines. Riots broke out when the order came to run and jump into them when sirens sounded. Observing the current state of bedlam in the city's streets where traffic, humanity and animals jammed the thoroughfares, it wasn't difficult to imagine the chaos that must have erupted.

I thought I'd save a bit of money by purchasing a couple of third-class train tickets to Madras. What we didn't realise was that it meant being confined to catching a third-class train, which took three days to complete the journey, as it was frequently shunted into a siding to allow expresses to pass. Some halts were for five or six hours, during which time everyone climbed out to cook and wash. We were in a compartment designed for six people, but were joined by ten others, made up largely of a policeman and his entire family – wife, mother, sister, children etc. – with another family holed up in the lavatory. What had made it all worthwhile was the passing of double locomotive-powered expresses thundering along the adjoining track at full speed with whistles blaring. Standing in the gap between carriages one was only feet from the driving wheels and could momentarily feel the heat radiating from the engines as the ground shook in a whizzing swirl of steam and dust. It was a strong reminder of carefree days back in Ireland when walking along the railway line on a Sunday afternoon hunting for wild strawberries. Back then copper pennies placed on the tracks to be flattened had to be closely watched when run over by a passing train as they flew off, and spotting where they landed could only be done by lying close by. Here one just clung on to anything to hand, iron or human.

From Madras we crossed the one-time jungle, now stony desert, of Bangalore. As it was a traditional garrison town the main square was a military parade ground, with almost continual activity of one sort or another to the sound of military bands. Fearsome-looking Sikhs armed to the teeth marched backwards and forwards in and out of self-created dust storms. The tiger-skin drums being beaten to keep step were enormous and added greatly to the spectacle. But there was not much else to see and, with ears ringing, we headed for Goa and a rendezvous with Barney, my hippie friend from Singapore. The station's forest location and the dusty track to the village were surprising. When a large, dilapidated church of cathedral proportions loomed up out of the jungle, the impression was that the Portuguese had not been gone long. St Francis Xavier's decorated tomb was the centrepiece, but tendrils of bougainvillea were snaking in through the windows and along mud brick and plaster walls, while dusty dark portraits of anonymous saints scowled down from above.

We found our way to the beach, but locating somewhere to stay was a bit of a hunt. Eventually the local priest rented us a store-house. We found out he was also the local money-changer and doctor. Stumbling across Barney was to find him only a shadow of his former self, quiet and listless. It was no surprise when, one morning, the priest asked me to identify his corpse, which had been retrieved from the sea at first light. No papers, passport or money, just needle-marks on his arms, indicated that he had probably gone swimming when he shouldn't have. I felt a momentary pang of sadness for the chap I'd once known, but it was clear his spirit had actually departed some time before I'd reached Goa. The deadness in his eyes had told me this. On arriving in India the first sight of an ox-cart laden with dead bodies as it made its way round the edge of a street market had been a shock, but it wore off as we adjusted to the country's pace of life and such scenes were found to be commonplace.

Barney's demise signalled that it was time to leave and catch a train for Hyderabad, with an onward connection to Benares. I understood Hyderabad to be the Crewe of India, but did not expect the thick smog blanket, nor that the changing of trains would include changing stations. Visibility was no more than 50 yards outside the station in the murky light and before us swarmed a sea of pedal rickshaws. We were a group of about 12 Europeans who needed transport to the other station and were quickly taken in hand by the rickshaw wallahs. All bags were grabbed and piled on to three machines which then shot off into the gloom, causing two Americans to become hysterical. The effect on the rickshaw drivers was one of great amusement and it was obvious there was nothing for it but to join in their game, whatever it was, so our line of four rickshaws set off, weaving like a giant centipede through what appeared to be complete traffic bedlam. Darkness fell and what street lighting existed was reduced by the filthy air to only a faint overhead glow, but the boys seemed to know exactly what they were about – either it was a large-scale robbery or they were just attempting to race the more heavily laden baggage couriers. Then, below the smog, appeared the lower portals of a railway station and before it the three baggage rickshaws with beaming drivers. Needless to say, reward rupees flowed, particularly from the American wallets.

All India appeared to have to journey to the Benares ghats at some point in a lifetime as well as to be cremated. On the train a tape of *Sergeant Pepper* was played to some singing pilgrims, which shut them up for a while, until one commented that the sitar player was comparatively inexperienced – he could only have been playing for about ten years. That shut me up. Highly decorated oxen pulled wooden carts laden with entire families along clogged roads, the children wide-eyed and clearly agog at the scenes all around. Colourfully painted pedestrians weaved their way through the mayhem, burdened with containers of ashes to be tipped into the Ganges. We rented a room within walking distance of the river and I'd tried to get Maria to gargle in it to cure a sore throat, but she wasn't enthusiastic after we'd watched two vultures picking at a corpse as it floated by.

On reaching New Delhi Maria finally received news and money, which meant she had cash and was able to get the Swedish embassy to provide a passport. We celebrated by going to see the Taj Mahal by moonlight. On the way a fellow visitor told us that during the recent Pakistan–India conflict it was deemed necessary to drape camouflage nets over the white alabaster dome so it could not be used as a navigation aide by the enemy – particularly at night. The ongoing madness of India never ceased to entertain and surprise – so different from Java and the Malay Peninsula.

Maria offered to repay me for the help I'd given her by financing the next leg of our journey home via Kabul, Tashkent and Leningrad. I was up for it but, unlike her, having a British passport, I needed particular visa clearance from the Soviet embassy before the In-Tourist Office would produce other required travel permits. The embassy and the In-Tourist office were a couple of miles apart but refused to communicate by telephone. The diplomatic officials stated that specific In-Tourist travel documents had to be produced before the embassy could provide a visa, but refused to be of help. This Catch-22 predicament continued for days until, from Maria's point of view, the ground opened up and swallowed me. The last image of my friend of many months of adventure was to be that of her walking away from the hostel we were staying at with the camera we'd sourced in Singapore slung over her shoulder, as she had headed off to photograph something while I wrestled with my Russian visa problem.

An Australian came into the room and said, 'You'd better sit down, mate.' Seconds later my mother appeared in the doorway and embraced me with a loud 'Dah-ling'. My mind numbed with surprise, we sat in silence for a long moment. I just didn't know what to think or say. The feeling she was an unwanted presence hovered for a few moments, but was pushed aside as the reality of the situation sank in. I'd been wandering totally free in the world for a year but was aware there would inevitably have to be a return home to face life. The best needed to be made of the moment, as getting cross over her turning up would achieve nothing. The short-term solution was to do what she expected – revert to the role of a dutiful son and give up the battle of trying to continue home as planned with Maria.

Leaving the hostel, we looked up the British naval attaché friend of Bill's and visited his residence in a smart Delhi suburb. When I returned to collect my things there was no sign of Maria; she and the camera had vanished. We never met again. Mother wanted to see the Taj Mahal and visit Bodhgaya as she had always been an admirer of the Buddha and harboured a yearning to visit the site of his enlightenment. During the first-class train journey back to Agra she fell into conversation with a middle-aged doctor on the subject of India's break with Britain and the subsequent agonising pains of Partition. He was most complimentary about the legacy of the Raj and what a happy 'marriage' British rule had been, while I silently came to terms with my changed circumstances. After Agra we headed for Jaipur, as she had known the Maharajah during the war in Cairo. As we entered the palace they fell into each other's arms and wandered off to another room, deep in catch-up talk over what had happened to so-and so, leaving me to stare awkwardly at a group my own age. My now rather worn tweed jacket, white cotton trousers and sandals contrasted rather strongly with the tiger-skins, chandeliers and cool London fashion of gold belts, chains, high-collared shirts and Cuban-heeled boots. Conversation was attempted but never kicked off and, rather rattled at this failure to engage with my own generation, I wandered over to a window to watch some monkeys being ineffectually chased by a gardener.

8

My Army Application and Mons

When we returned to Delhi flights to Tehran were booked, and after an exceedingly difficult time at the airport we managed to pass security. The scribble made in my passport on arrival in Calcutta months before apparently concerned Maria and erupted as a serious problem. As she was not present I was prevented from being allowed to pass through a barrier. Just lifting her photograph out of the document had not sufficed. With no obvious way forward, my mother pulled a splendid Memsahib act, a beaming senior Sikh appeared and the crisis was resolved without my taking any part in the conversation.

Tehran was cold, windy and depressing. The street dress code of men in three-piece suits of varying colours and women in Western dress of the late 1960s just didn't look right when compared to the world of the Indian dhoti and sari I'd been immersed in for the previous four months. The Shah's crown jewels and the hall filled with gifts presented to the Iranian court in the 1870s by European heads of state portrayed a unique, momentary snapshot going back into a period of world history, the legacy of which had now almost vanished.

From Tehran we flew to Istanbul, specifically to visit the Hagia Sophia church/mosque, but a dark pall of acrid smoke spreading over the city from a burning oil tanker moored in the Golden Horn rather spoiled the Byzantine atmosphere we were expecting. Then it was on to Rome.

On arrival at Uncle Jack's apartment in Trastevere, the happy atmosphere that had developed while travelling melted away – 'something in the air' had begun to materialise, and finally emerged into the open as a two-part bombshell.

There were two matters. Desmond, her youngest brother, to whom she had made over Castle Leslie in Monaghan six years before, had run into financial difficulties and begun to sell off parcels of farmland. He had already sold over 300 of the best acres and was now pressing her to purchase the Victorian farmyard and some surrounding fields within the demesne wall. She was planning to do so and register all in my name with the capital earmarked for purchasing Renville. This completely unexpected news came as a deep shock, as I'd dreamed for years of one day farming by and potentially under the sea – but there was more.

An opportunity to take up a commission as an officer in the Blues and Royals, my godfather Peter's old regiment, was on offer if I could get through a qualifying course. When I went back to London all would be explained by somebody I didn't know yet, a colonel presently commanding the Household Cavalry Mounted Regiment at Knightsbridge.

Bill had been away at sea and I guessed he was equally stunned on hearing of her decision about Renville, but it seemed there was nothing to be done, as a point of no return had been passed – my mother had committed the capital and the place had been sold to someone else.

Time was needed to digest these developments properly, and I travelled alone on the final leg of the journey to London by train in very low spirits. Days after reaching my mother's flat in Cleveland Square, Colonel Denis Daly technically came for a social lunch, but in reality to talk through the various tests and exams ahead of me before I could attend an officer training course at somewhere called 'Mons'. It was clear my mother was most enthusiastic about the concept of my having a go at taking up a commission, as she felt it might keep me out of Ireland until the current bout of social turmoil where I would be farming in Ulster had settled down. Back in Istanbul all had been fine, with not much serious thought about the future, but during the journey home the reality began to dawn that I'd no real idea of how to counter the military proposal now put forward. The Jaipur experience had been a warning that I'd slipped wildly out of touch with my own generation over the year away and that there might be a lot of catching up to do.

Shortly after the colonel's visit Harold Harris, my mother's book editor at the time, came to lunch and suggested that Bill and I motor down to Newbury with him in a couple of days to visit Nicholas Elliott ('Lightbulb'), who, for some unexplained reason, he thought would be most interested to hear about my travels. We turned up for an exceedingly good lunch, with the old boys spending most of the meal reminiscing over the clandestine goings-on in wartime Cairo during the months leading up to the battle of El Alamein. The topics jumped about somewhat in a light-hearted fashion and were hard to follow, but I began to understand vaguely that during the war my mother had been involved in intelligence matters. To confirm a particular point under discussion, Elliott left the room and returned with a copy of Winston's history of the Second World War. He read out a passage that quoted a captured German general called Von Thoma as stating, 'Rommel was led astray by a duff map', which made everyone laugh.

Lunch was followed by a short walk in the garden alone with Elliott, and the usual questions were asked about what I was thinking of taking up as a career. He was fully aware of the Army idea my mother was pushing and advised that I would be bound to have an interesting time, as the travel experiences in America and Australia would be a great asset. He appeared unaware of my Maria-entangled months wandering in south-east Asia and I didn't enlighten him – I suspected my mother had edited that chapter of my adventures out of her mind. During the journey back to London I asked for clarification on some points I'd not understood at lunch, particularly the activities of 'Rebecca', who appeared to have been a player of some sort – was it the same 'Rebecca' that had been mentioned at Chartwell years before? This query was greeted with great amusement by Harris, who confirmed that it was. He explained that a copy of Daphne du Maurier's novel *Rebecca* had been discovered being used as a code book by a captured German listening post in the desert, with a corresponding marked copy coming to light in Cairo, where my mother had been involved, when a deception with devastating consequences for Rommel had been carried out.

Within days an envelope of army application papers arrived and Colonel Daly came round to give me another briefing. The deciding factor for acceptance to the officer training school at Mons rested on the outcome of a three-day period spent at the Regular Commissions Board (RCB) centre at Westbury. As soon as I established my identity with a birth certificate, a date for the test could be fixed. Surprisingly, it proved to be a very difficult document to unearth. As my passport was blue and British I naïvely went to Somerset House, only to be advised that because the document stated that I'd been born in Dublin I should search there. Furnishing the required details found in its pages to the correct department in Ireland drew a blank. Eventually my mother took over and in a week a certificate arrived for me, only with a shorter surname (omitting the 'Leslie' part) and the date of birth recorded as two months earlier than the details I'd been forwarding and had used in life so far. Perplexed, I wandered through to where she was working on a book manuscript and asked for an explanation. Without looking up she said, 'Oh darling, it's just that I couldn't decide who to marry at the time and it meant that you could have your birthday parties in the school holidays.' Totally stuck as to how to continue the conversation, I withdrew, quietly filled in the paperwork with the new details and posted it off to the MoD.

In some ways my mother and I were quite close, but there were frozen areas that were impossible to penetrate. She'd never told me she had once been married to a Tsarist Russian colonel for 11 years before marrying Bill, and I'd been left to find out aged 16 by reading about it in a newspaper. I'd been aware of the stress she suffered in having to cope with Bill's periodic post-war nightmares, suspecting that the strain had something to do with her own migraines and asthma attacks, but though she was physically frail I'd learned that mentally she was made of iron. On one rare occasion she had opened up about how the noise of her parents endlessly arguing at night had brought her childhood to a premature end, her knees knocking in fear as she listened on the stairs to the terrible shouting and screaming below. When her mother's health began to fail it became her role to look after her sickly younger brother Jack, but there were gaps in what she disclosed, and this was one of them – I'd come to learn that one just didn't ask.

It was now May 1970. In the year I'd been away many friends had moved, and re-entering the social life I had previously led in the capital just didn't happen. In early June an invitation for a coming-out ball arrived from a distant cousin in Suffolk and I was persuaded to go. The dance proved to be a sort of set-up in that my hostess, Lady Myra Fox, unknown to me, was fully aware of my army entry plans and had arranged for me to share a room with a chap who had recently been through the RCB exam. As the date had just come through for my own test session in two weeks' time my room-mate was able to talk me through what to expect by telling me what was being looked for by the interviewing colonels, sergeant-majors and NCOs. There would be a wildly mixed bunch of fellow candidates and a failure rate of about 65% was normal.

A tea-party at the Ritz was arranged to celebrate my newly discovered 21st birthday in June, just days before going to Westbury, and the nightmare of politely greeting a sea of strangers of 'approved stock' created a desire to pass the coming test come what may, so that the Army could be used as a route of escape. The three days of examination were bemusing rather than confusing. It was my first proper military-style 'incarceration', but Elliott's advice to draw on travel experience proved sound. Nervousness and apprehension didn't clog up the brain, allowing clarity of vision to watch out for the tips given. At a one-to-one interview with a splendid Colonel Fletcher the conversation turned early to pike fishing in Ireland and firmly remained there. I failed in the command task to get all my team and equipment over the series of obstacles in the time frame allotted, but it didn't seem to matter. The test could only have been on how one coped with impossibility. There was just one discordant note, when I was unexpectedly bounced into giving a ten-minute talk on adventure-walking. Colourful descriptions were given covering my time in Timor, Bali and crossing from Malaysia into Thailand. I was asked to repeat the bones of it to two officers I hadn't seen before, who didn't come across as particularly amused. One commented that there was nothing in my file about having recently been in south-east Asia, and somebody might want to 'have a little chat' in days to come. Other than that all went well, and I returned to London with the intention of looking up the one attractive girl with striking red hair I'd met at the Ritz party.

Time went by and a letter arrived announcing I'd passed the RCB test, followed by one from the Regimental Colonel of the Blues and Royals, Field Marshal Sir Gerald Templer, inviting me to tea at his house in Wilton Street. By coincidence he lived directly opposite where my new friend Virginia was lodging with her aunt, the Countess Birkenhead. In the two-week interim I'd visited a number of times in an old car which was a bad starter and prone to occasional oily outpourings in the street. Arrival for tea at the appointed hour coincided with a Harrods delivery van and a new colour TV. Lady Templer invited me into her drawing room to help move furniture while the Harrods men placed the still boxed receiver where it was wanted. They departed, explaining that they didn't do installations, just as the Field Marshal appeared. I recognised him instantly but couldn't immediately remember why. After a warm hand-shake and a friendly scowl he said, 'Now, your job is to get this thing going.' New shoes, a freshly tailored suit and a starched shirt proved not ideal to be wearing on a warm June evening while wrestling with a heavy object in a confined space, surrounded by fragile china ornaments. Catching a pause, as I wasn't sure how to address him but needed to know where I might find the aerial cable, he said, 'It's Colonel, but you're not in the Regiment yet. If you do make it through Mons I've got a job for you.' He then went on to explain that he had a family grave at Ardrahan in Co. Galway he wanted me to keep an eye on.

While we were talking, the penny dropped as to where I'd seen him before. He'd been the fedora hat-wearer talking to my mother when she'd let go of my pony's leading reins, back when I was seven. I asked if he had been in the west of Ireland in about 1956 and he confirmed he used to drive down from Ulster on gardening trips. My heart missed a beat when he mentioned Castle Taylor and I guessed what was coming. The grave in question was that of his uncle, a member of the Shaw-Taylor family, who had been murdered by the IRA in the early 1920s. Castle Taylor had subsequently been abandoned by the family, who had departed, leaving the walls of the old Norman keep to gradually disappear under a carpet of ivy and the surrounding stony parkland to revert to gorse or hazel thickets. It was a good fox covert but otherwise an exceedingly gloomy place. The unexpected conversation did wonders to put me at ease and keep me from making a muddle of the TV wiring task, and the great moment of switching on arrived. There were anxious moments while the valves warmed up, then some final tuning and we had a cricket match on the screen. Lady Templer

Oranmore Castle in Co Galway, 1990, with the bay I used to sail around alone in the background.

Castle Leslie in Co Monaghan. (Castle Leslie Archive)

A pause during Uncle Jack's funeral at Castle Leslie in April 2016.

My grandfather, Shane Leslie, in the 1920s. A keen
forester.

1950 at Castle Leslie. Aunt Agnes (Hungarian), Grandmother Marjorie Leslie, Denis
Daly, Uncle Jack, self on radiator, cousin Shaun, mother, uncle Desmond, unknown
lady and Bill, who owned the car.

Peter and me picnicing in Oranmore bay.

With my grandfather about 1956 after uncle Jack had made over Castle Leslie to my mother.

Wyndham Waithman, my dear friend who mentally armed me with the tools for survival in life.

The SS *Dun Aengus* steamboat
in which I learned to read.
Wartime career partly spent
servicing a secret flotilla
of weather ships based in
the Atlantic. (Tom Kenny
bookshop, Galway)

Oranmore Castle.
Sea storms had been
blasting its walls for
centuries. In post-war
austerity, the new roof
was made from road
tarmac as there was
nothing else available.

ABOVE: Wonderful Violina who introduced me to her magic rainforest world in American Samoa.

LEFT: Maria Bergen, my Swedish travelling companion from Singapore to New Delhi.

Nicholas Elliott ('Lightbulb') who turned out to be rather more then a good joke-teller.

Urte Appel. Had me fooled into thinking she was just a friendly lady until the scarf slipped.

Rattler, my lead hound, who ran the pack and never let me down-except once.

The Dhekelia Drag Hunt moving off.

Peter (front left) and the future General Desmond Fitzpatrick (top left) with Hari (on Peter's right) recruiting Palestinian Arab support during the war.

Dining with Lesley Foxton and her parents in Larnaca. Shell oil Intel proved an elusive goal but became close to Lesley.

and I made polite conversation over buttered toast while her little dog chewed the cuff on my sleeve, and then it was time to depart. I thought Colonel Gerald would remain lost to the cricket, but he saw me out and, after a reminder of the grave duty instruction, had scowled across the road at Lady Birkenhead's house, muttering, 'I hope it's the niece?'

Days later an unfamiliar voice on the phone summoned me to Lansdowne House in Berkeley Square with a request to bring my passport. I arrived at the advised time and was met by two grey-suited civil-servant types sporting security badges clipped to their ties. A slightly bigger one was attached to my lapel and I was invited to follow them to an interview room. My curiosity rose, as there seemed to be nothing military about the building we were in other than at the entrance, but the voice on the phone had indicated it related to something in my Army application. Thoughts emerged that it might be to do with the column labelled 'educational qualifications' on the form where I had written down all the O Levels I'd sat for, not ones I'd actually passed. Five 'O's were a fundamental requirement but I'd only managed to achieve three: Scripture, Economics and English Literature. Maths and English Language, the basics, had proved totally elusive and, in reality, not on offer. What was odd was that if it was actually an issue, why now and not much earlier?

The passport was handed over to one chap who promptly left the room. The other produced a notebook and, after asking if I would like a cup of tea, suggested I give a résumé of the Asian chapter of my travels, covering the period between Australia and India. For the next eight to ten minutes I gave a simple from-here-to-there outline, with occasional anecdotal descriptions of wanderings through Indonesia, Malaya, Thailand and the brief expedition into Cambodia, all the while moving a thumb around the tabletop to emphasise the geography being encountered and negotiated. The man stopped writing and I assumed he had deemed that what I was saying was irrelevant to what he was looking for. We sat in silence for a moment then he slowly closed his notebook, stood up, asked me to remain seated and went out. Considerable time passed before the two men returned, by which time I'd become somewhat bored. But they too seemed to be in a bad humour. I was asked to go back over the moment

I had met the Thai group at the zoo in Bangkok. Why did I think they had taken an interest in me? Why did they think of asking if I'd been to Moscow? What was I wearing at the time? Knowing Thailand was under a state of martial law, had it not occurred to me to check in with the British Embassy? Now everything I said was being noted. More questions. Anything anybody had said? What Americans had I met? What had they been doing? Where? It went on and on. Eventually lunchtime brought an end to the grilling. But it wasn't over. I was told I needed to come back the next day at 10 am when my passport would be returned, but some matters needed to be checked out first. I said I was sorry if I'd caused some sort of hoo-hah, but my mother's friend Mr Elliott – I described him as a retired civil servant type much like themselves – who had known her in the war in Cairo, had expressed the view that a bit of travel early on was a good idea before getting stuck into a career. Another stony silence, a bit more scribbling and then my escorts relieved me of my lapel label as they showed me out and, for the first time, one gave a faint smile as he repeated, 'Elliott, eh?' in the form of an unanswerable question.

On the walk home I really began to sweat about the passport. An official at the Petty France office had been very short and unhelpful when I'd phoned requesting advice on the procedure to have a date of birth corrected in a passport and so had not pursued the matter. What if these guys spotted the inaccuracy and confiscated the document? What if the lie about O Levels was unearthed? It was hard to see a way forward through the myriad complications.

The next morning the two were joined by a new face and things went much better. The passport was returned at the outset and this immediately raised my spirits. Feeling bullish, as the O Level matter also didn't appear to be on the agenda, I asked the newcomer if there was a particular concern, and this led to being asked for an opinion on the ideological forces fuelling the Vietnam conflict, something about which I knew practically nothing, other than what I had picked up in America that it was simply 'Communism' versus 'the West'. Sensing it important to keep control of the conversation as much as possible to avoid the lurking porkies surfacing, I used my reply to steer towards commenting on NATO and the Cold War, as about that I'd one view which could be expanded on with true feeling and confidence, TSR2. It worked and at last I was on firm ground. Pointing out the cancellation of the supersonic Tactical Strategic and Reconnaissance-capable fighter-bomber, the abilities of which had been dinned into me in great detail back in 1965 by a schoolfriend's father, still made no sense. During the autumn term of that year I'd been asked to stay with Mr and Mrs Burke as their son Nigel was a contemporary at Milton Abbey. Mr Burke was the chairman of Superflexit, the firm making the wiring for the aircraft, and the school exeat weekend had coincided with the announcement by the Prime Minister, Harold Wilson, that the project was to be closed down. Even as a schoolboy of 16 it had seemed to me an absolute tragedy to have scrapped such a fantastic weapon, particularly mad as the country had borne the development costs to the point where it had proved capable of breaking the sound barrier flying on only one of its two engines. A questioning pause triggered a nod to continue and I'd gone on to say that I understood it was an aircraft capable of being armed with a nuclear bomb and flying undetected below the Russian radar at twice the speed of sound, hence the '2' in the name. Though it seemed beyond possibility TSR2 had proved it could deliver all that was claimed and, in Peter Burke's view, expressed repeatedly in the strongest terms over the entire weekend, the project's cancellation smacked of Communist intrigues and Socialist rotten eggs at the very heart of the Whitehall establishment. He was convinced of it, as he had been in the thick of the fight to keep the project alive from conception through to cancellation. Otherwise, I said, having been away for a year I was rather out of touch on world affairs. I had yet even to return to my home in Ireland, but my family wanted to keep me out of the country until the disturbances in the North subsided. A long silence followed, ending when the newcomer stood up, smiled, shook hands and left. My ID badge was removed and, as a parting shot, advice was given to 'get fit'.

An Army medical was followed by lunch at Birdcage Walk beside Buckingham Palace and an interview with the Household Cavalry Silver Stick, a sort of colonel-in-charge. Conversation with Colonel Ian Baillie was slightly awkward at the start but turned totally in my favour when the subject of fox-hunting came up. On discovering I'd been galloping after hounds in the west of Ireland since childhood he opened right up, declaring he knew Lord Hemphill, the current Master of the Galway Blazers, and wanted a detailed description of stone-wall jumping, including size and number negotiated on an average day. Conversation eventually returned to talk of the next phase, which would be to attend the Officer Cadet course at Mons and what intake I would be joining.

A few days after lunch with the colonel (it transpired he had the nickname 'Toad') I motored down on my own to the training school at Aldershot on the appointed date, realising that a very new and potentially daunting chapter in life was about to start. The establishment turned out to be a collection of Second World War H-formation wooden barrack huts beside a large parade square. A reception clerk pointed out the cafeteria where the new 'Arnhem' intake was gathering. The group had grown to about 80, including about 15 Africans, when a summons came to go outside and form up in ranks – something I and a few others had obviously never done. Uniformed NCOs pushed us into position and when all was in order to their satisfaction a sergeant-major sporting a pace stick under his arm appeared. With a voice that filled every corner of the square, backed by a machine-gun-style delivery, Company Sergeant-Major Roger Thompson spent the next half-hour telling us he'd 'never seen such a ramshackle collection of sorry souls in his entire life but not to worry, in the coming weeks he and the PTI Sergeant-Major would be taking us apart mentally and physically, turning us from the shambles we were into leaders of men'. With that the parade 'dismissed'. The ex-school corps members and NCOs attempting to become officers knew what to do, the rest of us didn't, and so another shambles of shuffling bodies broke out. Assigned corporals descended like terriers, first barking instructions as to the correct procedure when receiving the dismiss order before escorting us to the barrack rooms where bed spaces in groups of four had been allocated. The minutiae of bed-roll preparation and folding were explained and then it was time to collect kit. The pace increased and by the time the evening meal arrived a sense of bewildered exhaustion had taken hold. Soon afterwards I made my bed and went to sleep. It proved to be a big mistake.

Dressing at dawn the next morning the nightmare continued, as we were all supposed to 'fall in' on the parade ground correctly dressed in our new army clothing. I had no idea of the right way to lace drill boots, assemble belt brasses, sort webbing, or deal with ankle puttees. Most had made preparations the night before under NCO instruction and my appearance on the square was simply that of a scarecrow with clothing and equipment hanging unclipped or untied, a source of amusement to my chums and the directing staff alike. Much screaming and yelling from the corporal while I was sorted out in the shelter of a barrack block and then it was off on a road run for a couple of miles. The new footwear immediately began to form blisters and the variation of fitness levels between us all became quite evident. The run was followed by the order for a racing change into drill kit and it was back on the square. The early afternoon gave a bit of respite: there was classroom work with lectures on signals and command structures before we fell into the clutches of Sergeant-Major Keating and his gymnasium kingdom for a dose of pull-ups, press-ups and rope climbing, all to the screamed dirge of what low life we were. Some telegraph poles were presented and introduced as our new best friends who liked to be taken for road runs, the longer the better. Then the energetic part of the first day was over and we went back to the barrack room to practise the art of polishing boots and metal when not nursing sore feet. The next day was a repeat schedule but with improved turnout rewarded by a drop in tolerance by the junior NCOs and roared warnings from CSM Thompson that life was going to be hell.

Wearing two pairs of socks proved a way of dealing with the blister problem, but the telegraph pole runs were a worry. It was all I could do to get myself through the present daily physical activities and I knew I just wasn't fit enough for anything more. On the third day I fell into a stream and had to keep going for hours in wet clothing, which resulted in a slight cough developing. By day 8 it was becoming serious, not helped by taking part in a two-mile run with one of the telegraph poles. It went better than expected as I'd teamed up with a wonderfully built guy from Ghana whom I had been able to help during the classroom periods, but my luck ran out shortly afterwards during the afternoon drill muster.

Everything suddenly appeared to go blank, followed by oblivion. As I regained consciousness, the face of the sergeant-major loomed into view. An ambulance took me to the Cambridge Military Hospital, Aldershot, and a wheelchair to an NCO ward. As an officer cadet it was my rank qualification.

The significance of a towelled bed did not become apparent immediately, but after a massive and extremely painful injection profuse sweating began. Every now and then the towels were changed but for the first few days I was not aware of much going on. Gradually the routine of doctors' rounds and Matron's inspections began to kick in. There were about 30 beds in the ward, with two bathrooms at the end. All my fellow patients were sergeants or corporals of varying seniority and age. It was basically a chest ward, but a couple were also being treated for head wounds from dealing with rioters in Northern Ireland. It was explained that I'd gone down with a pretty serious case of double pneumonia and it would take some weeks to make a full recovery.

This new incarceration was unexpected but, as I drew accustomed to the routines, life gathered a pace of its own and became not only entertaining but also deeply educational from a military point of view. It quickly became clear that all the nursing staff and doctors were in fear of the Matron, a tall handsome woman of about 30 with long fair hair and a northern accent. What she didn't know was that one of the sergeants with his head wrapped in bandages had witnessed her getting drunk in an NCOs' mess outside Belfast and performing a table-mounted striptease. He was wondering if she might recognise him when the bandages came off. This news created a wonderfully subversive 'atmosphere of expectation' and did much for general morale.

There were two tables in the centre of the ward. On one was a map of the world from the game *Risk*. On the other was a doctored map representing the Moon. The game was ongoing with the added aspect of earth-based super-powers being able to build up missile caches located on lunar bases. The days turned into weeks and a radio provided news coverage accompanied by endless analysis concerning the Jordanian Civil War and King Hussein's battles with Yasser Arafat's Black September PLO. I learned much from my fellow NCO patients on Britain's confrontation with Indonesia, the Malayan insurgency, ENOSIS in Cyprus, BAOR and NATO as well as the current Northern Ireland conflict. Eyes were opened as to how vital the role of the apparently humble corporal could be in the chain of command. Pearls of wisdom on pitfalls to be avoided as an officer were inadvertently dropped by the older chaps and absorbed so, by the time I was discharged, confidence in coping with the rigours of Mons was on a much better footing. After six weeks' absence it was decided I had missed too much of the current course and should join the next Salerno intake, starting in January. It was now early October. As an Army 'Direct Entrant' I was under MoD control, on a small rate of pay with nothing to do for three months other than go back to Ireland and get fit out fox-hunting. I returned home to find it was possible to hunt four days a week. My mother had three fit hunters, both packs of hounds in the county were going well and on days off time was taken to get properly fit running up and down the Clare hills.

Just before I left London Harold Harris had come to supper at the flat and grilled me on just how much I'd been following world affairs when in hospital. I'd given him a résumé of my fellow patients' take on the crisis in Jordan between the King and the PLO, Nasser's death in Egypt and the risk of Sadat, a suspected Soviet plant, being his successor. He and my mother had a short talk mentioning Yvonne Sursoc in Beirut, but I thought nothing of it at the time other than recalling that she was the mother of some boys I'd once tried to drown in the lake in Monaghan when they came to stay because they 'spoke funny'.

I returned to Aldershot in January 1971 physically prepared for joining the new Salerno intake, ready for what was to come. This time I paid attention to the corporal detailed to supervise turn-out and concentrated on making early friends with the stronger African cadets. Stevie Nyambe from Zambia and Johnny Johnson from Sierra Leone were in my barrack-room section and we formed a team from the word go. Johnny walked with a slightly rolling gait as he was muscle-bound, and struggled with English but proved excellent company on the pole runs. He sat closely beside me in the classroom and in return did my kit in the evenings.

This left me time to visit the NAAFI hut where tips on what was coming could be picked up from staff and better-informed fellow cadets. I would then return to the barrack hut and relay to my room-mates the gems of wisdom I'd learned. Johnny's skin was coal black, he wasn't very tall and his barrel-shaped torso gave him a bow-legged appearance, particularly when hanging from a door frame by one hand, which he liked to do as exercise. Mid-term in the course there was a three-day leave period and I invited him and Stevie to stay at my mother's flat, as they had nowhere to go, forgetting to warn my father I had guests staying when he arrived in transit from Ireland to go skiing. He'd risen in the early morning to go to the lavatory, only to be confronted by the sight of a naked Johnny hanging by one arm in the bathroom doorway. He froze. Johnny scratched an ear with his free hand, dropped to the floor and wandered back to my sister's room where I'd billeted him. I met Bill later in the kitchen with tears in his eyes as he whispered a description of what he'd observed in the dawn light.

The run-down to the Commissioning Parade began after a final exercise in the Brecon Beacons, all mainly in driving rain, with the final week spent on the drill square preparing for the great day. During the last rehearsal all was going well until Concorde flew over at tree-top level on a test flight. The sight of the long white unmarked fuselage and thundering engine exhausts at such a low altitude was as stunning as it was unexpected. The parade disintegrated totally, with all the African cadets running petrified for the shelter of nearby trees while the deafening sound drowned out cries for order and dressing.

The Commissioning Ball organised in a London hotel that night proved a bit of a disaster, as I unwittingly invited my red-headed girlfriend. The Africans fell on her flowing locks without hesitation as hounds would a fox, compelling us to leave early, she dizzy from a relay of tight embraces and me not ever having had an opportunity to venture on to the dance floor. Some leave followed to give time to get fitted out with various uniforms which would be needed on travelling to Germany to join the regiment, and having visited the various tailors at Windsor and London I returned to Galway for a few days.

It was April. As building works were going on at home I stayed nearby with dear Peter. He was thrilled that I was joining his old regiment, 'The Royals', which had amalgamated with 'The Blues' only a year before. He talked me through faded photograph albums mainly featuring him in various mounted cavalry contexts dating from the end of the Great War through to the end of the Second World War. On 18 April 1971 there was a census in the Republic of Ireland and I had to sign the form recording all who had resided in the house the night before. In doing so I noticed that his date of birth on the form was in 1897. He'd been commissioned in 1916, gone off to fight in France and had been wounded in the hand by a sabre cut during a night-time mounted skirmish with an enemy patrol. The Royals had been deployed to Ireland in 1920 to clear up the chaos created by the Black and Tan militia and then, after a period on the staff at Sandhurst where he ran the Aldershot Drag Hunt, he had been seconded to the Nizam of Hyderabad. The silver centrepiece on the dining-room table represented a mounted Royal Dragoon officer in the dress of the Trans-Jordan Frontier Force, which he was commanding when the Second World War broke out. Peter mentioned various people I might meet in times to come, as not all his old friends had fully retired, and in particular told me to make myself known to 'Spud' Lewis, who had served with him for many years from the Great War onwards.

There was just time to visit my grandfather, who was in poor health in Brighton, and while I was there I was advised by Iris, his wife, to look out for a Desmond Langley who, she said, had suffered terribly from wind as a baby. It was clear Shane was dying and it was likely to be our last encounter, so the time spent holding his hand was savoured while listening to ramblings about the forest at Glaslough and adventures he had had with his beloved brother Norman. The latter had been killed in 1914, but on my arrival in neat officer-style attire the old boy had momentarily mistaken me for him.

Along with two other new officers I joined the regiment at an old Luftwaffe complex of buildings located at Detmold in the Harz mountains of West Germany. Lothian Barracks had somehow survived the war and now overlooked an expansive concrete tank park. An acting adjutant greeted us and, having explained that our arrival had fallen between the disciplinary reigns of 'Plank' and 'The Twitch', went on to warn that the regiment was in a state of considerable flux – after the coming weeks of annual firing and tactical exercises on the Hohne, Soltau and Lüneburg training areas, the Chieftain battle tanks were to be handed over to the Lifeguards. Some senior LG officers had already arrived to gain experience of the role of heavy armour in supporting NATO forces along the nearby stretch of border with East Germany. Our first appearance in the officers' mess was a daunting experience for the three of us when Colonel Eyre, who had recently taken over command, entered the anteroom before lunch and all of the assembled 30-plus officers sprang to their feet and clicked heels in unison. Greeting me, he asked if I had a specific connection with the Blues and Royals and I said I had a friend, Thomas Messel, whom I was looking forward to meeting up with. A stunning silence descended temporarily, with the atmosphere turning ice-cold. The colonel suggested I visited his office without delay and walked on into the dining room, followed by the officers in rough order of rank, with much giggling and tittering breaking out. One put a hand on my shoulder and muttered 'Not a name to drop, dear boy'. Over lunch I listened as a tale was re-told further up the table of Thomas colliding with a railway bridge in a speeding Chieftain, the second of his troop of three tanks shedding its tracks trying to turn while straddling the railway line, followed by the last making it over the embankment, only to sink in a giant slurry lagoon on the other side – and all in a matter of minutes. The tale triggered laughter everywhere but left me feeling somewhat uncomfortable. Later, Colonel Jim explained that my file had been sent to Windsor for some reason, which was why he knew nothing about me and had not even been forewarned of my arrival.

A major called 'Boot' descended and instructed that I would be a jump judge at the Rhine Army Horse Show being held over the coming weekend, but before that I should get busy familiarising myself with the tank park as I would be taking command of three machines on an exercise the following Monday. It was quite difficult working out who everyone was really called, as a blizzard of names like 'Sleepy', 'Plank', 'Dim Bulb',

'Enoob', 'Dozy', 'Fluffy', 'Betty', 'Sunshine', 'Toad', 'Smiling Death', 'Black September', 'Hook', 'Jumbo', 'Coops', 'Spud', 'Dodo' and 'Boomer' floated about continually in conversation at the top and middle sections of the long table, depending on who was absent. Keeping as low a profile as possible seemed vital while waiting for the arrival of 'The Twitch', who threatened a rough ride while establishing himself as the regimental disciplinarian.

Most of the next two days were spent hiding in the tank park, exploring the internal workings of the three 62-ton monsters I'd be responsible for in a few days' time. The news that I would be doing so had come without warning, but it wasn't a joke, and to compound the difficulties it appeared to be bad form to talk shop in the mess. On enquiring about relevant reading material I was handed a copy of *Flashman at the Charge* by George MacDonald Fraser, with the advice being to just take a cue from the book character when the time came. Though fiction, the 19th-century tale of outrageous military behaviour was a welcome distraction while trying to keep out of sight.

Tips given during my hospital incarceration only months before proved invaluable and I quietly got to work with a Corporal Morris, beginning with how to recognise the front and rear of a tank internally, the fundamentals of radio equipment procedures and the synchronisation of gunnery commands, which were complex because of the differing types of ammunition. The main 120 mm armament was a vast naval gun loading a variety of high-explosive projectiles powered by 2-ft-long bags of cordite charges. Along with a commander, each tank crew had a gunner and a loader as well as a driver, and I would have responsibility for three machines, so there was a great deal to learn about who was responsible for what, and all in three days. The key was going to be getting the crews on my side for when inevitable mistakes were made and, with much humour, the troop members talked me through what to do – at least, what they would be doing. The learning curve was extremely steep, but I felt if I kept my nerve things would work out. By Friday night the coming weeks didn't look quite so terrifying, as relations had got off to a good start with the crews. The following Monday and a general move to the firing ranges was another matter, to be worried about later.

Saturday morning arrived and it was time for the Rhine Army Horse Show. My designated jump was eventually located, and I settled down for the day. The temperature rose and a thirst developed but I'd brought nothing. Then out of nowhere appeared a lady who sat down with a basket of sandwiches and a cool bottle of Moselle, which she offered. She was German, handsome, friendly and spoke English. We talked mainly about modern-day German music, and she offered to lend me a record if a friend didn't show up and if I could give her a lift back to Hamelin. Whoever it was didn't appear, and at the end of the day we set off in an old car I'd purchased. During the drive 'Urte Appel' told me about the 'Mojos' who carted the NATO tanks up and down the border, so there was always a concentration opposing the Warsaw Pact forces posturing on the other side. She thought it ridiculous because another band of Mojos, related to those in the West, handled the armoured transportation for the Eastern forces and all the drivers knew where everyone else was at any given point in time. 'Mojos' was the name she used for the stateless people left homeless in central Europe at the end of the war who had found semi-military roles to play when the Cold War stand-off erupted. She assured me they would appear in their blue uniforms, black field boots, breeches and funny cornered hats whenever tanks had to be transported. Another bottle of Moselle was half consumed in her apartment when she reached over to pull down a window blind against the setting sun. It was then that I saw it: an Adam's apple. It hadn't taken long to spot and get a feel for the transvestites of Sam Leong Road in Singapore, but this one was good and I'd genuinely been fooled for some hours. Fortunately things hadn't developed too far and it was still easy to escape without drama. The worry was being in a block of flats and maybe inside a giant nest of goodness knows what. Pleading a sudden massive migraine, I fled down the stairs to the car, which fortunately started. While attempting to sneak back into the mess I was caught and enlightened that 'Fräulein Appel' was a well-known security risk. I should expect an avalanche of mail which had to be handed in on receipt. So it proved.

On Monday morning the Mojos arrived at dawn. A command structure of whip-carrying officers dressed as Appel had described fanned out across the tank park. The regiment's war machines were lined up in rows and deftly loaded on to their transporters which, on a signal from the top chap in a slightly different-shaped hat, standing on a podium of his own, roared off in groups of four. The dance-like exercise of marshalling the transports in front of their parked charges and having the weighty iron monsters clamber on to their chariots at the wave of a whip was mesmerising. The cycle of roar, silence, clatter, clatter, clatter, silence, roar and honk was repeated until all that was left were exhaust fumes hanging in the air and marks on the concrete pan where 30 battle tanks had sat parked up only two hours before.

Luck gave me a senior NCO who was the squadron's gunnery instructor on top of being a thoroughly nice person. He made a point of getting me up to speed with the complexity of the orders expected of a tank commander by his gunner, loader and driver when on the move: spotting targets, calculating ranges, deciding what type of projectile to fire while the unfamiliar interior of the machine swivelled independently from the turret and the 8-ton breech danced up and down inches from a knee. I quickly discovered that sometimes the driver was not always below in front but might be on the left or on the right, so the instruction to move 'forward' might have unexpected results. Thanks to a huge gyroscope buried somewhere in the bowels of the vehicle's chassis, the gun could be kept trained on a target, enabling repeat firing as the tank manoeuvred across undulating ground. Heavy though it was, I learned to brace against the cupola ring when giving the order to fire as the whole vehicle jumped and rocked violently when the main armament discharged and tons of steel hammered back against the recoil.

'Annual Firing' over, it was time to move on to the Soltau plain and regimental role-play in a large NATO exercise in full swing. Lifeguards arrived and a Major Simon Cooper was embedded in my troop. Over the days on exercise I'd come to the conclusion that my tank driver Trooper 'Chico' Evans was very bright and good at explaining how things worked – or should work. This included picking suitable observation points, techniques for helping keep a tank hidden, plus cooking in the field, and so I left him to bring Simon up to speed.

The Soltau training area was a large plain of low sandy hills, scrub, forest and the occasional bog. The combination of dust, noise and a fast-moving exercise involving a number of armoured regiments was bewildering at times but, thanks to an excellent squadron leader, never too much to handle. Eventually the exercise came to an end, the Mojos returned, took our machines home and everyone set off for a jolly in Hamburg's red-light district. The Reeperbahn not being particularly to my liking, and as I didn't yet feel properly bonded to my fellow officers for such an expedition, but, wanting to spend some time with a kindred spirit, I motored up to Travemünde on the Baltic coast, hoping that Maria, my friend from a now former life, might catch the ferry across from Gothenburg in Sweden. We had corresponded after parting in Delhi and I suddenly felt in need of company. Sadly, she couldn't get away at short notice, and I ended up joining a bunch of drunken students around a beach-party bonfire.

Over the next two weeks the chaos of two armoured regiments swapping places reigned supreme. Most of the officers I'd known for only a short time left for new postings almost immediately the exercise was over, with only a skeleton staff remaining to pack up the mess contents. Two wooden crates had apparently been incorrectly labelled and I didn't think twice about obeying an instruction to adjust the stencilled posting addresses to 'BFPO 53', as it meant nothing to me. After the silver had been taken away a large cup came to light, and I offered to deliver it to Windsor by car while motoring to my new employment at the Royal Armoured Corps centre at Bovington for a troop leader's course. The next day, just as I was about to set off, a major I didn't know well sent for me and told me my grandfather had died, and I was being given two weeks' compassionate leave. He went on to say I should use the time to put my affairs in order, as there had been a change of plan and I was not going on the troop leader's course but coming with him to Cyprus for two years instead. This double whammy came completely without warning, and was quite hard to take in for a moment. My grandfather's death was an acceptable blow as I had expected it, but the concept of relocating for an extended period to an island at the eastern end of the Mediterranean, having hardly been home, was something else. I'd only just begun to find my feet socially after the year out jaunting round the world, and would now be away again for even longer. When I asked why the troop leader's course was being skipped, my apparent new boss replied that he understood I was a capable horseman and that would be my new posting's main requirement.

Motoring direct to the west of Ireland before Shane's funeral in Ulster provided the chance for a few days with old Peter. He was most amused to see the silver Waterloo Cup, which had remained in the boot of my car and now sat on his dining-room table for a few days, as in the past he'd won it three times. Then it was time to head north and join the funeral party in Co. Monaghan.

Shane had been born an Ulster Protestant and had converted to Roman Catholicism in his youth, so his wake was a somewhat confusing affair involving a real mix-up of orange sashes and saffron kilts viewed through clouds of frankincense thick enough to make the eyes water. For two days he lay in the drawing room in an open coffin, dressed in his Gaelic Chieftain finery, with countryfolk and gentry alike filing solemnly past before the final service and burial.

9
Germany, Cyprus and Beirut

On returning to England I handed over the cup, which nobody had missed, and stepped into a military aircraft bound for Cyprus. By now it was June 1971. The day's journey finally ended on reaching RAF Pergamos, located a couple of miles from the southern shore of the island, which was destined to be home for the next two years. Knowing next to nothing about the island apart from what had been gleaned from a book on the Crusades thrust at me just before I left home, there appeared to be a lot to read up on. Within a couple of days a rough understanding of the two Sovereign Base Areas 50 miles apart had been grasped, one an aerodrome for massive Vulcan bombers at Akrotiri, the other an enormous hospital at Dhekelia, which it was the squadron's role to guard. The vintage Saladin and Ferret vehicles of which we took command dated from the 1950s and were riddled with metal fatigue, as they had been rumbling continually over the back roads of the island for two decades. The Saladin's 4-inch gun was effective and easy to use, enabling a good loader to have three shells in the air before the first landed on a target. The only trouble was that one of the six huge wheel stub-axles tended to part company from the suspension wishbone assemblies without warning, causing the 7-ton vehicle to suffer total steering and brake failure. A number of buildings in the Greek villages dotted about the Goshi-Troulli training area as well as in the Sovereign Base had been flattened before a method of detecting spider cracks in vital points was devised. The big bonus was the access to unlimited supplies of duty-free drink, which was to prove an asset of considerable significance over time. The two wooden crates I'd been instructed to re-label back in Detmold came to light. Lots of paper-shuffling ensued as 36 cases of Dom Perignon came to light and then quickly disappeared from view into the mess storeroom.

Soon after arriving I was summoned to appear in front of the Dhekelia base commander, Brigadier Bob Windsor-Clive, who explained that one of my responsibilities would be to take on the role of hunting a pack of drag-hounds kennelled beside the Saddle Club stable block. Having shown me the polo field, kennels and views of the Mediterranean in various directions, he stated quietly that we would now be going to meet the real boss of the base, Colonel Olliviere, who commanded the hospital. I instantly took to the middle-aged red-haired Irishman, who invited me to come to his house for tea later that day. There I met his wife, who asked me to come out on hound exercise the next morning at 5 am. She would organise everything and assured me the orange blossom was not to be missed. As I came to take my leave the colonel requested that I come and see him in his office in a few weeks after I had settled in. Returning to the mess I found that everyone had come to the general conclusion that, with a 7 am start, the daily operational duties could be completed by 1 pm, leaving the remainder of the day free for us to head for the beaches. The process of renting an apartment in Kyrenia, a town an hour's drive north across the island on the coast facing Turkey, was also under way, so there would be somewhere thoroughly 'off base' to retreat to.

The next morning the 5 am date was kept with the colonel's wife at the Saddle Club, where I met the hounds, a soon-to-depart huntsman and a one-eyed polo pony known as Bobby-Fritz. The morning's ride revealed an almost biblical scene of ox-powered wooden waterwheels and fallen Roman-era pillars lying among olive and orange groves, complemented by a backdrop of arid rocky hills or twinkling seascape – the breathtaking views were so unexpected it was impossible not to linger, and I only just made it back to the vehicle park in time for morning parade. Quite a pleasant routine developed over the coming days, learning the names of hounds, horses and places to go on pre-dawn exercise before racing back for squadron duties.

The first weekend arrived with news that we had access to an apartment in Kyrenia for a year. Knowing nothing more than that it was a Greek enclave in the northern Turkish sector, we motored off to find out what the town was like and have a look around. The journey proved slightly complicated in that first a route had to be negotiated around the divided outskirts of Nicosia, the Turkish zone entered through a military checkpoint, on the United Nations 'concession road' used to climb up over the Buffavento pass and exiting into the once Venetian but now Greek port. As British officers we were not restricted to using the twice-daily UN-escorted convoys as long as we were in uniform. On arrival all were automatically invited to sign in as members of the Harbour Club, a restaurant with a commanding position overlooking the waterfront from which sundowners could be sipped on a terrace. Numerous beaches stretched out in either direction along the coast, imaginatively named 'three-mile', 'five-mile', 'six-mile', while a line of ruined Crusader castles decorated the mountain peaks behind that made up the spiny backbone of the island's panhandle.

Through the Harbour Club watering-hole we soon came into contact with local ex-pats, including an English couple busy raising and restoring an ancient Greek ship that had sunk just outside the harbour entrance around 100 BC. Above the town and tucked below the cliffs of Buffavento mountain, sporting a superb Crusader castle on its peak, lay the small Greek village of Bellapais, completely unspoilt and untouched by time. One could sit for hours drinking coffee under the orange and lemon trees of its little square while watching golden eagles soaring high above. A number of houses were already let as holiday apartments and, as summer approached, others filled up with shed-loads of jolly girls looking for fun in the sun. By the second weekend I'd acquired the makings of a water-ski boat with mooring space on the harbour front, not realising it was going to make me very popular.

We were all soon organised, as Kyrenia was the hub when it came to recreation. Troops manning the Turkish roadblocks began to recognise our cars on sight and waved us through, so reducing the average travelling time to and from Pergamos to around an hour. In general life looked good for the two-year stint that lay ahead – until a message came to report to Colonel Olliviere. I presented myself at his office and he asked his assistant to leave us alone, inviting me to sit by a window while he explained 'a delicate matter'. There was no warning of what was coming, but after a short preamble about family and his surprisingly detailed understanding of my mother's wartime exploits in the Middle East, he revealed that

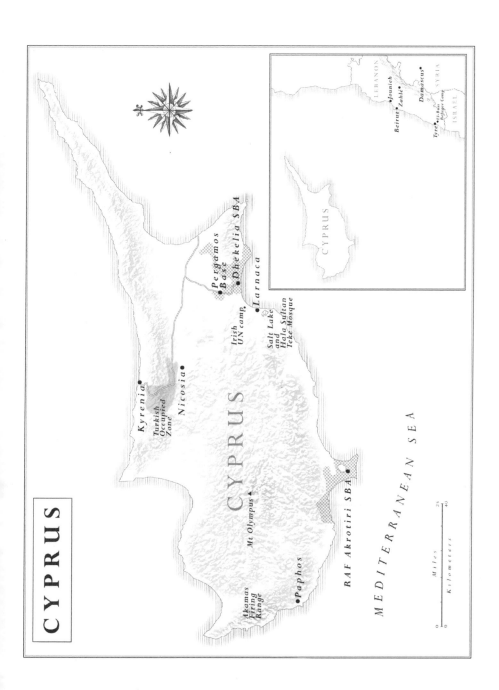

CYPRUS

MEDITERRANEAN SEA

Paphos

Akamas
Firing
Range

Mt Olympus

CYPRUS

RAF Akrotiri SBA

Kyrenia

Turkish
Occupied
Zone

Nicosia

Irish
UN camp

Salt Lake
and
Hala Sultan
Teke Mosque

Larnaca

Pergamos
Base

Dhekelia SBA

Miles   25

Kilometers   40

0
0

LEBANON

Jounieh

Beirut   Zahlé

Damascus

SYRIA

Tyre   El-Buss
       Refugee Camp

ISRAEL

CYPRUS

there was something extra I was going to have to fit into my life. I was to pick a convenient moment to visit my mother's friend in Beirut, Lady Cochrane ('Yvonne Sursoc', whom Harold Harris had been talking about in London), and make my way to the city's Mayflower Hotel. He gave me a contact name at the Ledra Palace Hotel in Nicosia who would provide flight tickets etc. All I had to do was use the leave period to be myself, my mother's son, and listen carefully to what Lady Cochrane and the people she introduced me to had to say concerning the new Syrian regime and Israel. Basically, all that was wanted was help in gaining clarity on the intentions of the Assad cabal that had recently seized power in Damascus with Moscow's backing. Anything of interest should be carefully recorded and notes handed over on return to Nicosia. The explanation for absences could be portrayed as to do with having a liaison role with the Lebanese Army over mountain training. There was no pressure other than keeping everything he had said totally confidential, and it was up to me to pick my travel dates, which should be sooner rather than later. Finally he said I should find an opportunity to go down to Akrotiri. It was important I familiarise myself with the airbase socially – 'I might find being able to refer to it useful as a conversation topic.' The words were said in a way that hinted there might be more to come. The meeting terminated with a repeated warning about confidentiality and, with military formality returning, I saluted and left.

As I reached my car, a few moments were spent assimilating what I'd just heard the colonel say before driving over to the kennels and sitting for a while with the hounds. The feeling was that a new turn of some sort in my life path had appeared and needed to be negotiated with care. I had been trained to be a soldier with responsibility for the welfare of men, but was now being asked to play a secondary, rather strange role for I did not quite know whom, though a finger of suspicion pointed at the joke-teller Elliott in London. Back at the base Brian, my boss, on being given an outline summary of the meeting, appeared amused by my predicament and, as we tucked into a bottle of Dom Perignon, advised me to keep the colonel's wife tactfully but firmly at arm's length. The matter of occasional absences was no problem as militarily there was nothing of a taxing nature to do, the twice-daily patrol of the Sovereign Base Area surrounding Dhekelia Military Hospital being the routine role for the squadron and its elderly armoured cars.

Army exercises in the moonscape of the Goshi-Troulli training area had to be kept to a minimum because of the age of the vehicles, with the only real excitement being when firing the Saladin 4-inch guns on the Akamas peninsula. Once out on the ranges there was very little time between the placing of old military lorries and Land Rovers to be used as targets and firing at them before Greek daredevils emerged from behind rocks, determined to tow the mechanical carcases away for salvage before they were hit. Luck blessed me with an extremely efficient corporal-of-horse who kept all in order so there was free time to run the kennels and start to plan for Beirut.

An invitation arrived to take the Saddle Club polo ponies down to Akrotiri for a match, including bringing the hounds to amuse the Pony Club with a special meet. Mounted police patrols checked the perimeter fence surrounding the runway, while a second, much more secure compound was guarded in a very different fashion by unseen Americans behind much wire, gravel ditches and lights of various kinds. It was code-named 'The New World' and I gathered it was where the nuclear missiles carried by the Vulcan bombers were stored. A senior bomber pilot told me the patrols over northern Turkey lasted 16 hours or so and were exceedingly boring, with the five-man crew having to sit in cramped conditions while flying their armed aircraft back and forth along the Black Sea coast, escorted by Lightning fighters. (Rumour had it there was room for only four parachutes.) The 200-metre-wide band of low scrub between the wire keeping wildlife off the runway and the main security fence was a perfectly contained area for hound exercise, while providing an excellent viewpoint as the laden monsters heaved into the air.

One early dawn I timed things so as to have a really close-up view. Crackling thunder announced an imminent take-off and it was just possible to pick out the oscillating tip of an aircraft nose cone as it emerged from a dark cloud of exhaust at the far end of the runway. The movement before lift-off was reminiscent of the times in India as steam locomotives thundered by and the four unsilenced jet engines under full throttle passed close overhead – the noise was enough to make the chest cavity vibrate. The reaction of the hounds was odd, with some lying down while others bolted – much as the Africans had done when Concorde appeared at tree-top height.

The big moment for the Saddle Club drag hunt arrived. The line-layer galloped off, only to get lost in the Bishop of Akrotiri's vineyard, near the air-base sewage works. Things went wildly wrong when the hounds bolted after a hare that ran round one of the settlement ponds before heading back towards the wood behind the stables. Inevitably the pack took a short cut, cooling off with a dip on the way, but all would have been well if a long row of tables had not been set out ready for a post-hunt pony club breakfast. By the time I arrived and regained control the disaster was complete, with sewage-coated hounds scoffing the last of whatever had been set out in bowls and trays. Fire hoses were deployed as an immediate remedy, which fortunately provided a certain entertainment for the children, and a second, more controlled 'chase' was rescheduled for the evening.

Back in Dhekelia, life settled into a steady routine of early mornings spent on hound exercise, the occasional drag hunt or polo match, armoured car patrols with the occasional mini-exercise in the training area, afternoons and evenings being spent in Kyrenia.

As September advanced and beach life slowed, I began to think about venturing over to Beirut as instructed. The Ledra Palace contact produced plane tickets and, having made myself known to Lady Cochrane in advance, I flew over, the journey taking 20 minutes but going through a one-hour time zone, so temporarily life went backwards. The Palace Sursoc was a magnificent four-floor building of white marble located in the old part of the city, with a commanding view over the harbour. Lady Cochrane, Yvonne, appeared well briefed on my mission, and wasted no time in giving me an earful from her Falangist Christian point of view about what was going on between Jordan, Egypt and Syria, repeating the colonel's view that Moscow was a new puppet-master pulling strings from behind the Middle Eastern stage. Her son Roderic and I began to slip out at night to restaurants when he was supposed to be swotting for

A Levels, and through him I was introduced to the best places to eat.

I'd no idea at first just how highly respected and influential the Sursoc family was in the city, but it soon became apparent. Yvonne took me to numerous receptions, introducing many old associates from my mother's wartime days when she was editor of Beirut's *The Eastern Times*. This led to a number of sticky-cake tea parties with elderly ladies, but it soon became clear that Syria was a dark and ever-present shadow nobody really wanted to talk about. Though the new Assad regime had been in place for less than a year there had been much ruthless internal consolidating of its grip on power in favour of one particular minority Islamic sect, and this was causing an increasing sense of discomfort among the Christian community that made up the bulk of Lebanon's political structure. I became a known face – on return visits to the restaurants without Roderic or with new friends the proprietors continued to give me a warm welcome, uncannily providing good tables and champagne often 'on the house'. An old turquoise Alfa Romeo was stored in the palace basement and the temptation to get it out was hard to resist. However, time was limited, Roderic had an elder brother I didn't want to cross and a line had to be drawn.

The Mayflower Hotel reception had a note for me with a number to ring. I called and introduced myself to a female voice that gave an instruction to wait in the foyer. About 30 minutes later a dark-haired, very white-skinned girl appeared and introduced herself as Mandi Stieger, an associate of the Nicosia ticket supplier. She explained that she worked at the casino along the coast at Jounieh and invited me to come up, as the floor show was worth watching. It became clear quite soon that she, too, already knew a lot about me and, after a few pertinent questions, went silent. Then, with a slow exhalation of breath and adopting a different manner entirely, she said, 'You don't have a fucking clue, do you?' I was now even more in the dark and just sat lamely staring at her. After a long, rather embarrassing silence she suggested we went for a walk. While strolling along the waterfront Mandi explained that Beirut was presently filling up with new Russian faces unknown to London. MI6 had been blinded by the treachery of their man Kim Philby some years before, with all established intelligence agents compromised, and though replacements were arriving the process to 'bed in' took time. My British-Army-officer-on-leave credentials and additional social association with the Sursoc family were perfect for attracting Russian attention and drawing operatives out for identification – it was a dream come true for the intelligence fraternity. All I had to do was just be myself – she was almost echoing the colonel's words. If I was picked up in a restaurant or nightclub by anyone describing themselves as a salesman or being particularly pushy, I should suggest going to the casino. She would take things from there. Laughing, she said they would most probably say they were from Bulgaria and sold tractors – no imagination, but I should be wary, as they would be skilled at steering conversations. The next night I went up to Jounieh for the floor show and was in for quite a surprise. After a scene when four grey horses slowly pulled a chariot across the stage, galloping on a moving belt, the curtain fell and spotlights illuminated two cages descending from the ceiling. Each contained a gold-body-stocking-clad female gymnast swinging on gimbals. With a shock I realised one was Mandi. Her act was followed by two baby elephants running down the aisle and up on to the stage, which revealed a jungle scene as the curtain rose. I left, sadly, before the performance was over, as I had an early flight back to Nicosia the next day.

I returned to Pergamos to great news. The cases of Dom Perignon had been written off as lost, and all we had to do was to drink the stuff. A mess rate of £2 a bottle was fixed and we started to have it for breakfast. A fellow officer introduced me to a Cypriot girl he had become fond of, and at her house in Nicosia I met Marion Slonim, a middle-aged rather formidable matron who not only oozed authority but turned out to be a master in the art of double-speak when in company. On giving me an address she asked that I made a point of making contact in the near future, the invite being given more as a polite instruction than an invitation, as she also let slip she knew the man who'd handled my trip to Beirut.

Back at the Dhekelia Saddle Club other developments began to unfold as the New Year advanced. Another brother officer had become friendly with the English nanny-cum-mistress of a local Greek tycoon who kept a large yacht in the marina at Larnaca. Through the duty-free booze supplies 'Miss McD' kept its bar healthily stocked, the deal being that we could party on board as the yacht owner, 'Dimi', was also amused by taking part in the occasional polo match and drag hunt.

News of our visits to Larnaca marina reached Colonel Olliviere and I was summoned. Braced for a dressing down, I was surprised by a friendly reception and instructed to try and get to know the Shell Oil refinery manager who lived in the town. Mr Foxton was of interest as he had access to the company's entire Middle East intelligence. On being advised that he had an undergraduate daughter the task took on a different hue and over the Christmas period I met Lesley, who turned out to be extremely attractive, bright and studying at Nottingham University.

Journeys became frequent along the road to Larnaca town, about four miles from the Pergamos base, and led past Wolf Tone camp, where the Irish United Nations contingent was located on the outskirts. Wonderful ancient Panhard armoured cars with huge tortoise-shaped body shells mounted on small wheel suspension units could be seen when passing the gate. A lucky break provided a way of bringing my troop of soldiers to have a good look when I met Michael Goode, a lieutenant in the Irish Army, while he was enjoying a weekend's leave in Kyrenia. An arrangement was made whereby I was to bring a Saladin and Ferret armoured car for his boys to crawl over on a Sunday afternoon while my chaps explored the inner workings of the Panhards. To give the event some structure, a friendly football match was held. The day went well and, the Saladin having departed with its Ferret escort, Michael and I retired to his mess bar for a drink. We'd hardly sat down before his commanding officer entered and with a roar demanded I leave the base immediately, shouting, 'You're in the wrong bloody Army.' It was around 6 pm and the news of paratroopers opening fire on a crowd in Derry had just come through. Nipping back to Pergamos I found Brian listening to a radio and making a grim thumbs-down sign as I entered the room. It was 30 January 1972 and over the following days the media christened it 'Bloody Sunday'. We looked at each other but didn't speak, as there wasn't anything to say. Like me, he had an Anglo-Irish background and we both knew there would be major consequences to the appalling news if it was being accurately reported. On hearing that paratroopers really had been involved, we both flinched in despair, as we knew they were the last troops that should have been deployed. A massive mistake had been made somewhere that would be incredibly hard to rectify. The one comfort was being able to share the shock with a senior officer so that it didn't become a weight as the world media exploded in outrage.

A request arrived from Lady Cochrane asking me to a function in Beirut and plans were set in motion for a second visit, with Marion Slonim organising the travel arrangements. At the Sursoc residence an elderly Jordanian called Hari introduced himself and invited me to his house at Zahleh, located on the other side of the mountains in the Bekaa valley, as he had served in the Trans-Jordan Frontier Force under Peter back in the 1940s and wished to entertain me. In his beautiful sloping walled garden with mountains as a backdrop I was shown a photograph featuring him standing with a bunch of armed Arabs, Peter, and another British officer sporting a solar topee and a pipe, whom he called 'Fitzpatrick'. Hari arranged for a visit to Baalbek the next day, insisting it was an opportunity not to be missed, and while exploring the Greco-Roman ruins and the great temple of Jupiter a couple of men in unfamiliar green uniform made a point of engaging me in friendly conversation. We mooched around the largely deserted ruins, climbing on some of the larger fallen capitals for photographs, and I was invited to visit Damascus, as they turned out to be Syrian army officers keen to show me round their country's capital. A ticket for the border checkpoint printed in Arab lettering and scribbled on by one was given, plus an address to make for.

It sounded like fun and fairly innocent, so I returned to Zahleh to explain to Hari I'd met some army chaps, so would be gone for a couple of days. Next morning, I caught a bus to Damascus. The border crossing was no problem, thanks to the pass, and I met up with the Syrians within hours of reaching the city. They organised a place for me to stay and had a car. To keep track of time I'd taken my Pergamos wall calendar with me to Beirut and, unpacking, stuck it on a convenient nail on the wall. It happened to feature the famous shot of Raquel Welch dressed in animal skins in *One Million Years BC*. As I returned from my first venture out it was gone. That evening the image of a Western woman was on the front page of the street newspapers. Her face seemed familiar and I bought a copy with the help of my minders, who became very interested in why I wanted it. Closer inspection revealed that it was a photo of Bernadette Devlin, an emerging Irish Civil Rights leader, heading a demonstration. The surrounding Arab print was meaningless but the event was obviously important to record, so I tore out the page and stuck it on the nail where the image of Raquel Welch had featured only a few hours earlier.

This action caused my hosts to ask for a résumé of what I knew was going on in Ireland. A sketchy explanation of what I thought the article related to was given – though I had no idea what the Arabic script said. We had an early night and, my room being close by the Mosaic Mosque, the next day started with a deafening wail of the muezzin being broadcast from close quarters. Visits to impressive temples were punctuated by stops for sweet mint tea, when questions as to what I actually did in the British Army were gently fielded. Conversation increasingly turned to Ireland and my view on issues underpinning the current state of unrest, with the atmosphere around the two men tensing as we entered the inner courtyard garden of an old building. The centrepiece was an ornate fountain beside which a shiny-faced gentleman in civilian clothes sat cross-legged on a cushion. He did not rise but indicated to me to sit, with the jolly minder acting as interpreter. There was a little small talk before I was asked why was I not in Ireland fighting the British, as he understood I came from a politically motivated family that had been instrumental in igniting the conflict.

The question came as a shock, and I realised with alarm that lots of little snippets I'd given over the previous day concerning my grandfather's involvement in the resurgence of Irish nationalism had been grossly misunderstood. Shane's American activities back in the time of the 1916 Easter Rising, friendship with Michael Collins and the 1920 Irish War of Independence had been rolled up into an assumption that I was like-minded concerning the current state of unrest, but the Syrians were much too far down the line now to be told that there was a gap of decades separating the two periods of civil strife. It was very clear that to have tried to correct the massive misunderstanding would have caused loss of face and, judging from the heavily sweating state of the silent fellow standing behind my interviewer, people round this man on the cushion were probably shot for less. The way forward appeared to be to express a view that eventual UN intervention would be a likely development. There was no reaction to my comparing the Ulster conflict with what was going on between Palestine and Israel, with interest remaining fixed on knowing more about what was stimulating the Irish strife.

Becoming uncomfortable at the way the conversation was heading and wishing to terminate the interview, I pre-empted what I felt was coming by stating, without going into details, that I was involved in a matter that would be deployed in the fullness of time. Though a work of total fiction it did the trick, smiles breaking out all round immediately that particular bit of the translation had run its course. Some juicy dates and tea were consumed, and then it was clear the meeting was over. My minders appeared delighted with the way things had gone as we returned to the guest house, where I collected my bags, including the Devlin cutting, and made for the bus station. There they saw me off with pats on the back, not realising a promised future return to Damascus wasn't ever going to happen.

Brochures at Baalbek advertising a forthcoming requiem being given by Ella Fitzgerald for Louis Armstrong in the coming June had been picked up on the way home and a couple of tickets booked, as my sister was shortly coming out to Cyprus on holiday. It was a perfect excuse for a second visit to the site, as some leave was due, and though a trip into Syria was definitely out there was clearly still a great deal yet to explore around Lebanon.

Orange blossom permeated the air everywhere during the months of April and May, lying particularly heavily in valleys in the early dawn hours and making hound exercise a struggle because of the soporific effect of the scents exuded by the groves of fruit trees in the dark hours. Horses' heads dropped, hounds trotted increasingly slowly until open ground provided ventilation and the chance of a breeze. Lines of string and wire coated in a sticky substance strung from trees set up to capture birds migrating from Africa to Anatolia were pulled down with a hook attached to the end of my whip. The Cypriot ex-patriot community in London appeared to be the main market for the subsequently bottled creatures. The other natural spring phenomenon was the sheer volume of hedgehogs suddenly appearing on the roads at night.

With a somewhat full schedule of roles to juggle between slotting in visits to Beirut, being an armoured car troop leader and running the Saddle Club hounds, there was little time to absorb more than just a sketchy impression of events in the news. This fact was brought home rather abruptly one morning on hound exercise when I found the colonel's wife was in considerable distress. Eventually she told me what was bothering her – 'the suffering of the poor boys on the hospital top floor'. The 'top floor' of the BMH was a secure area not reachable by normal lift. There was a helicopter landing pad on the roof, and occasionally a 'casivac' chopper with badly wounded soldiers serving in foreign parts clattered in from Akrotiri. That I knew. What I didn't know until then was that the hospital catchment area covered the entire Middle East as NATO's central store of antidotes for all known nuclear, biological and chemical weapons. A proxy war was being fought in Yemen, with British SAS troops active in the shadows occasionally being burnt by chemical agents being covertly deployed. Through her husband, who was in charge of the antidotes and their administration, she had a good idea of what was going on.

In Kyrenia some new visitors appeared. One confessed he was nursing a bad liver, having spent 'too long in the desert', but his suntanned, heavily scarred torso told another story, with steely blue eyes warning that questions weren't an option. It seemed that a lot was going on between the big powers at the bottom of the Arabian Peninsula, though it was a little difficult to understand exactly what. A Lightning pilot based at Akrotiri had started to visit Kyrenia on a regular basis, and late one evening his wife let drop that flying over the mass of uncharted desert called the Empty Quarter was highly risky, as no maps existed to enable a rescue if something went wrong. Everyone tried to avoid the territory if at all possible but, imitating someone taking a photograph, she went on to say, occasionally 'risks had to be taken'.

Leonie and my father arrived and were accommodated in the Kyrenia flat. As a leftie art student she didn't exactly fall for my army associates and took off within days for the Troodos Palace Hotel, a threadbare ex-colonial establishment high up on Mount Olympus above the winter snowline. The wide staircases, worn carpets, high ceilings, large creaking bedroom doors and old crones servicing chamber-pots on a 24-hour basis resembled many an Anglo-Irish home we both knew and it became a bit of a joke naming various places in a similarly dishevelled condition, with equal lack of heating. Then it was off back to Lebanon for the Baalbek show.

Passing through Beirut and giving Mandi a routine warning of where I was dining, we visited one of the restaurants I'd been to with Roderic. During the meal a couple at a nearby table joined us in conversation about the forthcoming Fitzgerald concert, which they confessed they had overheard being mentioned. In explaining how I'd acquired tickets I let slip the fact that I'd been in Damascus a couple of months previously. This casually given information triggered a reaction, subtly hidden, but detectable. Suspicions were confirmed that they were what Mandi and others were looking out for when the 'Akrotiri' lollipop (sanctioned mention of a role in the airbase security) was deliberately mentioned in conversation as a place of work. Hardly discernible, the distance between tables narrowed slightly. It wasn't the first time the game had been played, but if there were other eyes about they weren't ever spotted. The proprietor fussed and made a point of supplying a house dessert and champagne for free as a finale. We left him explaining the entwined history of Beirut and the Sursoc family to the couple. Next day Leonie and I explored Baalbek, and in the evening, backed up by an amazing *son et lumière*, Ella Fitzgerald sang a spectacular if tearful requiem for Louis Armstrong beneath the giant pillars of the temple of Jupiter.

Returning to Pergamos, I was met by two grim-faced plain-clothes policemen holding a letter addressed to me stamped TOP SECRET in red, which had been opened. I was instructed to read the contents and give an explanation. It was from my Uncle Desmond in Ireland. The social fallout from Bloody Sunday was still resonating around Ulster, north and south, with barricades defining no-go areas for police going up in the hard-line Catholic communities of Derry and Belfast. He, Desmond, had been in touch with General Tuzo about the crisis and his Cambridge undergraduate son Mark had been temporarily arrested by paratroopers in the Falls Road. Closer to home at the edge of the estate, which at that point also marked the border with Northern Ireland, the Comiskey family, whose tenanted house was right beside a jurisdiction-defining bomb crater in the road, were finding life difficult thanks to the build-up of security forces on both sides of the unapproved crossing point. I looked at the policemen, they looked at me. Eventually one asked for an explanation for the presence of an apparent nest of Russians on the Irish border. It was impossible not to laugh. A description was given of the family in question who resided in one of the gate lodges of my uncle's estate. 'Old Joe' (Comiskey) didn't speak to but lived with his son, 'Wee Joe'. 'Wee Joe' was the estate stockman who couldn't count. His unmarried sister Winnie kept house and must have had something to do with various small children who ran about. There was an epileptic dog so fluffy its tail couldn't be determined from its head until it moved, and another sister/daughter whom the village had nicknamed 'Arkle' stayed periodically when not 'working' in London. The name Comiskey had no Russian connection and was common to that particular border region. A hotter point was my uncle's expressed opinion concerning accidental incursions by British troops across the border into his woods as security tightened. The associated helicopter activity was having an impact on his efforts to open the castle grounds as a cross-country riding venue for paying guests from America, and had forced him to send a letter of complaint to the general in command with whom he had once been at school. Looking at the policemen, I said that none of this was my problem.

The current state of affairs in Ireland had erupted while I'd been in Cyprus. Lectures at Mons only the year before concerning military support of the Civil Power had featured film footage of the Malayan insurgency, with subversive Communist elements being Chinese. I'd been instructed how to give the order to fix bayonets should a street disturbance get particularly rough but didn't think such a move would currently go down too well in the Falls Road. Requesting that I forward any further 'news from home', the policemen closed their notepads and left. It was almost midday, and the pre-lunch Dom Perignon was on me as the details of the letter were gone over and re-analysed, with everyone wanting to hear more about how 'Arkle' had followed in the footsteps of the famous racehorse to 'earn her colours'.

In July a number of the more experienced NCOs disappeared back to the UK on short notice to attend a special course of some sort. Nothing much was thought of it until newspaper reports featured Centurion tanks fitted with bulldozer blades having been deployed in the streets of Derry to clear the no-go area Bogside barricades. 'Operation Motorman' was announced as effective in breaking the Republican stand-off, but information gathered from returning soldiers revealed it to have been a close-run thing at times. The boys had known nothing like it and the chatter in the vehicle park lasted for weeks. Then an exercise period with annual firing on a range fell due and the dear old Saladins rumbled off to the far end of the island to blast even older Land Rovers and lorries to bits, catching fire and losing wheels on the way.

On my return, activity at the polo stables picked up pace and an extra line of loose-boxes became a pressing requirement. Beside the base where the squadron was stationed lay the abandoned remains of a top-secret Cold War era radio listening post. With the surrounding security fence in a state of complete collapse, a fellow officer felt there was nothing wrong in doing a deal with a local Turkish builder who agreed to erect a new line of stables at the Saddle Club in return for being allowed to dismantle what remained of the buildings. I had already begun to pick at the steelwork to extend the hound exercise area, as it all appeared to be up for grabs. The only access lay across some fields and cactus scrub so lorries carting everything away drew no attention until a competing Greek contractor complained to the Sovereign Base authorities that he was not getting a slice of the action. As nobody could find the site marked on any map because of its D Notice classification the issue was passed to higher command at Akrotiri. I watched in horror as poor Mikie, the officer, found himself facing a court martial. Fortunately he was totally innocent of any financial misdeeds and was exonerated – the main fact being that, due to the still valid strong security classification, no evidence could be produced in open court to confirm the site's actual existence. It was a worrying time for us all until the end but was followed almost immediately by the ghastly Munich massacre in September, which had come without warning. A state of high alert was declared until the question was clarified as to whether it was a one-off event or heralded the beginning of a larger campaign.

By October the situation had calmed down and a few days of unspent leave were used helping a stunning brown-eyed girl who had shown up in Kyrenia to search for the war grave of an uncle buried somewhere on the island. At one point we were near the Larnaca salt lake and a visit was made to the grave of Prophet Mohammad's aunt, Umm Hanam. Though the little mosque, Hala Sultan Teke, was the third most revered site in Islam it was rarely visited, a place of perfect charm and solitude surrounded by whispering palms. The flamingos wading along the shore inspired my companion to talk of her swannery on the south coast of England, which prompted me to describe migrating whooper swans landing on the bay outside my bedroom window back home in Ireland. I didn't expect the sudden bout of homesickness that erupted, but it did as I sat by the salt lake reflecting on the world I'd left behind and almost forgotten about.

The arrival of 'A' Squadron, Blues and Royals, for United Nations duties at Nicosia coincided with that of a large agricultural machinery dealership of obscure origins, which proceeded to throw jolly receptions supported by large quantities of caviar. Copious amounts of it soon appeared on mess tables at low cost and life through the Christmas period of 1972–73 picked up considerably, with it being viewed as a form of Cold War 'collateral bonus' as it was obvious from where it was originating.

Spring progressed and wild flowers blossomed just about everywhere. Peter, to whom I'd been writing frequently, came out on a holiday, stating, 'Whatever I was doing was going down well,' and, sighting my elderly Renault, suggested an upgrade was in order. My mother chipped in and a life-style-changing metallic silver BMW 2002 was purchased.

Just before Easter there was a message from Mandi to get over to Beirut – and bring some warm clothes. It was an odd request, but I was to make my way up to the snowline settlement of Beshara, near where the last of the great cedars were still to be found. On arrival the instruction was to contact a Lebanese major called David Nagby at the military station and go on ski patrol with him. The long single ski-lift took us up to the mountain crest where views of the Bekaa Valley spread out to the east. The mission was to observe what was going on in the sky where the air crackled with the sound of jet fighters manoeuvring in tight circles. Nagby pointed out some that he identified as Russian MIGs being flown by Egyptians attempting reconnaissance flights over Israel a little to the south, but were being seen off. The mountain slopes were long and gentle and we were always in virgin snow while descending to villages from where Nagby never failed to organise transport of some sort back to the camp.

One day after a long ski we were returning to our hut when an old man approached the major and spoke anxiously for some minutes in what sounded like Arabic. Nagby instructed me to change out of my ski kit quickly as he had to go somewhere in a hurry and needed me along. In his Renault 4 we drove down a twisty mountain path, stopping every now and then to either talk to somebody, check a signpost or read a map, eventually arriving in a hamlet perched on a steep mountain slope. Halting by a wooden structure with steps Nagby got out of the car, took an unfamiliar stubby automatic from a bag in the boot, inserted a loaded magazine, cocked it and handed the weapon to me, pointing out the safety catch. My puzzled expression was answered with a wave of his free hand and one word, 'Dogs'.

A terrible smell greeted us as we went up the steps, passed through a hallway and entered a long barrack-like room full of white hospital beds. The light was fading fast, but it was clear that the room contained many dead or dying human beings. The stench was horrific but the sight worse. As my eyes adjusted to the gloom it became clear that the ward occupants were either elderly or badly disabled men. Some figures were motionless, while here and there an arm or leg rocked to the background sound of general moaning. It was immediately obvious from the flecks of spittle round their mouths that everyone I could see was in an advanced state of dehydration. Nagby went to the far end and began to visit each bed in turn. Quite what he did was unclear but slowly the moaning began to subside. I didn't want to know. Momentary eye contact with a middle-aged man beside me was broken by Nagby moving between us. He was the last and the room went silent. Then we were out. There was a flight of steps to a lower floor. He descended a few, hesitated, listened, shook his head, drawing a line across his throat, and gestured towards the car. Though it was now almost dark he did not switch on the lights as we drove back up the mountain and used the hand-brake on the rare occasions when we needed to stop or slow down, leaving me to sit in stunned silence with the pistol on my lap. Eventually he spoke: 'Druze. Those wretches were Maronite Christians. In war the weakest always get left behind. This business is going to end badly and Syria is behind it.'

For me it was all too much and I asked Nagby to drive me back down to the Mayflower Hotel the next day. Gradually the state of shock subsided and we had lunch. During the meal I was fairly free with answers to questions as to what I'd been doing up to then in Lebanon, giving details of who I'd met, where I'd been, and I sensed that he was intrigued by the Sursoc association. Then Mandi arrived and he departed after a short separate conversation with her in the foyer. She suggested that, as I had a day spare before having to fly back to Nicosia, why not come with her and visit Lara, her co-dancer, who was 'off sick' at home. We'd be travelling along the coast and it would be an interesting trip, with lots to see. Needing something novel to distract me from dwelling on the recent ghastly experience, I agreed and we set off for Tyre in the south. Just past it, wedged between the road and the seashore, she parked outside an opening in a long wall of galvanised iron. Inside, it was clearly a Palestinian refugee camp where a warren of narrow metal-walled alleys with open drains had to be negotiated, with sullen, filthy children staring in silence. The lack of happy laughter usual among a group of five- to seven-year-olds was striking.

Then we were at Lara's abode. She was a little shy at being seen in her tin shack as I'd only ever really known her as a gymnast cavorting in a semi-transparent body stocking. Here she was hobbling around in dirt with a bandaged ankle and all beauty hidden under stained, dull clothing. Lara's English was moderate and the girls soon lapsed into 'Lebanese'. While they talked, cried and hugged I tried but failed to engage in any way with two barefoot small boys who had appeared in the doorway. Then it was time to leave and renegotiate the maze of alleys. The camp skyline was 8 ft in every direction, the height of a sheet of corrugated iron on end, and represented the horizon once inside the boundary 'wall'. There was no view in any direction, just the metal sheeting, which created a feeling of being trapped like a rat in a barrel. Relief was tinged with guilt when we exited back on to the roadway and the smell of fetid drains reduced in intensity.

On the way back to Beirut Mandi confirmed that it was one of the main refugee camps in Lebanon, Lara's home and where she'd grown up. Her outstanding figure had got her the nightclub job but Palestinians had no employee rights and could be ruthlessly exploited. I talked about the incident the day before with Nagby in the village and she opened up a little about what appeared to be going on. Druze militia, armed by the new Assad regime's Russian weaponry, were beginning to drive isolated Maronite Christian communities out of their traditional mountain hamlets. It was a worrying development, but not for me to become concerned about. That evening I flew back to Nicosia for what I decided was the last time, knowing I would probably never see Mandi again.

The de-brief with Marion Slonim was complicated and tearful because of the mixture of experiences encountered in so few days, and reuniting with the hounds in pre-dawn darkness came as a welcome relief. Finding further consolation in squadron life which remained its steady, sleepy self, with only the occasional breakdown of an armoured car interrupting the monotony, I realised I had had enough of Lebanon and the twilight world I'd been operating in – some internal spark had died.

It was then that Colonel Desmond Langley ('Boomer'), Colonel Baillie's replacement as Household Cavalry 'Silver Stick in Waiting' and the 'wind-sufferer' my step-grandmother had asked me to look out for, came on a routine visit to the squadron. He requested to see me and said that my Short Service Army commission was going to run out in a couple of months. The colonel appeared as confused as I was but it seemed that as a 'Direct Entrant' (?) my Queen's Commission had begun to run from the first day's attendance at Mons, which had been in July 1970. However, a suggestion had been made from some source – here a curious pause, with him looking up and fixing me with a questioning stare – that I be invited to sign on for another three-year term of service. Did I have other plans or need time to think the matter over? A fairly quick answer would be helpful as my next posting would not be with C Squadron, which was due to go on a tour of duty in Northern Ireland, but at the Guards Depot at Pirbright, training young soldiers. We were all becoming aware of the fact that the end of the Cypriot sojourn was vaguely drifting into sight, but the question, simple as it was, still came as a shock. The colonel then asked, 'What was my connection with General Desmond?'

'Who?'

'General Desmond Fitzpatrick, Deputy Supreme Allied Commander in Europe. He seems to think you have been wandering around in Syria,' boomed the colonel. 'Have you?' Recalling the wartime photograph I'd been shown in the house in Zahleh on the way to Damascus it dawned on me that the other pipe-smoking officer standing behind Peter and labelled 'Fitzpatrick' might be the senior NATO general now being referred to. My numerous letters home to Peter containing details of various adventures on the mainland had presumably been passed on to his old wartime chum. An effort was made to explain the role of my female contacts in Beirut and Nicosia but the conversation completely fell apart when the Syrian Army entanglement was referred to. The only way forward was to suggest a word was had with Colonel Olliviere at the hospital. At this point my squadron leader intervened and quietly explained the seniority of Colonel Olliviere's position alongside that of the overall Sovereign Base Area commander. A pregnant silence followed, indicating that it was clear that the colonel was either satisfied or didn't want to hear any more and, with a reminder to try and decide what I wanted to do, the meeting came to an end.

Sitting alone in my room afterwards, I realised my future entailed choosing between shortly leaving the Army and returning to a totally unknown situation in Ireland or venturing on into an equally unknown military environment. It was like coming to a fork in the road of life, with no signpost or guidance as to the way ahead. As I bumbled over to Kyrenia that evening with my mind very much elsewhere, the waterfront social scene didn't feel attractive, and I headed out of the town up into the foothills of an overhanging mountain to think things over. The news from home was dire, but despite the political chaos the family lawyer had been sending a stream of land purchase contracts for signing as my mother stepped in to prevent the old Leslie family estate she'd given away from being totally sold off. Somehow the idea of diving blindly into the Ulster inferno, having lived abroad for three years, had disquieting undertones. My squadron leader, with whom I'd had a career discussion after the meeting with the colonel, advised that the next posting on offer could be fun. Though 'Pirbright' was the Brigade of Guards' main training centre and regarded as the 'Footies' Heaven' from a cavalry point of view, it being basically an enormous parade ground where sergeant-major drill masters reigned supreme, it was also an interesting meeting place where all seven regiments of the Household Division intersected. I'd be most likely to find many old friends and make a lot of new ones. In his opinion, with luck, I'd probably go on to Knightsbridge and the Mounted Regiment at Hyde Park Barracks after about a year. Watching the setting sun illuminate the distant Turkish mainland and turn nearby hilltop Crusader castles into black silhouettes, I decided the best option was to continue with the military adventure.

Shortly after this episode a fellow troop leader back at Pergamos appeared one morning on parade, sporting a cut forehead and two circles on his neck that gave a strong impression of the end of a double-barrelled shotgun. His badly damaged, blood-stained but still just drivable Saab was parked outside the mess building. Over the last of the Dom Perignon, Carlo described how he had fallen asleep while driving back across the plain from Nicosia in the early hours and crashed the car on to its side over a bank. In doing so he had cut his head. Needing help to get the car upright he'd made for a distant light, but the profuse bleeding impaired his vision and, on reaching a house, he'd had to feel about for a door but entered through an open window by mistake. He'd found himself in a bedroom, a light had gone on and a girl had begun to scream. He still couldn't see much but the next thing he knew a gun was being pressed hard against his neck by an irate male and there was a lot of shouting in Greek as the room filled with people. He guessed that if he had not been in British Army uniform he would probably be dead. Luckily the uniform counted for something, and the assembled company walked him to the car and helped to push it back on to the road. Initially we all laughed as we imagined what the chap's 6 ft 4 ins blood-covered frame and physical similarity to that of an Apache brave would have looked like to a young woman when he appeared in her bedroom in the middle of the night, but as the laughter died away we realised that the incident was a warning of how far we had all drifted from the military norm, and return to reality might be painful.

It was shortly followed by another jolt in that early summer of 1973, when my world momentarily caved in one morning in Kyrenia as a voice, familiar but totally out of context, began to call my name from along the waterfront. If I'd been quick I'd have dived into the harbour to hide in the floating garbage, but it was too late as I'd obviously been spotted by Molly Cusack-Smith, Oonagh-Mary's mother and the ultimate west of Ireland dragon. Her unexpected appearance was more brain-numbing than surprising as she advanced along the quayside dressed in an extraordinary sort of kaftan, barefoot and with hair up. Though it was not yet 9 am she'd accepted a brandy sour before launching into a tale punctuated with much loud laughter of how she had been in the shower on a Greek ferry when there had been a fire and the order to abandon ship. There had been no time to dress, only enough to grab her bag and a bottle of gin before being forced into a lifeboat wearing only a towel. A rescue ship had deposited her at Famagusta on the other side of the island and from there she had made her way to stay on an old friend's houseboat, moored 20 yards away along the harbour. Then her mood changed and a ghastly anti-British tirade began, followed by accusations that I had let everyone down, not just my family but also Oonagh-Mary, whom she accused me of abandoning. The verbal onslaught increased in tempo as brandy sours were downed, greatly amusing my military chums who were sitting about in swimming gear leaving me to take it all on the chin. Fighting a myriad traumatic childhood memories, I saw the only obvious course of action was to walk her back to the houseboat, arrange to deposit a large amount of gin with her host and volunteer for extra duties back at Pergamos while she remained on the island. The drama was contained, mainly by the booze supply, but the experience set alarm bells ringing, acting as a further blunt reminder that there was another real world with sharp edges outside the carefree one I'd been coasting along in.

When an advance party of the squadron taking over arrived it was the final blow, with the dreamy time coming to an abrupt end. 'The Lancers' had been on a long tour in Northern Ireland and were very much in warrior mode when it came to troop training, security, military exercises and threat assessments. It was quite hard to explain that the armoured cars being handed over were very fragile elderly vehicles, with journeys being made only 'when necessary'. The traversing mechanism used to turn the turret of my Saladin had recently just dropped off as the vehicle was manoeuvring round a parade square during a ceremonial squadron drive past a visiting VIP on a raised dais. It meant that the gun barrel didn't turn with the vehicle body at a corner, remaining at 90 degrees to the direction of travel, threatening to knock Brigadier Robertson off his stand. Fortunately a good foot purchase was found at the last minute and the turret was heaved round roughly into position for a salute as we passed.

A party thrown to introduce the newly arrived officers to the Larnaca yacht scene didn't go well, as they were more interested in the arcs of fire of the Greek defensive rooftop machine-gun posts dotted about the suburbs than meeting the town's restaurant owners and side-street shirt-makers. My yacht-catering friend took me aside on board and confessed in an emotional outburst that she was very frightened about something politically subversive her employer and his business partner friend were up to. She wasn't sure what exactly Dimi and Nicos were actually planning but it was big, very big, and she was scared – she was torn between staying on and returning to Yorkshire, but the comfortable lifestyle enjoyed for many years was hard to give up. A suggestion that something 'political' might be afoot was made in the last meeting with Marion Slonim but was rejected as 'meaningless tittle-tattle' and caused us to part on rather cool terms. (Within the year I was to be proved right when the men, Dimi Dimitriou and Nicos Sampson, attempted a coup to depose Archbishop Makarios, with disastrous results for the island as it triggered a military invasion from mainland Turkey.)

Eventually the day came to leave the island. After the round of emotional goodbyes in three towns the inevitable taking leave of the hounds arrived. It was the moment I'd been dreading for weeks and was pure agony – compounded by deep affection for Rattler, my lead hound and trusted friend. Feet turned to lead as I approached the kennels and sought him out. Tears flowed as we sat together, and this may have given him a clue something was up. The flick of an eye before he walked to a corner and curled up carried a look I'd never seen before – a farewell. Somehow he seemed to have sensed that we were parting and had made the break. He'd ruled the pack and, though a dog, a strange bond of trust had come to exist between us that was now over. Taking the cue, I left and drove off to load the BMW on to a Piraeus-bound ferry. It was a journey weighted heavily with emotion as the reality sank in that a magic two-year chapter of my life had come to an end. Watching the Cyprus coastline shrink and then gently dip below the horizon in the evening light, more tears flowed. In the morning I knew I would be looking forward to what lay ahead in life, but as darkness fell feelings for beloved Rattler back on his island dominated all. A short stop at Rhodes the next day allowed for a little sightseeing and then we reached Athens.

10
Pirbright and the Junior Guardsmen's Wing

Two weeks' leave was due and the plan was to spend some of it journeying back across Europe via Corfu. There I met a female cousin looking for a lift home who offered to help with the driving. We caught a ferry to Brindisi in Italy and stayed overnight with Uncle Jack at his Badia in the mountains south of Rome, with the next stop just short of the entrance to the Mont Blanc tunnel. The following day was a long haul, not reaching Paris until the early hours. Being unfamiliar with the city layout we became completely disorientated in the Bois de Boulogne and ran into a camp of blue-uniformed riot police. There seemed to be hundreds of them, generally short, stocky types in high boots standing round burning braziers. Batons and shields were stacked in piles and the scene closely resembled a snapshot of the American Civil War rather than the late 20th century. Attempts to find a hotel still open drew a blank and, with this lot in the park, sleeping in the car was not an option, so when an illuminated building was spotted down a side street we went for it. It turned out to be a brothel but the concierge was prepared to rent a room for six hours with an extra rather steep charge because I was 'accompanied' – corkage! We collapsed on to an unmade bed and, as busy corridor sounds faded and sleep descended, I muttered, 'This is a first for me.' My companion replied, 'Me too.' The next day we reached London and went our separate ways. A day was spent with my mother, briefly talking over family matters, but it was impossible to think properly about Ireland without being there and mentally I remained focused on the Pirbright adventure that lay ahead.

Arrival at the Guards' Depot coincided with a moment when over 1,000 guardsmen of various ranks were strutting their stuff on a giant asphalt drill square. As I had not taken part in a formal parade of any note requiring footwork in over two years, this sudden exposure to thousands of boots crumping back and forth in response to the barked orders of drill sergeants was extremely unsettling.

Bad news awaited me at the mess in the form of a letter from Cyprus. Stupidly, I opened and read it before doing anything. The description it contained of Rattler's decline starting after my departure was like a stab in the ribs. His usual place on morning exercise was padding along at the front of the pack, but he had begun to drop back as the days passed until he showed an unwillingness even to leave the kennels. Then one morning he'd been found curled up dead in a corner. Sitting in my new lodging with suitcase and car still unpacked, I could do nothing but weep. Then a knock on the door brought back reality.

The moment had come to be 'on parade' in the anteroom and introduce myself to over 40 fellow officers without any form of warm-up – like an actor making a first-time stage entrance in a play. With butterflies in my stomach, I took a deep breath before facing a pre-lunch drinks gathering in full swing. Surprisingly, some chaps were familiar from school, some I'd met in Cyprus and others in London before ever setting off round the world. And so, with much friendly badinage, a new chapter of life began under the guiding hand of Colonel Michael Hobbs.

My job was to command a platoon of 60 junior Guardsmen aged 16 and 17 who had to be trained separately from mainstream recruits because of their youth. Some boys came from service families, others were from care homes or regions of high unemployment, looking for a way of improving their prospects. There were two groups requiring particular attention: those set on escaping from a fairly grisly home life, the psychological scars of which were quite apparent; and the already mentally institutionalised ex-care-home fellows, who had nowhere to go. The first few days were taxing while adjusting to an office-bound existence that was very different from my life-style of the previous two years. The work was challenging, with endless documentation to be dealt with, and from the outset it was clear that a disciplined routine needed to be adhered to.

Being back in the UK I found the evolving situation in Northern Ireland hung over everything. As officers and NCOs came and went to Ulster on tours of internal security duty, tales of daring-do and woe floated about, with the evening TV news bulletins bringing home the reality that we were all players of a sort in the unfolding drama as the year changed to

1974. Recruits from Argyllshire and Ulster were watched more closely than the rest, to make sure they were correctly motivated. Spontaneous locker searches sometimes produced caches of live rounds being secreted from the ranges. On one occasion, along with a pot of bullets, an orange sash came to light, owned by a 17-year-old lad from Belfast. The ingenuity of the boys knew no bounds when it came to supplementing rations, or when night patrol exercises skirted villages and occasional towns adjoining training areas. Double-decker buses were often provided as transport vehicles when larger centres of population had to be negotiated during a fast-moving exercise, and this proved quite a headache from a map-reading point of view thanks to the danger from unmarked low bridges in unfamiliar territory. The chaos involved in turning round a convoy of four or five buses in a restricted roadway, particularly at night, might provide entertainment for some, but not myself.

Factors emanating from the outside world impacted on occasion to break the routine of mess life, parades and compiling training programmes. It was then that I heard of Sasha's death, but the pain was eased by the distraction in November 1973 of Libya's Colonel Gaddafi triggering international upheaval with his oil embargo, which lasted until March 1974. During that time faded booklets of fuel ration cards were issued to car-owning officers like me, giving food for thought as to where the world might be heading if the mainstay pillars of society became further destabilised.

To escape the atmosphere of gloom and doom during the 'three-day week' era, Princess Anne's marriage to Captain Mark Phillips was celebrated with a wild party in the mess, ending up with my share of the clearing up and a redecorating bill of £140. On an annual salary of £1,300 it was quite a facer, but it had been a memorable night.

Ongoing news from home did not improve and two years on from Bloody Sunday the atmosphere in the Republic remained raw. The collapse of the Sunningdale Agreement, which had promised to introduce power-sharing, had not gone down well with Loyalist hard-liners, and there was a sense something was going to give. It did. In May bombs went off without warning in Monaghan and Dublin, killing 33 people. A new depth in the conflict had been plumbed. Family letters described such a different point of view from the opinions expressed by chaps returning from recent tours in Belfast and Derry cities that I found it impossible to utter a word without running the risk of taking on the entire mess in argument. Remaining silent was the safest option, frustrating though it was.

The luck of serving under Michael Hobbs, a superb commander of men whose leadership skills touched everyone, meant I strove to give my best, the demanding work being balanced by repeated attendance at the *Rocky Horror Show* and singing along with Tim Curry as the musical worked its way along the King's Road.

In the autumn of 1974 the promised posting came through to the Mounted Squadron at Hyde Park Barracks in London for a two-year tour of ceremonial duties, with my last task at Pirbright being to command an advance party convoy of 30 vehicles from Pirbright to Otterburn training camp in Northumberland. A 4 am start meant that it was going to be a tiring day. The NCOs forming the party explained that the usual routine was to break up the procession of Land Rovers and laden trucks into groups of five and rendezvous at a predetermined spot known to all drivers. Inevitably I fell into a sound sleep, only to wake as the Land Rover was being parked up in an unknown terraced street. The driver, before inviting me in to have tea with his mum, advised that we were on the outskirts of Durham and not far from Gosford roundabout, where everyone would be gathering in due course. With not another military vehicle in sight, there wasn't much to be done but make the best of the situation, so I accepted. Tea, cake, agonisingly slow polite conversation about the mining industry's demise, and we were back on the road. Reflecting on the episode afterwards as the Land Rover rumbled on, I realised I'd just been given a unique insight into the current forces disturbing the nation at grass-roots level. The entire convoy was found at the Gosford roundabout, marshalled and ready for me to lead off on the last leg to Otterburn.

As we arrived in darkness the camp gate was found to be blocked by a police car with its blue light flashing. The road ahead was taped off as a designated crime scene, and so a rear entrance via the ranges had to be found without the help of a detailed map. To add to the difficulties a strong gale was driving rain hard against the windscreen, reducing visibility to almost zero. Once we found a way into the camp it was only to discover there was nobody to report to, just rows of unlit, locked huts. I returned to the police car on foot, as most of the stores in the vehicles represented food supplies for 1,000 soldiers for a fortnight and a good deal required immediate refrigeration. A caretaker with keys was unearthed who, while opening up the kitchen and accommodation units, told me the camp commanding officer and his wife had been shot dead earlier in the day – but he did not know who was responsible. Then he departed, leaving me alone in a hut of my own with just the howling wind and a TV for company. The one channel that worked featured a play called *The Cheviots, the Stag and the Black Black Oil*. Scottish grievances over treatment down the centuries and the feeling that the new wealth coming from under the North Sea was rightfully Scottish were being presented with a blatantly anarchistic slant. From somewhere a negative anti-establishment stance appeared that had been completely absent during the Durham tea party earlier in the day. I still did not know who'd shot the commandant, why, or even if they had yet been detained. The wind rattled the door and window continuously and it ended up being a long, lonely night. Next day the main party arrived, I made my farewell and didn't hesitate to head off south for two weeks' leave.

The year at Pirbright had taught me much about leadership. Sensitive young men from all backgrounds had to be guided through the difficult transition period between adolescence and manhood, while the large numbers of NCOs and officers on the base meant regimental standards of turnout and parade performance had to be kept up to the mark. Although my immediate superior had been an absolute martinet and a nightmare to work for, the experience of serving under an outstanding commanding officer more than compensated.

With ten days' leave I headed for the west of Ireland in the BMW, as I had received news that Wyndham and Peter were in poor health. There was something deeply comforting about being able to discuss aspects of regimental life, as if I'd joined a private club with my two oldest friends the members, but sadly it was the last time we were to be together, as both died the following year.

The quick trip to Castle Leslie on the return journey sounded a warning note that the future might not be entirely a sea of calm, as the old retainer left in charge of my newly purchased property was doing what he could, but stated that my Uncle Desmond was tending to forget what land he had sold. The farm was badly run down, and needed fencing, manuring and stocking, but the main difficulty was with groups of unrestrained horse-riders careering about across the grassland. Added to this was the shadow of the current Troubles, which weighed heavy as a number of killings had recently taken place within the village environs, leaving me with much to think about as I lay in bed in the old nursery where I'd once slept happily as a child. There was a large bay window that looked out over the lake but now, instead of a singing silence, it was upsetting to hear the rumble of car bombs going off 12 miles away in Armagh. Even the rooks in the ancient wood appeared to be unsettled by the distant rumbling sounds carried by the night.

11
Ceremonial Duties and State Visits

Leave over, it was time to shelve thoughts of Ireland and report to Hyde Park Barracks. Colonel William Edgedale, my new commanding officer, outlined the next few months' activity, which was going to be tough because of the need to have 'passed out' on the riding course required before taking part in mounted duties, and time was short as a state visit loomed in Scotland. The riding master took things in hand very quickly and showed no quarter when it came to yelling and barking expletive-decorated instructions to mount from the ground on to a stirrupless saddle wearing knee-high jack-boots, cuirass, sword and helmet. Swinging a leg back and over the pommel of the sheepskin-covered standard army issue equipment was quite a challenge at the start, particularly as the horse involved was usually a good 16 hands. But eventually the day came when approval for Queen's Life Guards and other duties was granted.

Almost immediately a nasty and highly contagious respiratory infection known as Strangles hit the Knightsbridge stables, sending the entire barracks into quarantine. As it was potentially lethal for horses if not dealt with correctly, a massive logistic problem arose, as a full Sovereign's Escort for the state visit to Edinburgh of King Carl Gustav of Sweden was due in weeks and over 80 horses were going to be out of action. The crisis peaked as the day arrived for my first actual duty at Horse Guards Parade as Captain of the Queen's Lifeguard. Video footage had been available to study the procedure and I'd watched a few guard changes, but on the day that it was my turn everything was suddenly different. At the last moment the entire Guard was instructed not to ride but to bus down to Whitehall and go through the ceremonial motions on foot. There was no precedent to study in detail and it seemed in order to execute a number of natty foot manoeuvres I'd picked up at Pirbright. Things appeared to go fairly well, with my extra parade-ground antics carrying the day with the viewing public, but it became clear that it was not the case with a number of senior officers who had heard about the change in routine and had gathered to watch from a window. The phone began to ring, culminating in a visit by the very unamused adjutant who set out the ground plan for the Life Guards officer taking over from me the following morning but equally in the dark.

My punishment, on coming off guard, was to escort the BBC presenter Valerie Singleton and her *Blue Peter* film crew on a tour round the stables. Again, no script or guideline was provided, so answers to questions were purely my own and totally off the cuff. There was much on the adjutant's plate at the time and the matter was quickly forgotten until four months later, when warning came through at lunchtime that a programme featuring life in the barracks was being broadcast that evening on the BBC. Nightmare followed, and more sense-of-humour failure. My answer to a question on training band horses to like music did not come over well, as I had frequently slapped a gloved hand or boot with my whip. The repeated *whack, whack* of leather on leather had not been edited in the slightest, causing the adjutant and colonel to receive some interesting letters. Small though it was, the incident was quite a sharp lesson on how contact with the media was a minefield that needed careful handling.

The date was fixed for the Mounted Regiment to box up and head for Scotland. Of the 200 horses, about half had been judged as clear of the Strangles outbreak and had been moved to Windsor for safety. The remainder stayed confined to Hyde Park Barracks and the shortfall was made up with partially trained remounts brought down from Melton Mowbray and others being shipped back from Germany. Luckily my charger, Rosinante, along with Sefton, another steady and experienced old hand (later injured in an IRA bomb attack), had not fallen foul of the infection. The regiment was quartered on the edge of Edinburgh at Redford cavalry barracks, dating back to the Victorian era. Access for exercise purposes was available in reasonably open country round the suburbs of Kingston, but no maps or designated routes were provided and it was a matter of using one's head when taking 'the watering order' out for exercise in the early morning. My turn came and I spotted a side lane that looked as if it led to some grassy hills. Unfortunately it didn't, but narrowed quite quickly, to end up with a gate leading on to a golf course. With the entire equestrian crocodile behind me consisting of 100 mounted troopers each leading a horse, it was impossible to turn round without first getting everyone through the gate and on to the course for a large wheeling manoeuvre to be executed. The excitement of the fresh grass and open space was too much for a couple of young half-trained animals and after a burst of bucking and rearing they broke loose, cantering off over the dunes with tails held high. Two corporals were dispatched to catch them before they disappeared completely among the knolls. I needed to get to a higher point of observation in order to keep control of events, as I could see little from where I was, and the chaos of the moment felt like what Balaclava and Waterloo must have been for some, right down to the apprehension and churning of stomach at the sight of cavalry speeding away into dead ground. Eventually the NCOs appeared with their captives in tow. Later in the morning a somewhat played-down report of the incident was made to Colonel William and the matter was forgotten – or so I thought.

The next day was the rehearsal, and all went well from the station through to Holyrood Palace. As commander of the First Division I was on point and responsible for the pace of the entire procession, so the importance was noted of a sharp cobblestoned bend at the end of Princes Street needing to be taken slowly to prevent mishap. Because the turn provided a good view of the passing pageantry a number of disabled people in wheelchairs were to be positioned there. Then it was the day itself. The King arrived, was greeted by Her Majesty the Queen, and the procession moved off according to plan, going into a trot on reaching the Royal Mile. At that moment a cannon on the castle ramparts overlooking the processional route fired the 1 pm salute, spreading immediate panic through the ranks of partially trained remounts. There was a great surge forward from the back of the division and a quick rearward glance revealed grey stomachs of rearing carriage horses, a helmetless Colonel William and the black flanks of troop sections in disarray. If any animal broke into a canter there would be no going back, only forward into a gallop, and the sharp turn was fast approaching. Good old Rosinante and Sefton saved the day: with them as steady chargers in pole position, Corporal of Horse Fox and I formed a snowplough action which contained the forward pressure of the panicking troop horses until we were safely round the bend, over the bridge and heading downhill for Holyrood Palace. The day could easily have ended up very differently, with a momentary vision of a Grand National jump at Aintree built of wheelchairs being taken head on. Colonel William's helmet arrived by police bike in time for the salute and all was well. Then the £3,000 estimate for golf-course repairs arrived and a very uncomfortable half-hour was spent explaining actual details of the morning's exercise drama, before a way of steering it into an insurance claim was found.

On my return to London a settled routine of guard duties, soldier training and horse schooling programmes filled the days. The IRA bombing campaign was relentless, with the vast plate-glass windows of the officers' mess overlooking Rotten Row rattling in their frames as shock waves resonated across the park from blasts in Oxford Street and shook the mess furniture. There was a general impression that when Basil Spence designed Hyde Park Barracks he had not foreseen a future demand for raised levels of security. On duty one Saturday night I'd been informed by the police that a suspected car bomb was parked across the entrance to the main stable-block fire exit. I was asked to evacuate all 200 animals without delay. Finding it impossible to contact any superior officer and realising an immediate course of action was needed to appease the police, I looked momentarily at the fire drill. The standing orders stated that troop horses be led out of the barracks into Hyde Park in head-collars. At 8 pm on a Saturday evening just before Christmas there was hardly a trooper to be found, and the idea of 200 loose black horses getting spooked in the dark by an explosion dictated that evacuation was not an option. The order to break out hay was given and the police saw the logic. Time ticked by very, very slowly as the bomb disposal team went about their work, taking almost two hours before announcing the 'all clear'. After that, when on duty, I took to eating under the portrait of Kaiser William, because his 8-ft-high representation as a colonel of the Royal Dragoons was positioned near a cosy concrete corner far from any window.

Sometimes the face of Tom Leslie in a long painting of Blues officers in 1857 would catch the eye, as he was visible from another corner where it was safe to sit and read. Tom was the link with home, where his Crimea medal with four clasps and a dented lead musket ball lay in a glass-topped box on the drawing-room table. He'd served in the campaign as *aide de camp* to the Chief of Staff, Lord Raglan, and had been shot in the thigh at the battle of the Alma. The dented Russian ball had been dug out and sent home to his mother with a supporting letter from Raglan stating that 'the boy was doing well'. Tom recovered and was present at the staff meeting on the heights overlooking Balaclava when it was noticed that the Russians appeared to be moving dangerously close to allied guns at the head of the valley below. The famous order was given to Tom to deliver to Lord Cardigan, who was positioned with his brigade of Light Cavalry on the valley floor. However, because Tom's thigh wound was not fully healed, he found it difficult to make his horse negotiate the steep incline at any speed, and ended up dismounting to lead it by the head. A frustrated Captain Nolan, nearby but not within earshot of the staff group as it conferred, intercepted Tom and grabbed the cartouche belt containing the ambiguously written instruction to 'take the guns'. History records what happened in the second valley, not visible from the heights, and Nolan mistakenly pointing up it when questioned for clarification of the order. Poor Tom eventually made it to the valley floor, mounted and galloped off in pursuit, only to have his horse killed, pinning him underneath it as it fell. When night came Russian women roamed the battlefield, slaughtering the wounded before robbing them and the dead. Luckily he managed to feign death, was overlooked and found next day by army farriers collecting forehooves for the quartermaster's accounting purposes.

On returning from the campaign Tom retired from the Army, driven by the teasing he was getting at his clubs, came home to Glaslough to plant up the walled garden with ornamental yew trees, then changed his name to Slingsby and went to live in Yorkshire. Odd though it was, his image quietly looking down from the anteroom wall imparted considerable comfort on lonely winter nights.

There was a change of government in the autumn as the Heath

administration collapsed under pressure from the three-day week. As luck would have it, my duty as Captain of the Queen's Life Guards at Whitehall coincided with the state opening of Parliament on 29 October, with Harold Wilson returning as Prime Minister. My role in the proceedings was to give the monarch a Royal Salute as the state coach and accompanying entourage of carriages passed through the arch at Horse Guards on its way from Buckingham Palace to the Palace of Westminster. The passageway would then be closed to all traffic by having the mounted guard walk forward in line. All went well and at roughly the appointed time a trumpet heralded the approach of the procession's lead division of cavalry moving at a brisk trot. A number of two-seater carriages passed, followed by further divisions of mounted troops in front of and behind the royal coach bearing the Queen. Then nothing. I felt there had to be more and a fourth division of 40 mounted Life Guards had not passed – or had I missed them? Silence descended, punctuated only by the tinkle of curb chains and the occasional hoof scratching a flagstone. Eventually, after what seemed an eternity, the clatter of fast-approaching carriages on gravel echoed through the stone tunnel and a small two-seater carriage shot past with a large white buckskin bottom sticking out of its open door, to the great amusement of the crowd in Whitehall. The rest of the procession followed at speed and then it was all over. The arch was formally closed and the Guard stood down to continue normal duties.

It had been a near thing, as I'd only been seconds away from giving the order to move the line of horsemen forward to block the arch and the advancing carriages would not have had time to stop or take avoiding action, as direction of travel was confined by the tunnel masonry. The pile-up that would have resulted didn't bear thinking about. On coming off duty I learned that one of Princess Anne's carriage horses had got a leg over a trace while going down The Mall and had had to stop. 'Boomer', as Silver-Stick-in-Waiting, was following in the next carriage and got out in order to find out what was going on. He then could not get back in when the procession started to move again, as there were no footmen on hand to hold the rocky little vehicle steady. As the Princess's carriage moved off his Gold Stick companion, Field Marshal Templer, pulled him in on his knees, holding on to him until they reached Westminster.

In early November a spot of leave fell due and was spent helping a friend move a narrowboat from Northampton to Oxford, rather than going to Ireland, as news was depressingly bad. The boat owner suggested we throw a party one weekend and each invite two friends. With an interesting library on board conversation topics had been wide-ranging, with thoughts coming to mind of Jane Forbes, a girl I'd met years before. A lengthy hunt for her phone number via a number of people finally led to a house in Chelsea. Emboldened by a couple of pints I made the call, offering an invitation to spend a weekend cruising on the barge, which included the possibility of exploring some Black Death sites and a few old churches. It had been a wild stroke but was taken up and the weekend boat party proved a surprising success.

Back on duty at Knightsbridge, the routine of life at the heart of the capital settled into one of horse health management, hunting expeditions to Leicestershire, battling with the internal security demands being created by the IRA bombing campaign – and seeing more of the girl I'd had the courage to contact after a gap of five years. A friendship fluttered into being that was to deepen and deepen as the months passed.

On Christmas Day I volunteered to be on duty as I was not returning home. The Queen being at Windsor, no full guard was mounted, and it was my role as Orderly Officer at Hyde Park Barracks to ride alone down to Horse Guards to inspect the troops manning the gate at 4 pm. The dire security situation and the fact that the hour's journey was made mainly in fading twilight was disconcerting, with just one comfort. The thickness of my frock coat's ornate frogging might give some protection from a bullet or shrapnel, but it was still a very lonely ride.

Any opportunity was to be taken to relieve the monotony of routine guard duties in the quiet periods between ceremonial occasions outside the hunting season. During one such occasion my troop of 32 horses was boxed down to Windsor for a change of scene. While there an instruction arrived to appear at the Royal Lodge in the park, as the Royal Windsor Bloodhounds had been invited by the Queen Mother to hold a meet in the courtyard. My new commanding officer, Colonel Morris, joined us as we hacked to the venue, where the Queen appeared on a chestnut, escorted by a groom. The Queen Mother came to the window and waved, giving the signal for trays of cherry brandy to appear and be downed before a peep from the horn signalled that we were off on the business of the day. A short hack and the hounds were shown a red T-shirt by a tree. One after another heads went down and the pack was off, emitting deep baying cries as they found the line the T-shirt wearer had taken 30 minutes before. We cantered, checked and galloped for about three miles until the pack was found to have run its quarry to ground by a giant equine statue. There we came across a black-skinned NCO being licked furiously by 20 bloodhounds weighing approximately four stone each. Sensing drama, I reined back and looked about to see if any members of the public were in the vicinity, as, I noticed, was the Queen. The colonel appeared to have lost a stirrup, as he was cantering round in circles some distance off, while the huntsman, a major, made hasty moves to collect the hounds and move on to the start of the next line to be run. A quick word later with the NCO, an ex-Royal Dragoon whose family had lived in Birmingham for three generations, revealed that the chap who was supposed to have run the line had pulled a tendon the previous evening and he was the next fittest person who knew what to do.

The following Saturday the troop was out in the park for a quiet hack after some arena schooling when a black estate car approached, slowed, then pulled over to let us by. Passing the vehicle in shirtsleeve order at a walk in the balmy weather, I looked down and acknowledged the driver's courtesy by casually waving the fingers of my right hand while keeping my thumb hooked in a pocket. There was momentary eye contact and then the car was gone. An NCO had been muttering something for a few seconds and then suddenly the sounds turned into 'eyes right, sir', but it was now, obviously, too late. It didn't take long for him to confirm it was who I'd begun to suspect it might have been and we trotted back to the stables thinking about what step to take next. It was 10.30 in the morning. The best bet was to take advice from Sally, Duchess of Westminster, another godmother who was conveniently also a periodic Lady-in-Waiting to Her Majesty. I gave her a brief outline of my predicament by telephone, and she told me to sit and wait for a call back. Ten minutes later the Duke of Beaufort rang and, having checked I'd a sheet of regimental paper to hand, dictated a letter. Minute detail as to folding and addressing of envelope was given and after a bit of practice a final document was handed to a duty driver for immediate delivery to Windsor Castle. As the Land Rover pulled away from the mess, destined for the royal residence with my freshly written letter, I noticed the time was still only 11.45, though it seemed like a century since the actual incident.

There being nothing else to do, I stayed with a friend for the remainder of the weekend and on Monday returned to Knightsbridge with the horses. There a message reached me in the stables that the colonel requested my immediate presence in his office. On entering and saluting I found him all smiles as he greeted me, asking for the details of why I'd apparently written a letter to the Queen and what on earth had I said? The adjutant, Peter Walker-Okeover, had taken up position behind the colonel with a millboard in hand. The only way forward was to come clean on what had occurred and state that I had felt it prudent to do something, having failed to salute in the park when only a few feet from Her Majesty. A demonstration was given of how thumb had remained in pocket and fingers waggled as an acknowledgement of her pulling over. At this the millboard moved up to the adjutant's mouth while the colonel asked me in a whisper to relate what happened next. I explained how I'd trotted back to the stables and wasted no time in telephoning my godmother to ask for advice on protocol surrounding such an incident. With a laugh the colonel looked over his shoulder to the adjutant, commenting, 'He called his god-mum!' followed by 'and?' While watching the adjutant, who was now biting the millboard with eyes focused on a point high above my head, I described in a few short sentences how Sally asked me to sit by the phone and have some regimental writing paper ready. When I referred to the Duke of Beaufort solely as 'the Master' the Colonel asked for clarification of whom I meant. The adjutant took his eyes off the ceiling and the board out of his mouth, and bent forward to explain in a quavering voice that really caught my attention that I was talking about the Master of the Queen's Horse personally dictating an instruction on how to phrase my letter of apology correctly. At this the colonel leaned forward over his desk letter-pad, put his head in his hands and muttered for me to get out of his office. Looking up to salute I noticed the millboard was back in the adjutant's mouth and his eyes were back looking at the ceiling. Some days later a letter came from an equerry informing me that the prompt course taken to correct the 'park incident' had been noted.

Then came sad, sad news. Spud Lewis, my godfather Peter's great friend, who had served with him through both World Wars, came up to the horse lines and told me the old boy had died at home in Galway. The information hit me unexpectedly hard. I'd suffered a bout of grief earlier in the year on hearing that Wyndham, my first and greatest boyhood friend, had passed away, but now something deep down seemed to snap in two – a little private world imploded. Leave to travel to Galway was sanctioned and I read at his funeral in St Nicholas's Cathedral. The two Union flags sporting the colours of the Connaught Rangers hanging from the ceiling of the Norman building added a fitting bit of colour to the old colonel's send-off, for which the remnants of 'the county' before me had gathered. In a way they represented the dying embers of a race of which I too was a member but which was shuffling towards extinction. Spud had once told me that back in 1920 when over in Ireland rounding up errant Black and Tan forces he had witnessed Peter carrying out summary justice on two serious offenders caught in the act of torching a hamlet, and worse, near Oranmore. The action at a place called Frenchfort had done much to calm the situation at the time and he understood that when Peter had retired there from the Bahamas an election was held in the village bar to decide who would be his gardener. This tale meant that the odd sign of recognition given me in the village at the parade to commemorate the Easter Rising finally made sense. I had grown up understanding 'the colonel' was well liked locally but had never known the underpinning back story.

As the winter of 1975 advanced the IRA terror campaign in London intensified. Near Christmas a group of bombers were unmasked and chased north of the Marylebone Road to an apartment block in Balcombe Street where, with two hostages, they held out for almost a week before surrendering. Setting off in the early hours one Thursday for Leicestershire and a long weekend's hunting round Melton Mowbray with the Quorn, Belvoir and Cottesmore hounds, I stopped to have a look at the siege, which was very much at its height. Dressed in uniform, gloved, field-boots, Sam Browne and service dress hat with its thick band of gold braid, I was able to walk through the various police cordons right up to the arc lights and sound broadcasters. There a conversation with two senior Met officers did not go well. I expressed a view that until 'work started on addressing the social problems in the Derry and Belfast ghettoes there would just be an endless flow of ideologically brainwashed foot soldiers such as those presently holed up in front of us – more of the same.... The nettle to be grasped wasn't in London.' Sensing a negative reaction I departed.

After about two weeks, because of Christmas, there was a summons to visit the regimental colonel at his new apartment overlooking the Royal Hospital. The old Field Marshal stated that the opinion I'd been reported expressing to the police officers had rocketed through the establishment. As a fellow Irishman he understood my line of thought and felt I was probably right, but I'd touched on policy only just being introduced at staff college level. It was obvious my time would be far better served by retiring from the regiment and moving into a position to take advantage of my unique family situation back in Ulster, so I was to write him a formal letter of resignation. A year should be spent cooling off somewhere before returning home, where a more constructive employment role would undoubtedly materialise. It was a little hard to follow the old boy's line of thought, as he was in the habit of expecting one to understand deeper meaning behind the words spoken. I was left with the feeling he didn't view my retirement as 'service over', more a new phase beginning. With all the staff promotion courses and exams I'd missed over the years I was beginning to wonder what lay ahead and found his taking charge of the situation a bit of a comfort. It was obvious Ireland was where I was inevitably headed and now a line in the sand had been clearly drawn. What I didn't realise was that there was a string attached to my army departure. It had been buried in the Field-Marshal's words and was to manifest itself from a surprising corner in the near future.

The required letter was written and accepted, leaving me with six months to serve. The remainder of the hunting season at Melton was pursued with vigour and one troop horse, Zetland, was worked up to be fit enough for the famous 'Melton Chase'. There were over 100 competitors on the day who all surged forward as a single mass at the sound of the starter's pistol. The course of four and a half miles lay across well-known hunt country and it took concentration to avoid massive pile-ups, fallen riders, loose horses and at the same time keep Zetland focused on the next obstacle. He came down, slipping on sand spread across a road crossing, but I managed to catch, remount and bring him in 35th out of the 50-odd who made it to the finish. With one fatality and seven hospitalised it had been quite a race.

For over a year Jane and I had increasingly begun to enjoy being together and I felt I didn't want to live life alone any more. An array of unknown adventures eventually awaited me in Ireland and the thought of facing them without the support of a kindred spirit was bleak so, in February, I took the plunge and asked her to marry me, having skirted round the subject in a lengthy conversation with her father. On being informed of the news my mother responded by writing a letter describing the funeral of Frank Stagg, the hunger striker, which had recently taken place at Ballina in Co. Sligo. He had died in prison in England after starving for over 60 days and his body had been brought back to Co. Mayo in the Republic for burial. There was a Nationalist cry for him to be interred in a dedicated IRA plot somewhere, but the Dublin government wasn't having it and had deployed a detachment of soldiers to back up Gardai officers on duty to see the funeral went according to plan, with the coffin being encased in concrete. My old nurse's husband was an Irish Army sergeant present at the scene and had given her an eye-witness description of what happened. A large body of Nationalists who had travelled down from Derry became incensed at the sight of green uniforms and began to riot, throw stones and chant 'Free State Bastards'. The Irish soldiers were armed but, as a precaution, since they were inadequately trained for such an event, they had not been issued with ammunition. Order broke down when the food truck was rolled over and set on fire by the mob. It was only regained when rifles were used as clubs – which was done with vigour as the boys had lost their lunch. Without doubt, had the troops been equipped with live rounds there would have been a massacre. It wasn't exactly a welcoming picture to be given of the world that awaited us as newly-weds.

With the spring of 1976 came more ceremonial duties, State visits, 'the Trooping' at Horse Guards in early June and the Order of the Garter investiture at Windsor Castle. Harold Wilson was the newly elected Knight and when the ceremony in St George's Chapel concluded he followed the Queen out, walking on her left. My position was at the top of the flight of steps leading up from the carriages by the chapel door through which the procession had to exit at the end of the service and, being very bent and slightly unsteady on his feet, Wilson swayed to one side, stumbling over my jackboot toe-caps. He began to roll forward, and my free left arm was required for support at the very moment the order came to give a royal salute. This involved raising and waving the sabre in my right hand in a circular motion above his head before bringing hilt to lips and then making a swift downward motion with the blade, in this case, following along the contour of his curved spine. The ex-Prime-Minister swivelled his velvet-bonneted head upwards as I withdrew my arm, smiling a thank you on seeing the view down towards a forest of waiting carriages and horses legs. A momentary thought passed through my mind as to what Peter Burke, who firmly blamed Wilson for the cancellation of the TSR2 fighter bomber project, might have done in the circumstances.

With just weeks to serve, Jane and I were married at her home outside Henley on 3 July 1976. It was the hottest day of the hottest year on record, and my commanding officer (still Colonel Morris), a devout Hindu, and a number of regatta judges ended up in the swimming pool with many other guests. (That night, as we were flying to Rome for an Italian honeymoon, a band of Israelis were heading for Entebbe on a daring hostage rescue mission.) Hamish, Jane's father, had delivered a master-stroke when introduced to my mother shortly after we had decided to announce our engagement. I had arranged for them all to meet over a drink while I was on duty at Horse Guards, at which he confessed to having read and much enjoyed her book on Rodin, *Immortal Peasant*, which his mother had sent him when a prisoner of war. He and her brother Jack had been captured at the same time in 1940 and spent the entire five years of captivity together, sharing an interest in art and sculpture. Over the following years Hamish dropped the occasional snippet about incidents during the war years in Germany and the lengths he and his fellow prisoners had to go to in fighting the boredom. Jack was an unusual character who had played a role in misleading the camp guards over what escape plans might be under way. He had been deliberately set up to be identified by the Germans as a potential weak link in the Allied ranks and the plot had worked, in that a guard with a mutual interest in painting had been detailed off to develop a relationship through art. Jack played his role perfectly in 'accidentally' letting slip misleading titbits for the Germans to fall on. A series of 'designed to be discovered' tunnels was exposed, repeatedly drawing the search teams' interest away from the real undertakings and leaving all parties happy.

Shortly after returning from Italy an unexpected buck by a young horse had me carted off to Woolwich hospital for a couple of weeks of traction to repair a damaged spine. The forced isolation in a semi-monastic environment was a blessing in that it provided time to reflect on the massive lifestyle change that was about to take place, with a bachelor life ending and a future shared one lying ahead. In an adjoining room and undergoing the same treatment I came across Anthony Major, the young Grenadier officer who had escorted Winston's coffin down the aisle of St Paul's and on the great man's last barge journey along the River Thames. We were kept company by an elderly Pakistani general undergoing treatment for an elbow worn out because of over-saluting, who never stopped talking about his fear of an invasion by the USSR. From him we both learned a great deal concerning global politics, but for me it was coming rather late.

The final day of military service arrived soon after I was discharged from hospital and returned to Knightsbridge. In the evening I met up with my troop of soldiers in a pub for a last get-together. Finally, the moment came to rise quietly, nod to the boys and make an exit alone into the street and the night. The sense that six years of order and institutional stability had come to an abrupt end was unsettling, like being on a raft breaking away from a riverbank. There was nothing to do but take refuge in the darkness offered by Hyde Park and slowly walk round in circles for emotions to settle before returning to Jane and the apartment we had been loaned.

12
Cirencester and Return to Ireland

I had enrolled at Cirencester Agricultural College, and with a month before the term started Jane and I travelled over to Ulster to look more closely at the chunk of the Castle Leslie estate that was now my property. Having seldom visited during the previous 12 years most of the place was just a foggy memory and there was much catching up to do. Bill came up from Galway to explain what he'd achieved during my mother's period of ownership, while loyal old employees appeared, asking me to call in for tea. Nobody appeared to notice or remark on the frequent border patrol helicopters rattling almost overhead, the bullet-ridden road signs or the fact that there wasn't a clear idea where we were actually going to live when the Cirencester course was over in a year's time. Even the sunniest days seemed gloomy, with all the unanswered questions hanging heavily in the air. A courtesy visit to the local family solicitor was made, to find he had just intercepted the sale of a gate lodge and managed to procure it as a possible residence for me to live independently of my uncle when the agricultural course was over. The challenge of pulling the farm together into a viable operation looked stimulating and exciting, though the weight of dark unknowns in the shape of family politics was impossible to ignore. Ridiculous reminders of the *Rocky Horror Show* plot kept surfacing in startling clarity, with all the show's characters seemingly still in play. Though serious, the security situation was containable, but relations with the big house looked like a potential nightmare from which it would be wise to keep well distanced where possible.

To occupy her time while I attended farming lectures at Cirencester, Jane enrolled on a foundation course at Bristol Art College. Sally Westminster lived about halfway between the two points and provided a converted potting shed at her Gloucestershire home, so we lodged there under somewhat spartan conditions as newly-weds for the coming year.

During a few spare days before term began my mother arranged for

Derek Hill, the portrait artist, to do a painting of me in Household Cavalry uniform. He stayed with Sally in cool luxury, but for me it was to be three days of considerable discomfort. The summer heat had abated so the full-dress tunic was bearable, but Derek's grilling while I was a captive sitter was something I was totally unprepared for. The conversation between artist and subject began with him describing how as a vulnerable young boy he had been left in the charge of a Cairo *maître d'hôtel* while his parents went up the Nile. When they returned he was not the same innocent chap they had left a week earlier. In return for his 'exposé' Derek wanted to know if Jane and I had had a general 'tell all' conversation concerning previous encounters, dalliances and 'misadventures', or were there incidents I was holding back on? Trapped on the stool for over an hour each day, it was difficult to avoid being compelled to eventually contribute something juicy, so I hammed up the Urte Appel transvestite incident in Hamelin, but confessed that the sight of Christabel Ampthill coming out of the sea draped in semi-transparent headscarves had probably channelled my psyche firmly down the heterosexual path. He seemed riveted by this and the last sitting was spent describing details of our camping exploits, her peculiar scars and how we coped at night in bad weather. During lapses in the conversation my mind wandered a bit as the minutes dragged by and I tried to imagine what life might have been like if Jane and I hadn't married. It now seemed it would have felt very empty, with something big missing. The problem of feeling Irish in England and English when in Ireland hadn't entirely gone away, leaving a sense of being nowhere but now not alone any more.

The one-year course at the Agricultural College consisted of 26 retired officers and four other unfortunates. We had all made use of the TOPS grant scheme, which paid the fees and provided a generous weekly cash supplement. My interest was in grass management, drainage and beef production. Most chaps were going on to run farms of their own and, like me, already had an outline of what they were interested in focusing on. However, intensive farming of some type was a fundamental part of the course, with a Miss Johns appearing and proceeding to lecture us on pig-breeding. Methods of artificial insemination, assisted excitement,

The Household Cavalry Regiment 1975
FRONT ROW FROM LEFT: Col Morris (H.M. letter saga), 3rd Colonel Langley ('Boomer'), 4th Earl Mountbatten, 5th Colonel Gerald Templer, 6th Col. Edgedale (sorted Golf course damage bill)
SECOND ROW FAR RIGHT: Capt Walker-Okeover (millboard-chewing adjutant)
THIRD ROW, SECOND FROM RIGHT: Self.
(Rupert Ridgeway photos)

Self on Rosinante who saved the day at Edinburgh.

Hiro Kutsuzawa at Castle Leslie in 1990 escorted by Mrs Forshall, the 'Lambo' car agent.

Mrs Leonard Jerome. ('Sitting Bull') Winston Churchill's part Iroquois American grandmother – shared with my grandfather.

'Bee' Beamont (spent the war in the air) with Bill King (spent it under water) at Pentridge.

Bee taking off in TSR2. Broke sound barrier using one engine but aircraft deliberately destroyed by being put to use shortly afterwards as a gunnery range target.

Bill and *Galway Blazer 2* setting off from Devonport in 1968 to compete in the Golden Globe race round the world – 'The Voyage of Madmen'.

I argued over dinner with this nutcase in 1995 on how to shape goals of a terrorist campaign.

Early days of 'Pentridge Pots'. Jane holding up one
of our prize items.

The moment when Dr Paisley asked for my opinion on Sir Roger
Casement – traitor or hero?

Family heirloom. Smock did the rounds between the Jerome sisters, starting with Winston Churchill and ending with the last child, my great uncle Lionel.

Cor-Tynan road crater remained in place from 1971–2000, but was easy to bridge or by-pass.

Patrick Rattray opened up the London 1968 social scene and sister Leonie witnessed the Marianne Faithfull dining debacle.

My great-great-aunt Olive Guthrie presenting colours to a UVF muster in July 1914.

'Easter Rising' memorial in Oranmore village where I attended the 50th anniversary march past.

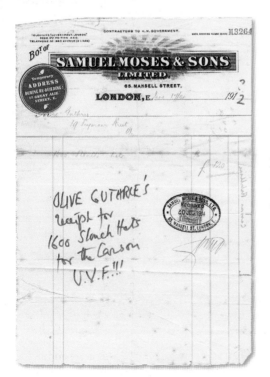

Aunt Olive's UVF outfitting bill dated June 1914. 'For Carson's Rebellion' scribbled on reverse.

Bourke Cockran at Castle Leslie in 1922 sitting with his American
wife, Anne, and her sister, Marjorie (my grandmother, in shadow).
My mother (8) on ground and Shane standing with his father.
(Castle Leslie Archive)

New York Herald. Height of respect
shown in Washington on news of
Cockran's death on 2 March 1923.

Bourke Cockran in 1906 when he
married my great aunt Annie Ide.
(Casle Leslie Archive)

gloved techniques for semen collection were all explained in excruciating detail and delivered with a dead-pan expression. There were moments of stunning silence when she paused for breath and all that could be heard was the creaking of tightly gripped furniture as we struggled to contain ourselves. It was as if she was throwing down a challenge of some sort.

The forestry management demonstration on how to fell trees resulted in the nearby main road being blocked for a day as a sudden gust of wind buffeted the mature dead beech into falling in the opposite direction from that intended. Another field trip was made to see how maize was harvested for animal feed. It was pretty clear that the driver of the state-of-the-art machine must have fallen asleep, as the self-feeding chain cutters had tried to gobble a telegraph pole. The result was a fascinating mess of twisted steel blades, with the harvester's now lifeless feeder arms giving the appearance of a giant dead crab having expired while attempting to devour something it shouldn't. The weeks moved into months of carefree bliss and then there had been a sudden jolt.

Early in the New Year 1977 the phone rang one evening and a man claiming to have met me in London asked if I would join him for a few minutes in the local village pub – he said he was just motoring by and would like a moment's chat. Entering the bar, I was met by two suited men a little older than me, but didn't recognise either. They introduced themselves as 'Dan' and 'Shaw' and wasted no time in explaining why they really wanted to talk to me. It was because my uncle's first wife, Agnes Leslie, was involved in some way with a theatre in Dublin and they said I needed to start visiting her establishment in Ireland as soon as possible. She had grown up in a pre-war theatrical environment in Hungary. I'd once overheard her describing how when at school she, being Jewish, watched with alarm as classmates began to disappear one by one when the Nazis started their weeding trawl through Budapest society. Fortunately the family had managed to escape to London and there she'd met and married my Uncle Desmond. After a turbulent married life with him, first in London and then Monaghan, she had reverted to the stage and, with others, founded the Project Arts Centre in Dublin. The proposal being made by the two men was for me to establish myself as a frequent visitor at her Arts Centre and then start bringing them along as casual past acquaintances. Their goal was to develop an innocuous reason for hanging out in the bar that would not arouse suspicions among the rapidly rising number of Russian diplomats attached to the Soviet Embassy in Dublin who were habitual visitors. As Agnes's nephew I had the perfect cover. Her one-person Brecht performances and satirical Weimar Republic sketches were very popular with Eastern Bloc diplomats, whose numbers were not limited by Dublin and therefore needed covert monitoring, there being no travel identity checks between the Republic and the UK. Finally Shaw gave me a dedicated phone number so I could advise of a time and place to meet in Dublin. It was Beirut all over again.

I felt annoyed by the way I'd been conned into the meeting, and as the security situation appeared to be going from bad to worse in Ireland this prospect of again being used to check out Russians was a completely unwanted extra headache. Then the Field Marshal's parting words referring to the finding of 'useful employment' came to mind, and it was clear Whitehall had not let go of me just yet. The best way forward was to agree to take the boys to a couple of her performances at the Project when passing through Dublin some time later and, having done so, leave them to it. After that it felt vital for survival for me to break totally with the British Establishment.

In June the Cirencester agricultural course came to an end and, having witnessed the nightmare situation of mad in-laws combined with the almost doorstep proximity of the ongoing IRA war, Jane applied for and was accepted for a further three years at Bristol Art College. Moving into the gate lodge in Ireland for the summer brought some surprises. The north-facing building commanding the main entrance to the estate didn't take long to prove a virtual fridge, as not one window caught the sun. No insulation and an inefficient wood-burning stove providing the sole source of heat were rounded off by the building's location beside the village sewage plant. But the *coup de grâce* was the noise at night of heavy cattle lorries negotiating an incline outside the gates. Between midnight and 2 am there would be a whoosh-whoosh sound as laden transporters towing trailers passed, heading downhill for the border just a mile further on. The sound was enough to disturb sleep and warn that in 30 minutes or so there would be a repeated but louder 'chu-chunging' as the returning empty vehicles changed down gears to climb back up the incline. It was the last straw that had Jane enthusiastically skipping off to Bristol in September.

I had been on the farm for only days when it came to light that the commercial forestry on the estate was in the process of being sold to the government and, because of the way the conifer plantations were located around the field pastures, it would have a disastrous impact on any practical ability to continue farming. When I confronted Desmond in what was our first proper meeting concerning agricultural matters, he stated that the sale was well advanced, with contracts exchanged and a deposit paid. I could contact his conveyancing lawyer, but he did not hold out much hope. Reverting to the solicitor in the town for advice, a clerk spotted an error on the copy I'd been given of the map of the forestry sale. Further study proved there were solid grounds to demand a conveyancing delay, which provided precious time to somehow find a way to unravel the entire deal. Deeply frustrated at the way things had developed in our very first week at Glaslough, Jane and I went down to Dublin to stay with an old friend from army days. In passing, I told my tale of woe and, as luck would have it, was offered help. The government owed my host a favour, as he'd been able to use his position as chairman of Guinness Breweries to finance payment of the Garda Siochana's entire national wage bill during the six-month bank strike a few years before from cash accumulating in all the Republic's brewery-owned public houses. He would have a word with the relevant minister. A fortnight passed and then news came through that the government was prepared to withdraw from the purchase, provided the deposit was returned. My uncle's reaction was to increase the price being asked, reduce the acreage being sold by 20%, demand to be paid up-front in full within a month and send insulting letters to my legal representatives. In order to achieve something concrete I paid the principal in advance, expecting co-operation and a speedy completion, but it didn't happen and he lived out his *Rocky Horror Show* role of Frankenfurter to the full: 11 years were to pass before he finally capitulated and signed the contract of sale.

Coming up with €60,000 at short notice had been a story in itself. My bank manager in Galway had sounded hopeful on the phone and I went to see him on a Monday morning. Hearing how the government department had co-operated, he advised that he might be able to arrange something within a couple of days. Just before leaving he asked for help over a problem of his own. A recently deceased bank customer had left instructions for a large sum to be paid to what appeared to be a proscribed organisation. He didn't know what to do. When asked why he felt my opinion was of value he replied that it was because it related to 'an old comrades' association of a military nature'. He couldn't say much more at that moment, but might have more details when we met next.

The capital borrowing was sanctioned and once the banking business was done we set about sorting out the other matter. All he was empowered to say was that the association concerned had a symbol of a skull sitting above two crossed bones. To me it sounded very like the 17th/21st Lancers and I expected him to confirm that the words 'Or Glory' would appear in a ribbon below. Definitely no words or ribbon, just a skull looking slightly to one side, mounted over two bones. To my horror the penny dropped: we were talking about the death's-head insignia of the Waffen SS, and it appeared that a recently deceased client of the bank in Co. Galway had left a large sum to its old comrades' association. It wasn't going to be hard to find out who, and then there would be some fun. Realising I'd guessed the significance of the insignia, the manager had gone on to say that the young widow of the deceased was a 'lovely girl', and it would be a shame if 'things got out'. That confirmed who it was, and what I knew of the late client was recounted. An earlier, well-insured wife had died alone suddenly in a Spanish villa. I'd once helped him to his feet at the scene of a road accident when a passing car had knocked him off 'Old Tipp', a popular fox-hunting hireling. What seemed at the time nothing more than confused mutterings of a dazed person now fitted perfectly as a string of German expletives. I recounted the episode to Bill, who confessed he'd always held slight reservations about the chap – he had claimed to have spent the war in Spain because he had bad asthma –

but it hadn't ever affected his ability to spend days galloping across the countryside on the best hirelings to be had.

The summer of 1977 progressed with the realisation that the unplanned bank borrowing caused by the forestry purchase was going to leave me severely stretched financially, with no working capital to stock the farm. The conifer plantations were young and badly in need of a first thinning, with no mature timber to provide cash-flow. With effort a slow market for poles was developed but it was hard work and time-consuming. Jane's departure to Bristol meant that a bachelor life in the lodge began, but before I'd had the opportunity to visit the Coach and Horses in the village on my own my sister, her husband and some musical associates came up from Galway for a few days. This meant that shortly after arrival there was an expedition to the pub 'for a pint'. We kept to ourselves at the end of the bar, but it wasn't long before one of the gang broke into song, a tin whistle came out of a pocket, a fiddle from under a raincoat and a bouzouki was retrieved from the lodge. It was my first encounter with the village drinking circles and I was feeling somewhat apprehensive about the reception, but I needn't have worried as the singer I'd entered with was recognised early on as the son of Tom Barry, the famous IRA flying column leader during Ireland's War of Independence with Britain. Pints began sliding down the bar in rapid succession, and some friends made that night proved invaluable in helping me through turbulent years to come. The next day the whistle-player's dog bolted after a deer, pursuing it across the border into Northern Ireland, and in the process of retrieving it I photographed Dave, the singer, standing astride a ditch defining the border, so he physically had a leg in each country. With the ice broken in the village community, it wasn't long before a deputation from the Glaslough Tidy Town committee arrived to ask for my co-operation in cleaning up the cast-iron railings at the estate's main entrance. Though the village was a mixture of Catholics and Protestants the population had always been healthily integrated, acting as a single body in such efforts, and the invitation to become involved was perfect. It led to making contact with old friends and new doors being opened as I asked about for farming help and advice.

The Earl of Caledon, an immediate Northern Ireland neighbour with whom my property physically marched, was an enthusiastic forester and started coming round to look at the young plantations I'd purchased, on occasion bringing a very knowledgeable Polish silviculturist who was nearing retirement. The first meeting with him was quite formal, but the second time I met Stanislav Fifer my hand was grabbed enthusiastically and for a moment I thought it was a prelude to an embrace. The old boy was almost tearful with emotion as he began to describe his admiration for my grandfather, who, he believed, was largely responsible for Polish surviving as his country's national language. Apparently Shane had campaigned internationally in the first decade of the century for it to replace Russian in Polish schools and had overseen a petition signed by thousands of Irish schoolchildren. Fifer gave me an address, and said that if I was ever in Poland I should visit the Muzeum Narodnowe w Krakowie, as the 1908 petition was on permanent display. Dealing with this totally unexpected outpouring as we took shelter from a rainstorm wasn't easy, as I'd hoped to recruit the man to help with the forestry management task that lay ahead of me. I knew Shane had been passionate about reviving Gaelic as part of his vision of Ireland's own national identity, but news of this international foray was completely new ground. To try and make something of the meeting, as I'd rather lost my line of thought, I suggested we visit a Scots Pine wood Shane had been particularly fond of. I needed time to steer him into volunteering to assist in sorting out the congested woodlands, and hoped the walk would inspire him to do so. Sadly, it didn't work. His management advice was invaluable – but it remained that, just advice. Though the distance to Caledon village was minimal, it lay across the juridical line, and with all the blocked roads the northern forestry contractors were not interested in venturing into the Republic, where there was no active timber market to speak of. In the end the impenetrable banks of woodland were opened up by a local man working with a voice-operated horse called Daisy, and the extracted poles became a popular 'must have' farm item in the neighbourhood.

Then the deer arrived: first in twos and threes, but soon in groups of up to 30. I'd no gun, but felt compelled to do something. Word travelled

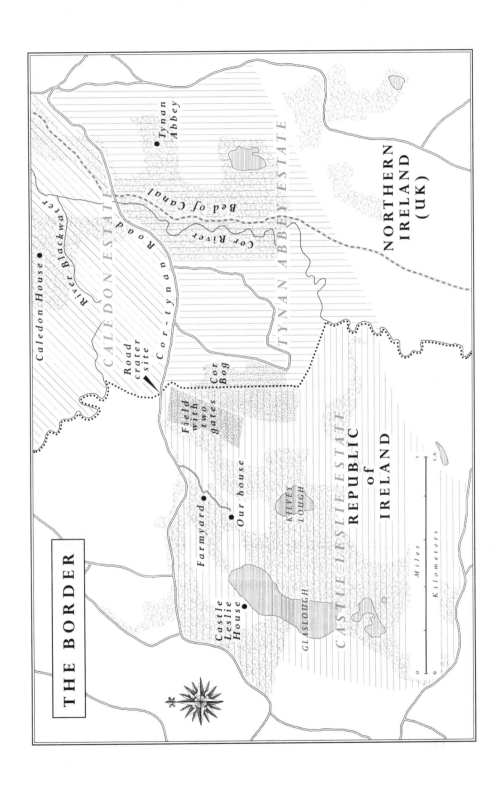

THE BORDER

Tynan Abbey

Caledon House

River Blackwater

CALEDON ESTATE

Bed of Canal

Cor River

TYNAN ABBEY ESTATE

NORTHERN
IRELAND
(UK)

Road
crater
site

Cor-tynan Road

Cor Bog

Field
with
two
gates

Farmyard

Our house

KILVEY LOUGH

CASTLE LESLIE ESTATE

REPUBLIC
of
IRELAND

Castle
Leslie
House

GLASLOUGH

Miles

Kilometers

0   1

0   1.6

and the town's parking warden arrived with a pump-action shotgun that took eight solid-ball cartridges, a belt of ammunition and a strange .243 rifle. The warden left the rifle with me after a little practice to make sure the telescopic sight, designed for use in poor light with rather wide lenses, was properly zeroed. It was an assassin's weapon, deadly accurate and capable of being effectively used even in moonlight. Safe arcs of fire covering popular grazing areas in isolated dells where groups of animals could be found at twilight were quickly worked out, so that culling could begin. Though 'lamping' after dark was frowned upon, the situation was dire, with now huge groups being observed moving from field to field on a clear night.

I laid into them as best I could, as social life was zero thanks to the Troubles, and with over a decade's absence from the county I just didn't have any kindred spirits to be distracted by. My most frequent visitors were the Gardai and a handful of elderly bachelor farmers looking for forest thinnings, who found it impossible to converse with Jane, a woman, if I wasn't home and she was on holiday from art school. One morning, when there were over 40 bloody carcasses hanging round the farmyard from machines and roof-beams, a Special Branch car roared up to the workshop door. I'd not yet had breakfast, had just gralloched and cleaned out five freshly shot buck, a rolled-up balaclava sat on my head and arms were bloodied to the elbows. My immediate reaction was to smile and offer the car occupants a pair of freshly removed kidneys, still warm and steaming in the cool morning air. A war was obviously raging all round me, but I was fighting a tough one of my own in the forests, and after one glance from the man in the back the car shot off without explanation. With the pressure I was under from the wildlife infestation I didn't care or worry. A game-dealer came for a few days' culling and bit hard into the numbers – his nine-inch curved gralloching knife fascinating the lads in the village pub, where he would sometimes use it to pick his nails after a day's work. Blood ran from under the tarpaulin covering the back of his laden pick-up, giving the smaller village boys great entertainment as they caught it in paint pots for use later in war games of their own making.

Eventually the Gardai Superintendent summoned me to his office at the top of an old Victorian building in Monaghan. After a preamble about being an admirer of my grandfather and his political activities in the early days of the State, he requested I stop borrowing unlicensed guns 'from lads round the town', as the paperwork for me to legally purchase one of my own would be sanctioned. Then the conversation turned to the security situation, and the extra effort patrol cars were having to make negotiating the estate road's potholes in order to check on my safety. Would it not be possible to move into the big house? Pointing out I didn't have a close relationship with my uncle, whose heir I was not as he had two sons, the policeman looked me straight in the eye and, apologising for saying it was probably none of his business, asked what exactly were my long-term intentions, as they seemed unclear. As I didn't have an answer the conversation lapsed into a slightly awkward silence. Then, thanking him for his concern and help in getting a rifle, I left the office but pulled over on the drive home to think about the point he'd made. It wasn't the first time somebody had questioned what I was doing in Monaghan, trying to settle down into family life, confronted by such a muddled set of circumstances, and each time insoluble worry clouds formed. They were temporarily dispersed by the beauty of the undulating farmland, the friendship of neighbours and the disciplined ignoring of the ongoing political turmoil, but the conversation with the Superintendent confirmed that my being at Castle Leslie was a serious issue as currently it had no real long-term purpose.

The autumn moved into winter and then the spring of 1978, with the routine of cattle-feeding, dung-spreading, harvesting firewood, battling with derelict buildings and containing roof leaks becoming the norm. With no social distractions and living alone, I fell asleep for the night in the pub more than once. The action-packed days of struggle to pull an under-capitalised farm together caused memories of a previous life to fade, and without a phone even contact with Jane was sporadic. The difficulty lay in the days being so filled with action involving machinery, animals, neighbours and contractors that there was hardly time to think or reflect. Sleep came fast, with sometimes the discovery on waking that I'd forgotten to take my boots off. The Superintendent's query continued to surface periodically but was countered by the view that, if my time at the family home was up it was up, and an event would dictate the moment.

The Troubles gained in intensity, as killings occurred nearer and nearer with increasing frequency, causing Lord Caledon's visits to become more discreet since he had taken up the reins of colonel of the Ulster Defence Regiment, a locally recruited paramilitary organisation designed to back up the Royal Ulster Constabulary. After Lord Mountbatten's murder not far away at Mullaghmore in August 1979 he asked what security precautions I took personally, being an ex-serviceman living in what was viewed to be a very dangerous environment. Pointing to some buildings in the distance across the border, I explained that word would come to clear off to Galway for a few days when there were 'bad articles' about – a euphemism for chaps up to something one didn't want any knowledge of. This caused a part-time B-Special to be instructed to find an opportunity to conduct an investigation. Somebody got wind of Stanley Hazelton's efforts, and he was shot dead at the foot of a farm lane within sight. The earl didn't visit me after that, and he died of a stroke the following May. At his funeral I met my other immediate neighbour, Sir Norman Stronge, whose estate in Co. Armagh was also in sight but in the North, like the third petal of a shamrock. Standing with a bunch of locals among tombstones as the coffin slowly made its way to the Caledon family vault, I was deeply shocked to be accosted by an old schoolfriend from Milton Abbey, dressed as a captain in full Grenadier Guards uniform. My local friends melted away with speed as Rhodri Wynn-Pope proceeded to ask after my sister and family, while I just stood rooted to the spot by the unexpected encounter. The episode was another stark reminder of the incompatibility of the two worlds I belonged to but with seemingly no way of bridging the gap.

Months went by and the succeeding earl came to live at Caledon. In the New Year of 1981 Jane and I invited him and his wife to dinner in the Coachman's House, our new abode, located at the end of a partially derelict Georgian stable block almost in the centre of the estate, where we had moved on Jane's graduation from Bristol. A date was set for 21

January, with the plan for him to drive to a point where the two estates met but were separated by the border, marked by an impassable crater in the road. This 'unapproved road' avoided a 15-mile road journey through a selection of security checkpoints. There they could park, walk round the obstacle and be ferried on in my car. As it was mid-winter the mud left by active cattle movements was pretty deep and the requirement for waterproof footwear had been overlooked. It was obvious I'd need to do something, so I knocked on the door of the nearby bungalow to ask for the loan of some boots. Dainty stockinged feet were dipped into well-used wellingtons and we shuffled across the frontier to my car. The evening proceeded normally until the end of the first course, when my uncle barged in to announce that Tynan Abbey was on fire and Lord Caledon needed to make immediate contact with the authorities in the North. A telephone had yet to be installed, so the call had to be made from the big house almost a mile away.

The news was grim. A body bearing close-quarter gunshot wounds to the head, including powder burns, had just been taken out of the Abbey, which was now completely on fire. My guests were not to return to their car but to proceed immediately to another border crossing point some miles away. We collected the countess and I drove them both to the Moy border crossing at Aughnacloy, where a large reception party of military and police was waiting at the far side of the bridge over the River Blackwater. As my dinner guests were being whisked out into the night a gloved hand came through the car window, which I'd opened in response to a thump on the roof. I was immediately grabbed by the throat and a voice I recognised from Pirbright said, 'Got you, you little shit.' At my reply, 'Fuck off, Richard', the hand released its grip and the balaclava-covered face disappeared back into the darkness. With no further interest being shown in me I turned round and drove home, calling in at Emyvale Gardai station on the way. There the duty sergeant was quietly reading a newspaper, and said he knew nothing whatever of any rumpus in the North.

Back at home the meal continued without further interruption, other than going outside to observe helicopter-mounted searchlights arcing around the sky. Next morning I went down to the border to return the wellingtons, only to find the old lady who'd loaned them somewhat upset. There had not been time for Lena to get back to her chair, having given me the footwear, before there was another knock on the door. She thought it must be me needing something else, but it was a group of hooded men with guns demanding the keys to all the cars outside. On taking what keys she had they'd gone, but when the RUC arrived later she stated that she 'thought it must be Mr King wanting something else', so had unwittingly placed me at the scene where the cars used in the atrocity had been hijacked.

During the day news began to break about the fire at Tynan Abbey and the double murder of Sir Norman and Jim Stronge. (The crime was destined to be recorded as one of the lowest points of the Troubles.) Gardai forensics teams combed the estate roads beside our home for tyre tracks and, examining a number of broken gate padlocks, slowly pieced together the fact that the escape route taken by the Abbey attackers was close by the house where we were all dining.

At a regimental dinner in London some time later I was cornered by Jim Eyre, my old commanding officer in Germany and now a general, who had been head of Army intelligence at Lisburn at the time of the incident. He told me that my face had been on his screen, as the Royal Ulster Constabulary suspected me of being the architect behind the Tynan assassinations. For a very long 45 minutes he'd struggled with the concept that I'd been a sleeper in the regiment for six years, but incoming facts had painted me in a very bad light. In response to advice that I should watch out for a Provisional IRA hot potato called Lynagh, the conversation took an awkward turn as I confessed I had already met the man. 'Big Jim's' eyes bored into me as I explained that there was a larger devil in the Glaslough area and he, Lynagh, had been leaned on to leave me alone by the local community because of the strategic value my land commanded, lying as it did along almost a mile of border with numerous crossing points. Smuggling had put food on tables round the village since 1924, enabling livings to be earned, whereas terrorism hadn't and didn't. Lynagh himself had come to my house to define the terms under which my presence would be tolerated, but warned that incoming foreign anarchist types who didn't know the form on the ground would remain a danger.

The disastrous start with my uncle over the forestry saga was destined to decline further, with a 'horse dealer' associate of his from near Belfast starting to bring groups of horses and riders for camping weekends. The kidnapping at gunpoint one evening of a visiting Belfast day rider just outside a building not 30 yards from where I was standing was the final straw that killed the enterprise, though I was blamed as somehow being a culpable party.

At this point a Frenchman wishing to spend a year in Ireland came to stay and earn his keep as an odd-job builder. Philippe had a useful second role in deflecting the persistent overtures by a well-heeled Northern businessman who was insistent on buying me out, but at a fire-sale valuation – 'the bigger devil'. The proximity of the border meant that I could count on the support of local cattle farmers and, thanks to Philippe who would act as a scout when word had it 'Tank' was in the area, roadside ambushes to attempt a 'conversation' were successfully foiled. The only mishap with Philippe was when he used an old oil barrel as a target to test the range of solid balls fired from a shotgun. I was standing some distance to the side of the barrel when a lead slug fell unexpectedly short, hit the frame of an iron gate lying on the ground, was deflected and banged up against my left leg. The shock and pain were nauseating but fortunately only severe bruising round the femur resulted, with nothing broken or cracked. A hospital visit warned of a big haematoma, subcutaneous bleeding and the likelihood of permanent muscle damage, but as the skin wasn't actually broken and didn't require stitching the injury wasn't classified as a gunshot wound requiring the Gardai to be informed.

The shooting incident was a total godsend. A nightmare situation had developed in that an expedition to see my mother in Galway for advice on how to deal with the multiplying family problems had ended up with my being cornered by Molly Cusack-Smith, who appeared minutes after my own arrival from a three-hour drive. She was hell-bent on having me hunt her pack of fox-hounds over the coming season, and wasn't taking no for an answer. My mother was obviously part of the plot, as she was immediately all for the idea, so for some weeks life had to be split between Monaghan and the kennels at Birminghame House outside Tuam.

I'd been totally steamrollered, with my own parents involved, so a way out of the situation had to be sensitively handled. Capturing the hounds' full attention would have been possible if the old dragon had not insisted on following on horseback when I walked them out in the mornings as they responded distractedly to her blood-curdling shrieks on what to do or not do. With the Wild West lifestyle of Co. Monaghan appearing to have travelled to Galway with a horrible twist, the only escape was Castle Hackett Hill, some miles off. Making for it with a tractor pulling the hounds' trailer and a couple of horses for me and a whipper-in became routine. The upper reaches of the mini-mountain were wild, fox-infested scrub, the perfect terrain for young hounds to be let loose to learn from their peers. While they did so I tried to cheer myself up by enjoying the landscape, which held something of interest in every direction: Tuam's cathedrals to the east, the riverside Norman keep and ruined Clare Abbey to the south, a ninth-century round tower to the west with Lough Corrib twinkling in the distance, and Castle Hackett brooding over all from the north. A giant cairn dominating the summit marked the reputed grave of Queen Maeve, at one side of which stood a high stone cross bearing the name of a General Bernard who'd had something to do with India. For me the hill was proving a unique sanctuary of peace and quiet while a way out of the mess could be found. Then Philippe's blessed trigger finger had done its bit.

In 1980, as social unease began to increase in intensity because of the stand-off between the Thatcher government and the IRA hunger strikers in the Maze prison demanding political status, Monaghan won the Best European Rural Museum Award. The curator had luckily managed to save the collection of artefacts when the town hall, where they had been on display, was set on fire during a riot. By unfortunate coincidence it had been the turn of a Westminster MP, Duncan Sandys, to be the European Minister of Culture representative when it came to visiting Monaghan town for the prize-giving. With the town hall out of action, the event was held in the St Louis Convent, where there was a room big enough to host the occasion.

The security situation required a large Gardai presence, and four heavily armed officers were positioned in an upstairs gallery facing the stage, where the ceremony commenced with curtains being drawn back to reveal a choir singing. Quite a large number of foreign press members as well as British and Irish were also allocated space in the fairly cramped balcony at the back, causing guns and camera gear to become somewhat tangled up. As the VIPs took their seats the curtains opened to reveal a Gardai officer armed with a sub-machine gun at each side of the stage. The choir sang on while the officers deftly inched their way into the folds of material and attempted to hide. After the welcoming and introduction speeches Sandys walked over and unveiled the covered exhibit that had been positioned centre-stage. A gasp was audible at the unexpected revelation of Miró's *Big Breasted Woman*, which needed a moment to take in. The nuns took it well, but for a while Duncan Sandys looked as though he was stuck between a rock and a hard place as he made polite conversation with the Mother Superior. Reaching bed that night I found my stomach-muscles were aching from laughter – the evening had been Ireland at its best.

When my uncle's daughter, my cousin Samantha, came home from a hotel management course in Switzerland and announced that she wanted to set up a horse livery business, life became further complicated. Out of family loyalty, storage for dung, hay, a tack room, water, electricity and transport were provided, but it was obvious that her enterprise was going to hit the buffers eventually because of a general lack of proper capital investment as well as strong market competition. Being fully occupied in running the farm and forestry it was easy for me to avoid being sucked into the maelstrom brewing, though, like flickering sun-flares, occasional strongly worded letters would arrive from her father accusing me, the family whipping boy, of somehow being responsible for his problem of the day. After a couple of occasions when the Gardai had called and asked me to clear out of the county for a period because of security concerns, it became clear that the time had arrived to think seriously about stepping back from the madness. The farm was working and the forestry was turning a corner into profit, but the domestic side of life had begun to make absolutely no sense.

Then, purely by chance, it came to light that my uncle had embarked on a scheme to sell the walled garden overlooking the lake to a Dublin developer. The purchaser was being granted permission to build houses and a restaurant within the walled four acres. I was stunned to the core. Tom Leslie's golden yews were still there, overgrown and unpruned but still a poignant reminder of someone who had once also loved the place. For me it was the end. If the walled garden, the aesthetic heart of the estate, went out of the family's hands there was no point in holding on at Glaslough – the magic spell that existed would be broken, with the estate's integrity totally compromised. Intercepting my uncle *en route* to complete the deal in Dublin, I made it clear that I was off if he proceeded with the sale. His wife was apoplectic. Days later he informed me he'd pulled out, as I'd requested, but was therefore now short of the 100,000 Punts the sale would have realised. He needed some sort of compensation and what was I proposing to do about it. When I asked if he would sell it to me he asked why, and was horrified by my idea of building a house located between the two greenhouses – the view over the lake from that spot being particularly spectacular in the evenings.

Stunned at being refused the option of purchasing the garden when it had been offered to a total stranger, Jane and I motored to Galway and told my mother I had had enough of trying to make a home in Monaghan – ignoring the omnipresent security situation, which was dire, the void between myself and 'the big house' had become just too wide. Sadness wasn't a factor. Jane was expecting a baby and her doctor across the border in Tynan suggested she made plans to have it in England as, if she went into labour in the night at Glaslough, it might not be possible to get to the hospital in time because of the number of roadblocks. I'd recently been woken in the early hours by someone from the village asking me to get his wife and child quickly to a doctor. On dressing and going downstairs I met a chap I knew at the door who said I was the only man who could negotiate the numerous checkpoints round Keady across the border at that time of night. His wife was stranded there with a very sick child. He couldn't go himself as he was 'wanted' in the North, so I agreed to help and sped off to the village about six miles away in South Armagh, weaving through four official and two paramilitary checkpoints on the way. Red Republican number plates combined with a British driving licence did the trick, leading to the child, who had suffered a cerebral fit, being safely delivered to Dr Gillespie's door at 2 am. He was waiting in a dressing gown but, being also Jane's doctor, was horrified on catching sight of me as the driver. The return journey was made through the same checkpoints, collecting an order for firewood at one before I climbed back into bed.

In the summer of 1981, therefore, I took a heavily pregnant Jane to stay at her mother's house at Hambleden, near Henley, a short walk from the River Thames. With the summer harvest fast approaching I needed to keep focused in Ireland without domestic distraction, and on my return stayed alone at our home in the woods. One night my dog woke me, whimpering at the bedroom door, an odd thing for her to do as she normally barked loudly at any sound of visitors. At the same time there was a noise of breaking glass downstairs. Voices outside warned me that there were people at the front and both sides of the building, but unlike my night-time caller of a few weeks earlier they didn't sound friendly or call my name. As I reached for a gun under the bed the garage door could be heard being opened, followed by a pause before somebody cried, 'There's no car'. At that more murmuring, long silence, then the sound of an engine starting in the distance. My bedside clock read 01.18/28/07. In the morning I found that a glass pane by the handle in the conservatory door had been broken. Luckily I was in the habit of taking the key out when locking it at night or I might well have had to confront an unwanted visitor. The garage had fortunately been empty because a cousin's car had broken down and I'd loaned him my orange 2CV. When I reported the incident the Gardai came and, after a cursory investigation for foot and tyre prints, Gardai Sergeant Hugh Coll told me to 'go on a long holiday as from right now'. There was no alternative other than to put most of my stuff hastily into store in the roof space, install caretakers and leave for the ferry to England.

All was well until 21 November, when a fire gutted the building, all but the roof. When Jane was told the news she went into labour and produced our son William, helped by Mr Pinker in the Lindo Wing of St Mary's

Paddington, while a gory childbirth death scene in *War and Peace* played out silently on a TV monitor. Moments after he'd arrived in the world I was left alone with my infant son while the doctor attended to Jane, and for a few minutes we just stared at each other. Meeting his quizzical expression before his eyes closed I made a promise I'd give him a more structured start in life than I'd had. It might be less exciting but that way a future career path might be easier to map out and follow.

Returning to Ireland to deal with the insurance assessor I was busy digging through the kitchen debris and rubble of fallen plaster one evening, trying to recover some crystal glasses, when three men appeared in the doorway. They entered the room between me and my gun, which had been left on a window ledge, making me feel the game was finally up. They were all big-framed men and hadn't taken their hats off, signalling that it was official business of some sort, and with the fading light from behind their faces were unrecognisable. One had an object in his hand, which he raised. I held my breath, but when he spoke all was well. They were three neighbours, and the raised object was a bottle of whiskey wrapped in brown paper. The reason for the hats remaining on was because they were a delegation who had come to tell me I was not to feel compelled to sell up the farm because of what had happened. 'You're not to go, you know why,' was stated with emphasis, as if I did so it would put long-established smuggling routes at risk. There then followed an instruction as to what was going to happen to rectify the situation. The insurance money was to be left on account at Pattons' hardware store in the town and the house would be rebuilt with no labour costs. At that the hats came off, the bottle was opened and the crystal glasses put to their designated use. Afterwards I sat for a while by the fire, reflecting on what an extraordinary interlude it had been, swinging from expectation of imminent death to gossiping humorously about neighbours' attempts to dodge customs officers. After the initial misunderstanding and another momentary bumping of the two worlds I'd felt totally at ease, but in my heart I knew my schizophrenic existence had run its course, painful and sad though the admission was.

I returned to Jane in England for Christmas and the New Year of 1982, leaving repairs to the house to proceed at an amazing pace with a group of totally unknown faces beavering away through the early spring. Anger over the Maze hunger strikes raged with increasing ferocity as prisoner after prisoner died in the prison hospital ward. There had been a general election in Ireland the previous June, when one of the hunger strikers, Kieran Doherty, had been elected as a Monaghan representative in the Dail Eireann, only to expire shortly afterwards. Disturbances became commonplace everywhere, night and day, round Monaghan town, with much flying of black flags, causing the Gardai to ask me to stay away on a more long-term basis and take my guns from the station, as it was expected to be burned down at any moment. On the nightly TV news it was clear that Thatcher was beginning to come under pressure from America's General Haig to give way to the IRA's demand for political status for the prisoners, thanks to increasing opposition to her stand being voiced by influential Irish American lobbyists. Glaslough and my farm was right in the thick of the turmoil, with all sorts of foreign agitators starting to appear in the two village pubs.

The future looked dire indeed, with no glimmer of light of any kind on the horizon. Safely back with Jane at her family home, I made a promise that I'd find a little abode for us somewhere in England, paid for by selling some land when the spring ploughing season arrived. Back at Glaslough to oversee things, hot tea was being delivered to a neighbour busy preparing a field for sowing when he stopped his engine and announced that 'Falklands has been invaded'. This was stunning news. The 'Faulklands' we both knew was a local townland area lying between the villages of Glaslough and Emyvale, about three miles to the west. Being on a hill we had a view east across the Cor Bog, south to Middletown and north across the border to Caledon. The elevated panorama overlooking Northern Ireland was completely empty of helicopters and any sort of logistic activity supporting a military incursion, so how the invasion had leapfrogged a couple of miles into the Republic was a bit of a mystery. No distinctive thud-thud of laden Sihanouk or C130 Hercules transports dropping supplies, not a thing in the sky, yet the excited chatter from the tractor radio described a major military operation somewhere to be in full swing. A bigger question: why was 'Faulklands' the target? There was nothing there other than the stump of an old castle and the home of 'JR', a well-known cattle dealer.

Gradually, the picture became a little clearer and a memory came to mind of Bill having mentioned some islands of a similar-sounding name but located in the South Atlantic where, in the twilight, he had sighted the unlit hull of an 1850s-era ship moving slowly on its own, far out of any shipping lane. It had made him feel perhaps not quite up to continuing his attempt to circumnavigate the world, but he had gone on to do so and later discovered he'd spotted the SS *Great Britain* being towed home to Bristol on a raft. Back at the house everyone was gathered round a radio and before long we were all in the Pillar House bar discussing what might happen next over pint after pint.

Nobody realised it right then, but very soon after the invasion of those little-known islands on almost the other side of the world the IRA hunger strike came to an end. The world's media had raced *en masse* from Belfast and the Maze prison hospital wing over to Whitehall to hear what Thatcher planned to do next. When she announced she was ordering a task force to be assembled and declared war against General Galtieri's invasion forces the cheering was deafening – this from men who only days earlier had been calling for her blood. Quietly, the hunger strikers stopped their protest. Nobody noticed. Nobody lost face – neither Thatcher nor the boys in their beds. Like her, they had stood their ground for a cause they believed in and not given way, but Galtieri had provided everyone with an escape out of the impasse that had had the world holding its breath for weeks. It transpired that most of the men rebuilding the house were IRA members 'not on the run or nothing', and as hints of details concerning the task force weaponry began to be made public I was proclaimed to be an authority on the Harrier jump-jet's capabilities and armaments, secret and otherwise. Everyone continually voiced views on what might be possible and how military hardware might be best deployed, this lasting until the house repairs were completed.

13
Dorset Village Characters

As the Argentine war progressed in the spring of 1982 I returned to Jane and our infant son to go on a house-hunting expedition in the UK, armed with a current copy of *Country Life*. First day, second house, and that was it. We'd found Pentridge House in Dorset. I made an offer which was accepted, provided we completed in a month, so I returned to Ireland to sort out the capital, while Jane went to her bank in London and, on the back of a fortunate old friendship with the head of the loans department, was able to organise bridging finance. The bank rate being a somewhat steep 19%, I needed to square the debt without delay, but discovered that the exchange controls put in place by the Irish Central Bank in 1979 to protect the new-born 'Punt' were still very much in existence. Land deals done, I had the cash in Irish currency to pay for our new home, but could not get it out of the Republic, leaving no alternative but lean on old border friends.

Jane came over to Ireland with our baby and spent the summer in the restored house while bullocks were purchased and 'moved through the farm' into the world of sterling. A few extra operations were conducted, one of which involved the laying of a purpose-made track to take the weight of articulated lorries laden with steel girders negotiating the crater in an officially closed border crossing. Two months later, with operations completed, Jane and I went to stay with her father in Aberdeenshire. There Hamish was the chief of the local Highland and Friendly Society, which paraded every August at the Lonach games. On the Sunday morning after the festival we attended a drinks party given by Professor R.V. Jones, a neighbour who famously 'bent the radio navigation beams' German bomber crews used to fly along during the Second World War. The party was also attended by what was obviously a group of army officers from a Highland regiment guarding the Queen 15 miles away at Balmoral – they were all immaculately turned out in matching kilts and tweed jackets. I was asked by one who introduced himself as the regimental intelligence officer for the Black Watch if I'd been in Ulster recently, as my face was familiar. Everyone reacted when I mentioned where I lived and said I had only recently motored over to Scotland. One had raised and crossed his forefingers, saying he'd been observing me through the telescopic sights of his rifle as dawn broke two months earlier as I guided a group of lorries over an improvised bridge at a closed border crossing point. As the vehicles, laden with steel, had been heading south into the Republic they posed no obvious security threat so the Army had not intervened, but I was asked what it was all for. 'Industrial building roof frames' was my understanding. The moment arrived for me to be introduced to our host, the Professor, so I assured my interrogators Jane and I would be off their patch in a couple of days and they could then sleep easy.

By October the capital-transfer-via-cattle job was complete and we loaded up what was left of our belongings and moved to Dorset. A last-minute hitch had arisen over lodging the Northern Ireland abattoir cheques to Jane's account at her London bank. A bank teller refused to accept three cheques totalling over £100,000, drawing my attention to the lurid 'Lurgan Abattoir' lettering in red print, stating that they were 'trade'. My argument that Jane's family were well known to the bank and the cheques were in sterling was falling on deaf ears, until a man in the adjoining till queue came to the rescue by moving over and engaging me in conversation. He turned out to be Peter Townend, the *Tatler* editor. His statement to the teller, 'It's all right, I know the family,' followed by a little wave of the hand, had an immediate effect on the clerk behind the grille and as I listened to my rescuer begin a summary of my and Jane's family backgrounds one eye watched the cheques being taken away for processing. At 19% bank interest rates I'd been in a hurry to get them lodged – I could have kissed the man.

Thanks to the fire, everything we owned now fitted into a Volvo estate and horse trailer. The day the *Mary Rose* was raised from the sea floor after 400 years, 8 October 1982, was also the day we arrived at Pentridge. It was a somewhat spartan existence for a time, but we didn't care as we were just grateful to have escaped the Ulster nightmare intact. The first

Sunday we went to the church on hearing bells ring, and as we emerged a heavy hand descended on my shoulder. An elderly gentleman bellowed, 'You've got my house', and then introduced himself as Dr Sargant. (He turned out to be the controversial psychoanalyst who had invented electric shock treatment for schizophrenia, and had caused alarm in America over his unorthodox methods when psychoanalysing Patti Hearst, the kidnapped media heiress.) Beside him a chatty lady called Margaret asked us back for a drink and we went round to the Owens' house where her husband Robert was planing a kitchen door. Professor Owen was a member of the Royal Society and told me he had physically captured and later interrogated the German V2 rocket scientist Werner von Braun at the end of the Second World War. Searching the slave camp factories of Mittelwerk and Nordhausen, he had arrested the man and come across his Nazi membership card during an identity check. The Americans weren't interested in it as a record of the man's past, so he'd kept it.

Some days later a Mrs Beamont knocked on the door and invited us to come to her house one evening and meet some other villagers. On being introduced to her husband Rolly, Jane commented on his tie, as it featured the British Isles. He told her it was quite rare as it was worn only by Battle of Britain pilots who qualified as 'The Few'. When I commented on a silver model of a familiar-looking jet fighter on a table, he said it was of the TSR2 fighter-bomber of which he had been the test pilot. I couldn't believe my ears! There we met Judith Gillespie-Smith, another professor who lived alone in the house opposite our gate. She wasted no time in starting to talk about how she lectured at Reading University on ways of containing desert encroachment afflicting countries in sub-Saharan Africa. In time we got to know her quite well and would often meet students from a variety of countries such as Mali, Ghana, Niger, and Sudan, who stayed with her for holidays. As an entomologist her lectures focused on insects, parasite control and ways of arresting the desert's advance, but her growing concern was the expanding presence within the university campus of Islamic Fundamentalist 'watchers', whose intimidation of African undergraduates appeared to be completely unmonitored. After our five quiet years of social semi-isolation this rich intellectual cocktail contained within the hamlet of 26 houses was heady stuff to absorb – but there was more.

Answering a knock at the back door I was confronted by two young men who introduced themselves in heavily accented English as 'Petyr' and his navigator 'Heini' from the Luftwaffe. They announced that their Tornado gearbox had broken – they needed help. Looking over their shoulders down the drive I almost expected to see a pointed grey nose-cone of some sort, but there was nothing there so I guessed something must have been lost in translation. Petyr went on to explain in rough English that he was looking for Rolly Beamont and had been advised that he met Air Force people only by appointment. Their Tornado had developed a fault on a NATO exercise and while it was being repaired at Boscombe Down he had come to visit Mrs David, his aunt, who lived in the village, as she was married to a tenant farmer of the Cranborne estate. I phoned Mrs Beamont and explained I'd a couple of NATO pilots on my doorstep who were TSR2 enthusiasts and wanted Rolly to sign a picture of the aircraft they had with them. I had overlooked saying they were Germans, and received a bit of a wigging later as the old Wing Commander was plagued by Luftwaffe veterans wishing to go over various wartime dogfights.

Shortly afterwards the local pack of foxhounds held their Christmas meet in the village, hosted by Mr and Mrs David on an area of land just beside our house. I introduced myself and was invited for a drink. So began a long and friendly association with John and Urte David. She had grown up in East Prussia and could remember the July plot when Hitler was almost killed, as the base where it happened was on her family's estate. Hitler himself used to visit the family and on such occasions it had been her role as the young girl of the house 'to bring in ze cooken'. I asked if she'd actually met Hitler face to face and she replied, 'yes', and not only him but 'all ze boys'. On the day of the assassination attempt she'd watched staff cars 'buzzing like bees' as they raced about. Then the Russians had come and she and her mother had been forced to flee westwards, suffering all sorts of ghastly dramas. Somehow she had made it to Britain and trained as a nurse. Her brother had escaped to Sweden at the collapse of Germany and was now a vet in Munich. (His son was one of the visiting Tornado pilots.)

Some time later Margaret Owen, of a Lithuanian Jewish background, fell ill with a severe spinal complaint and could hardly move. She needed nursing, and Urte insisted on doing so. Sitting for hours she, Urte, related to Margaret details of the terrible ordeal her brother had been through at the end of the war. From boyhood he had wanted to be a vet above anything else, but when the Nazis came to power they had taken control of secondary education, compelling all to join the party before being able to continue in any formal type of career path. So, in order to train as a vet, he first had to join the SS. At the collapse of the Third Reich the German people had turned on the SS, blaming them for the catastrophe befalling the country, and he had been beaten terribly. A hospital ship had taken him first to Sweden, from where he was subsequently transferred to Britain. On recovery he'd been repatriated and began a new life in Munich pursuing the career he'd always sought. Over coming weeks the identity of another one-time village resident was brought to my attention. Pamela Gouldsbury, the late wife of my immediate neighbour, a retired colonial police officer, had worked as a nurse in Malaya during the Communist insurgency in the early 1950s. Her book *Jungle Nurse* recorded how, on her own initiative, she had set up chains of self-help medical centres reaching deep into the tropical forests for the benefit of the aboriginal tribes, who were otherwise at the mercy of the anti-government terrorists. Her operations had proved fundamental to the 'Hearts and Minds' policy introduced later by General Templer, when he was put in charge as military ruler of the entire country. The Field Marshal had written the foreword for her book, published in 1960, describing her as a key player in the success of the campaign – the 'fedora hat' again! After five years of total immersion in the bogs of Ireland it was exhilarating to start rebuilding a social life among such a disparate collection of individuals – I felt like a hermit emerging into daylight after years in a cave.

We were in our new home only a week when two grey-suited men appeared without warning at the front door. My immediate assumption was that they were TV licence inspectors, but it turned out that they were Special Branch policemen. The Republic of Ireland red number plates on my old Volvo had apparently set all sorts of alarm bells ringing at a nearby

Royal Signals camp. Back home the registration number 3871 ID had been 'hot' for a while, as one of the previous owners had been on a wanted list. I'd thought it a cheap buy at the time and only afterwards had found out why. Somebody in the UK had done their homework and the officers asked if they could come in and have a word. We sat in my makeshift dining room, which had a door on a box for a table and two trunks to sit on. The house was yet to be carpeted and Jane was busy making curtains. A short résumé covering what had brought us to Dorset appeared to satisfy their immediate concerns but, as they prepared to leave, one of them, Peter Storer, advised that he would like to keep in touch and gave me his card in case something came up that I felt he should know about. It didn't register at the time, but we were destined to meet again after a couple of decades with a great deal to discuss.

As the months passed, social life at Pentridge picked up. Inevitably locations of old school friends materialised and new characters were encountered when not visiting the Irish farm. While dining in a large old pile nearby in the New Forest I unexpectedly ran into Terence O'Neill, an old family friend and long-standing hero of mine who, on resigning as Prime Minister at Stormont in the face of the erupting Ulster conflagration of the late 1960s, had retired to the south of England with his wife. Back in 1963, as the Unionist leader of Northern Ireland, he'd responded to the IRA calling an end to its war and disbanding that year by entering into talks with Seán Lemass, his opposite number in Dublin. They commenced work on introducing some all-island economic initiatives – but the reforms had proved too much for some Unionist hard-liners, who had forced him out of office in 1969.

We soon began to chew the cud on the outcome of Mrs Thatcher's stand-off with the IRA, and it wasn't long before the old boy homed in on Caledon, three miles from home, where he firmly believed the initial flashpoint of the modern round of Troubles was centred. The village had been the setting for a demonstration led by one of the first civil rights activists, who rallied a crowd to march in protest at the way some Catholic squatters were being evicted from a council house. Almost to himself he began to reminisce, 'Austin Curry was my undoing. His demonstration, small though it was, paved the way for all that was to come. It led to the Burntollet Bridge ambush and then Ulster was afire.' To lighten the atmosphere, Lady O'Neill interjected with a story of how they had once arrived rather early for dinner at Castle Leslie and on entering the drawing room had stumbled across the then Earl of Caledon 'rather far into the process of seducing a lady on the sofa'. The humour with which the old girl described the incident – 'We just went neatly into reverse, still arm in arm' – saved a gloomy atmosphere from descending. The evening was yet another reminder of the two incompatible spheres of energy that were still out there, somehow co-existing and rubbing sparks off each other: the same two villages, Caledon and Glaslough, separated by just three miles but, from a social viewpoint, divided by an ideological chasm reaching to infinity.

14

Irish Horse Wars, Japan, and a Fraud Case

Ⓢ

In 1985, the year our daughter Olivia was born, my mother died peacefully in her sleep at Oranmore in November, leaving Bill with a broken heart and her younger brothers with a sense of massive loss. As the eldest sibling she had been the main pillar of support in their lives since childhood, thanks to a sickly mother, and now, suddenly, she was gone. Jack was left to ponder on his future in Rome and Desmond to make the best of a somewhat diminished estate. Since the age of three Jack had suffered from ill-health, and my mother had helped steer him through life until he found his feet restoring buildings in Italy. Desmond had demanded in 1964 that he be made owner of the family home, without any experience or land management training, in the mistaken belief that intelligence alone would suffice.

A great family funeral took place with a full-blown wake in the gallery of the old family home, before burial according to her wishes beside the lake she loved so. Oddly, at the moment of interment a small tornado momentarily swept down the water, shaking the tree branches and scooping up clouds of dead leaves in its path. Though she was my mother, and a person to whom I was close, my grieving came later, allowing time to console Bill, but eventually I mourned, in private and alone, walking through the woods and fields with just the cawing rooks to comfort a heavy heart. Her woods, her fields, her great love.

As the dust of her departure settled it came to light that Jack was suffering badly from depression. It had been alleviated by my mother's twice-weekly 'family news' letters, which of course had now ceased, and then, to compound matters, the lease on his house in Rome expired, leaving him with no idea of what to do. After an anxious few months for everybody he came home to take tours round the castle – totally reinventing himself – while his younger brother's health went into a steady decline with the onset of emphysema. For me Jack had been a distant figure who appeared briefly every summer to express views on life more suited to another age, and I hardly knew him until he returned home to become the beating heart of the family after four decades of semi-isolation in Rome.

A healthy portion of an American trust that terminated on my mother's death was used to support my step-grandmother at her nursing home in Brighton, in order to prevent the sale of a large cache of Jerome family letters that had been the bulk of my grandfather's estate. These were brought to Pentridge to be added to the document collection that had built up round my mother's writing career. Reading through the boxes of manuscripts and letter collections, I slowly formed an impression of what Shane's hopes for Ireland had been in the early years of the 20th century, before the Rebellion and War of Independence. He'd envisioned a society of artists and poets that reflected the island's fifth-century 'Golden Age' but had found no way of connecting his dream with the need for it to compete on the world stage as a modern nation. His poetic descriptions of the Drumlin Hills of Monaghan and the linkages back to ancient times struck a chord and made me think that there was merit in what he'd been looking for, and that there might be some unique non-confrontational resource still waiting to be discovered. In time it appeared, but not before many years of being fully occupied with the farm in Ulster and bringing up a young family in the UK.

When William and Olivia were old enough to enjoy it a small sailing boat big enough for us all to sleep on board was purchased and kept on the Dorset coast. *Talitha* could float in ten inches of water, so not only beaches but rivers were accessible for picnics and camping expeditions whatever the tide, and as the years of bucket and spade slipped by we became closely bonded as a family.

Then came an event of unique proportions.

Without warning, one day in late November 1990 I was phoned from London by a brother-in-law of Jane's and asked if I could help a property developer associate organise a tour round Britain for a visiting Japanese politician who was looking to buy or lease a substantial country house. After a hasty briefing I drew up a two-day tour which roughly answered the requirement. It began with Mr Kutsuzawa and his accompanying interpreter arriving at Salisbury by limousine and being taken to Trafalgar House, a large Georgian stately pile outside the city, which was conveniently on the market. This was followed by an in-depth tour round the Houses of Parliament by a cousin, after which I warned there was a very full schedule planned for the next day.

It began at 7 am with a taxi to Heathrow and a flight to Dublin where a contact with government connections had arranged for Mr Kutsuzawa and his interpreter to be greeted in the VIP lounge on arrival. After a brief 'welcome to Ireland' ceremony we walked out to a helicopter and flew up to Monaghan, landing 20 minutes later on the lawn in front of the big house at Glaslough. There were two properties for sale in Ireland that fitted the Japanese requirement, but I thought a view of my ancestral home would amuse. As it was November, Desmond and family were in the south of France and the building was empty apart from the housekeeper, who owed me a favour as I had managed to open some doors that had frozen shut during a recent period of hard frost. A message had been passed to her that I was arriving with some friends for coffee at 11 am and would be in the house for half an hour. We landed by ancient, tall lime trees and, even to me, the place by its shimmering lake looked superb in the milky winter sunshine. Crossing the fountain garden we entered through the gallery door, on a glass pane of which Desmond had stuck an 'Area 51' warning notice. The significance of the joke connection to Roswell in New Mexico as a suspected UFO crash site was not lost on the Japanese, and commented on with humour.

In the drawing room, coffee was waiting. While dealing with the cups and biscuits I asked the party to look through the window to the terrace and told them that Jackie Kennedy had picnicked there with Aristotle Onassis on their honeymoon, and en route to stay with a fellow American at his castle in Donegal. The cased jade bracelet given to my grandmother by the Empress Dowager of China in 1906 was pointed out, along with the framed christening dress worn by Winston Churchill, which was sitting on a chair. This had an electrifying impact on both Japanese and I was asked to explain why it was in the house. To make things simple and easier to understand I took everyone over to a small painting featuring the three Jerome sisters, who had all come over to Europe from America in the 1860s to be married into British society. One had become a Churchill, one a Frewen and one a Leslie. Winston had been the son of the eldest, Jenny. The son of another, Leonie, had been my grandfather, making the two boys first cousins. 'Granny Leo', my great-grandmother, also Winston's aunt, had died in the house in 1943 and was buried in the family vault below the church that could be seen out of the window. The christening smock had done the rounds of all the sisters' children, ending up here in the house because the youngest, my great-uncle Lionel, was the last to wear it. All this took considerable time to translate. Next we moved on to the dining room for a run-through of the family portraits. Here a potted history was given using paintings looking down from the walls, covering Mrs Fitzherbert's secret marriage to the heir to the throne of England (later George IV), their 'adopted' daughter's marriage to an earl, down to Constance, her granddaughter, who had married John Leslie, helping him build the current house we were in.

With that we returned to the helicopter and flew down to Slane for lunch. Slane Castle was for sale and I thought might be of interest to the Japanese. During the house tour we came across an enormous portrait of King George IV and before I could say anything our host, the owner, stepped in with an explanation of how he was descended from a later royal mistress, the Marchioness of Conynghame, and, unlike my link to Mrs Fitzherbert, his family had benefited greatly from a royal patronage 'after-glow'.

The shortness of daylight in late November meant we didn't hang around and flew on to Abbeyleix, which was also on the market. With the pilot anxious about time we had only minutes for a quick peep into the main drawing-room, where I wanted to point out the ceilings, but the Japanese interest was totally captivated by a pair of Chinese urns. Then it was back into the helicopter and off to the airport before the light became too poor to fly. There was just time for a pint of Guinness as we caught our return flight to London. On reaching Claridge's I faced the two Japanese gentlemen in the hotel foyer and stated that though it had been a long day there was one important matter we needed to talk about, the Second World War, and perhaps it should be done now, maybe while having something to eat. For a moment the two men stood rooted to the spot, while the interpreter repeated his translation to confirm what I'd said, after which both began to smile broadly, bow and shake hands. Over a steak I put the case that we in the West understood how Japan had fallen into the grip of a small power-hungry cabal, which had led the Emperor and his people down a path to disaster. The hundreds of years of martial rule under the Shoguns had resulted in a population with little strength to resist or fight a new authoritarian onslaught. There was no resentment against the Japanese people, only General Tojo and his cronies. This synopsis seemed to go down extremely well and resulted in some firm handshaking. Somehow the massive cultural divide between our two societies had been tentatively bridged. The meal over, I went home to Dorset, leaving others to show the gentlemen aspects of London before returning to Tokyo.

The next month I was invited by Mr Kutsuzawa to accompany a female London house agent to Japan, as there were some important people in Tokyo keen to meet me and, again, all expenses including a first-class air fare were on offer. On 4 December we set off on a direct flight to Tokyo, with the tickets providing beds and champagne. As it was December and the night sky clear, it was easily possible to ascertain when we crossed over into what had recently been the Iron Curtain and east German airspace. The lights of towns and illuminated roadways just suddenly stopped. Occasionally a faint glimmer showed to the north but otherwise the ground below appeared as if covered with a dark blanket, though I knew it wasn't cloud. Time passed and we were over the immense moonlit stretches of the USSR, where the snow-covered Urals and meandering white ribbon of the frozen Ob river could be seen drifting by. Huge open-cast mines occasionally scarred the landscape, which otherwise didn't give up any secrets or signs of human activity. Finally, after ten hours and many time zones, a glow on the horizon accompanied by a slight change of course heralded the approach to Japan and our destination. On reaching our hotel, we had 45 minutes to recover before the first meeting, which turned out to be a briefing on the week's activities. Jetlag kicked in with a vengeance. It turned out taking advantage of the on-tap champagne had its downside and left me pretty woolly-headed for the next 24 hours – even the hotel carpets occasionally appeared spongy and undulating, with a simple step occasionally going a bit askew. The description of the city's wards and where we would be going was hard to follow, as we struggled over a meal of authentic sushi, raw seaweed and green tea that tasted like grass – and proved impossible to swallow without great difficulty. The first venue was the Setagaya Ward museum, where an introduction to Mr Kutsuzawa's uncle, the mayor, was followed by a tour around the municipal offices. After tea in the mayoral suite we were taken to view an array of Egyptian stoles, Pharaohs' clothing and endless stone slabs covered in hieroglyphic carvings.

The only other occupants of the chamber were a tight knot of elderly gentlemen who advanced crabwise in our direction, parted and encircled me and Guhen, the interpreter. A very small but dignified figure was introduced as His Royal Highness Prince Mikasa, and after a round of pleasantries I was asked to confirm I was a member of the Churchill family. My reply explaining how my grandfather and Winston were first cousins was translated in bites to the group. This prompted the Prince to raise a hand and state that he had an important question: 'Why, as a failed and discredited politician, had Churchill been able to exercise such influence over America and bring them into the war on his side with just one speech? He had not featured in Japanese pre-war assessments of Britain's possible leaders.' The significance of Jenny's father being an American was not grasped in my initial reply and I had to repeat the point, emphasising the salient facts. When the detail of the trans-Atlantic family link became clear the group went into a huddle and murmured excitedly for some time, with much deep 'aahhhh-ing', before opening up again for the Prince to announce, 'In Japan women do not have status. Why did she not marry an American?' It took time to translate how the fact that old Mrs Jerome was partly First Nation American excluded her daughters from entering American and British society on reaching marriageable age, which meant that they had to be taken to Europe to find suitable husbands. This was followed by a long silence. The facts seemed seriously to un-amuse the old boy and it was clear the audience was over when, after much repeated expressionless bowing on all sides, the party closed round the Prince and departed. On the way back to the hotel I asked the interpreter if I had offended H.R.H. in some way. He replied that 'being informed that Churchill was descended from an American Aboriginal had been a bit of a shock for His Royal Highness'. It was only then that it sank in that I'd been engaged in conversation with the younger brother of Emperor Hirohito, the Japanese wartime leader.

At a formal dinner the next night one senior gentleman introduced himself as 'Headmaster of the Military Academy' (I discovered later that this was the Japanese equivalent of Sandhurst). Disappearing half-way through the meal, he returned in full samurai dress and gave a just recognisable rendering of *Danny Boy*. Following this another elderly and surprisingly tall gentleman rose from his cushion, leaned forward and, nodding to emphasise the gravitas of what he was saying, announced it was highly significant that I had come to be dining with their society that evening, as it was the eve of the anniversary of Pearl Harbor, when his country had entered into 'a dark era'. This obviously required a formal response, but as I rose it was to find that my feet had gone to sleep! – shades of the Rio Grande episode when I squatted on the riverbank before scrabbling back into America. Making it to the centre of the room was a struggle, but I managed to give an embellished repeat of what I'd said in London about a bunch of opportunists grabbing power as Japan strove to catch up with the rest of the world after two and a half centuries of almost total isolation: 'It was quite staggering what the Emperor Meiji had achieved during his reign to fast-track his country into the 20th century, but now what could be construed as a temporary blip was well and truly behind us, with Japan looking to have a promising future as a major player in the world community.' This utterance, totally off the cuff, went down well, with saki appearing for a round of toasts.

The next morning we were taken to the Imperial Shrine of the Emperor Meiji, a large wooden building with no windows, just a mish-mash of beams from which were suspended giant gongs being beaten by monks. We advanced into the darkness until my escort whispered via the interpreter, 'Only the Emperor goes further'. It was becoming pretty obvious that a significant return gesture of hospitality was needed, and when there was a moment I telephoned the British Embassy for advice. I ended up speaking to someone who seemed fully aware of my presence in Tokyo and what I'd been doing over the past few days, but instead of being helpful gave me a rocket about not following protocol guidelines. The only remaining hope was to call the Irish Embassy. On explaining the circumstances surrounding my presence in Tokyo and what my problem was, the Ambassador suggested I bring my Japanese hosts to tea at his home. The Irish Residence was quite a substantial house with a courtyard, and the reception given by Ambassador Sharkey could not have gone better, since when stationed in Rome as a junior diplomat some years before, he had been taken on bat-watching expeditions round the Forum by my Uncle Jack! As details of this conversation between me and Sharkey were translated, Mr Kutsuzawa became extremely excited and eventually entered into a long dialogue with the Ambassador, who happened to be a fluent Japanese speaker. I learned that bats were much admired by the Imperial family and guessed Sharkey was aware of this, which is why he had introduced the topic. That was our last day in Tokyo.

The following morning we were scheduled to fly to Kyoto and that night my female companion received alarming news from London which seemed to concern some business associates of Mr Kutsuzawa's involving high-end sports cars. Over the next couple of days she became somewhat wound up and distracted by long phone calls to London. Temple visits, walks in sacred parks, ritual meals and tea ceremonies came and went, but there was now a big shadow hanging over the last days of the trip. Eventually we said goodbye to Mr Kutsuzawa at Osaka airport, with him escorting us right into the plane. During the flight home via Anchorage I was told that, having successfully refurbished houses for a Japanese agent, the woman had been asked to try and source ten Lamborghini Diablo super-cars. The difficulty was that the entire limited edition had been pre-sold and were still in the process of being built at the factory in Italy. London contacts had advised that the desired models could possibly be found by a company based in Ireland if a premium of $100,000 per vehicle was forwarded. On the back of a Bank of Ireland reference of the firm's financial credibility the required premiums for ten cars had been sent from Japan. This was all six months before, during the previous summer. The contract date for delivery was approaching, but advice had just been received that there would be a delay, with actual dates uncertain, and concern was mounting. Exhaustion after the Oriental adventure turned to relief that I was not involved, which made my return to Jane and Christmas at our cosy home in Dorset doubly comforting.

In the New Year the London house agent made contact again and asked if I would come with her to Ireland. She was going over to meet the directors of the car firm and would like my opinion as to their credibility, as none of her business associates was particularly familiar with the ways of the country. We flew to Cork for a meeting in what was described as the firm's office, but in reality looked like an unmanned and unheated insurance office. There we were met by an accountant who made no sense and repeatedly spoke to an associate in garbled Irish, supposedly about the location of the car files but – harking back to my days at the Oranmore National School and even through a heavy Cork dialect – I picked up words relating to the milking of a cow. On leaving, we made the taxi go as close as possible to a supposed 'bonded warehouse' which had been pointed out as the super-car storage facility. A rusty chain securing weed-encrusted gates was not particularly inspiring and on return to London the agent phoned the Lamborghini factory in Bologna, to have her suspicions confirmed that Lambo Ireland's dealership claim was a work of complete fiction.

When the firm's bank manager was pressed in a phone call to say where the cars were coming from, he stated, 'The Bank of Ireland had a private arrangement with the Mafia in the factory,' but having contacted Lamborghini directly she had broken the contract and the firm was no longer obliged to supply the cars. A Dublin lawyer was engaged and the Bank of Ireland named in a writ as a defendant, as the branch manager had used his position to trigger the deposit money transfer from Japan. Once the injunctions were in place the Japanese client in Tokyo was informed of the situation, which did not go down well, as it appeared the cars had already been sold on to important clients at much inflated prices. Cars just had to be found. It gradually became clear that there was something slightly peculiar about the Japanese cash, suspicion growing that it was 'hot' and being laundered through the exotic vehicles. Tokyo's Yakuza underworld started to be mentioned as involved, with hints that fingers were collected from people slow to repay debts.

Realising how little relevant documentation was available to brief the plaintiff's lawyers, it was obvious that somebody needed to make contact with the translator, Guhen, who had been engaged in the early days, to see if he had retained anything helpful. I still had his phone number and we met for a drink near Swiss Cottage. This led to a series of meals spread over time to gain his confidence, during which we discussed hypnosis, neurolinguistic programming, his experiences in Oregon with the Bhagwan in the 1980s and the difficulties of growing up afflicted by cerebral palsy in post-war Japan. I'd noticed the left half of his body was semi-paralysed and his physical handicap severe, but I hadn't known quite how horrific his childhood story was. By luck a Leonard Cheshire Home had given him succour at an extremely low point, turning him into a total Anglophile.

Eventually, two suitcases of relevant transcripts were loaned, with the excuse that fax paper had a limited life and required copying. The cache laid the whole story bare, and even revealed collusion between the Japanese principals in Tokyo and the defendants in Ireland. Unearthing instructions from Tokyo to legally box in their London ex-agent meant the engagement of more lawyers and an application for legal aid needed to be made.

It was just then that I was informed by the Gardai that the body of Marie Coulter, a tenant in Ireland, had been found in a ditch north of Dublin with her throat cut. The communication was followed almost immediately by an unexpected instruction to present myself for interview at a police station near Heathrow airport. The request was doubly worrying as it came on top of the rather strange demise a couple of months earlier of an Irish neighbour with whom I was involved in a heated land dispute. To avoid having John Douglas come in person to my home in the UK to discuss a right of way over which we were arguing, we'd arranged to meet at Stansted airport. I'd sent him a letter detailing the rendezvous point, date and time, but he had not appeared. Weeks later his corpse, bearing insufficient funds for the train fare to London, had been discovered outside the airport in some boggy ground, too decomposed to determine the cause of death. I entered the police station beside the main runway at Heathrow in a state of high anxiety. I was met by an officer who had been looking into the brewing Japanese fraud case, and this complicated matters further, leaving it difficult for me to act normally or speak intelligently, as it was unclear from what direction the expected blow might fall.

The double set of fears subsided only when the officer announced that all he wanted was my opinion about there being any connection between some of the Lambo Ireland personnel and another money-laundering scam being looked into. The meeting terminated when the officer looked at his watch, beckoned me over to the window and asked for silence as 'the noise of Concorde taking off played havoc with the microphones'. The soundproofing was so good and my mental state so jumbled from adrenalin that I'd not noticed the big jets slipping past the long window overlooking the runway every minute or so, but then it all changed, with even the floor vibrating. The thickest of double glazing didn't do much to dampen the sound of the engines at full throttle, as we were no more than 100 yards from the point where the aircraft front wheel began to lift – reminding me of the laden Vulcan bombers heaving themselves into the air at Akrotiri. 'Thought you'd like that,' my interviewer said with a wink, proffering a hand to signal that the interview was over. Somehow the ability to keep acting normally lasted until I was safely in my car, but then a reaction of shaking and cold sweating took over for a few minutes, ending only when a gate security guard knocked on the window to ask if I was all right.

Though I had no idea it was about to happen, the Lambo directors were arrested soon afterwards on grounds of conspiracy to commit fraud, which set legal actions in motion that were to lead to the High Court in Ireland. A new Dublin law firm was engaged to face the bank, which was determined to extract their man from the list of defendants as, because of the discovery of the extensive documentation, there was a chance of the plaintiff winning. The bank being listed as a guilty party was the big draw, attracting legal interest from many quarters.

To recover while the turmoil settled and legal proceedings were mapped out, I accepted a Monaghan neighbour's invitation to help crew his 56-ton trawler across the Bay of Biscay. We assembled at Bilbao and dined at a very obscure but brilliant eating joint the skipper had found before joining the Dundalk-registered *The Bonny Lass* at Bordeaux. The three-day crossing to La Coruña went according to plan and I made my way back to Bilbao alone by train, as I had a separate flight from the others. Not knowing the town too well but remembering the excellent meal we had enjoyed only days before, I returned to the bar and passed through a curtain to the small room at the back where we had dined. There was just one couple in the room, which had four tables. With my zero Spanish but fortunately recognised from my earlier visit by the waiter, I found ordering wasn't difficult, though the process immediately caught the attention of my fellow diners. Without much hesitation the man asked, was I from the Irish boat? He asked how the trip had gone and was given a rough outline of events. Then the girl, who had been sitting with her back to me, turned and with a piercing stare declared 'I am Basque' and immediately shot the question, 'Why are you on ceasefire?' An awkward silence followed, as I was totally stuck for a reply. There was something about her manner that made me think she had strong views about something, but it might be better not to ask what.

The way forward seemed to be to maintain face by painting a picture of a grand plan being compiled by Sinn Féin which was yet to appear in the public arena, and so I gave a totally fictional description of how Gerry Adams was steering his movement towards political dialogue – it was the logical way forward. She wasn't having any of it and became quite irritated, until I suggested the current cessation might not last. At that she immediately cheered up and asked if I'd join her in catching a late train to a festival in the mountains. It was clearly time to part company, and using the excuse of having an early plane to catch I made to leave. The waiter stopped me in the narrow doorway and began to talk excitedly in Spanish, holding me firmly by the lapels. Over his shoulder and through the window of the full bar a number of police in a variety of green, blue and black uniforms could be seen milling about in the street. The grip on my jacket easing, I turned to wave farewell to the couple, only to see the chap now sitting alone. My coffee cup and wine glass were as I'd left them and his was in front of him but the girl's place setting, including the chair, had vanished, as had she. The chef hailed me from the kitchen door and I returned his thumbs-up sign, saluted my companion of the last hour and slipped off into the night, thinking that of all the mad women I'd met in life she'd topped the bill so far. Five years later her photograph appeared in the *Daily Telegraph* under the headline 'The face of Hate, Maria Iparraguierre, the new Leader of ETA'.

15
Kazakhstan

Next, 1995: quite a year. In the middle of the Lambo fraud machinations a message had come through from Mr Kutsuzawa in Tokyo that he would like me to accompany him on another expenses-paid trip, this time to Kazakhstan in central Asia. His boss in the Japanese Upper House needed information on a proposed oil pipeline across China in which the government was considering investing. A Danish group were handling the details of a series of conferences to be staged over six days and he wanted me along as an adviser. Intrigued, I flew to Frankfurt, meeting him and a replacement Japanese–English translator as our mutual friend Guhen couldn't make it. In the evening before the flight a briefing was given by the Danish principal when a rough agenda was laid out of the goals to be achieved, as it was clear the visit was likely to be at inter-ministerial level once we got to Alma-Ata (Almaty). During the flight there was a further meeting when it was revealed that we were likely to encounter Russian opposition, as Moscow was opposed to foreign elements engaging with the newly independent Kazakhstan – particularly anything concerning the Caspian oil basin. As the Russians were as European-looking to the Japanese as the Danes were, it was my responsibility to keep Kutsuzawa advised as to who were the good guys and who the bad.

Alma-Ata airport was a fright, with lines of semi-crashed, sad-looking helicopters lining the tarmac and one of the huge entrance doors half-hanging off its hinges. The impression contrasted wildly with the distant, pristine snow-covered peaks of the Tien Shan mountains. An armed escort appeared and we were taken to a fine though dilapidated walled *dacha* set back from the road, with sentry boxes and guard tower. More Kazakh armed guards wandered about but were friendly and smiled.

In the evening the minister Mr Kutsuzawa had come to see made a courtesy visit. Askar Kulibaev was a short, stocky, middle-aged man built like a tank, resembling a pile of brownish-yellow muscle contained in a suit topped off with a turnip on which was drawn a face. He and Kutsuzawa formally shook hands as the translator did his stuff, but then just looked at each other with hands still joined. A moment passed followed by both faces breaking into broad grins. 'We might be brothers,' announced Mr Kulibaev as he put an arm on Kutsuzawa's shoulders. It seemed that on sight the two gentlemen recognised that they possessed similar facial features and eyelids, telling of a direct centuries-old racial link between Kazakhstan and Japan. After more back-slapping and a short summary of what was planned for the next day, he left.

Over dinner we were advised that Kulibaev was quite close to President Nazarbaev – his son was married to the President's daughter. As Minister for Urban Development he had charge of the country's oil exports and the dining room was to feature as the main venue for meetings. Like the entire building inside and out the long room's once elegant décor was tired, with shadows on the gold flocked wallpaper marking where full-length portraits had once hung. Small cavities located high up in two of the shaded areas looked like oddly placed air vents, but could possibly once have had another purpose, as each was big enough to contain a camera. We learned that it had been Brezhnev's residence when Secretary of State for Kazakhstan prior to becoming Party Chairman in Moscow, though the plumbing and electrics gave the impression of being of 1930s vintage, with extraordinary rusting tap arrangements in the bathrooms. The food was the same at every meal, slices of horsemeat, a drink called kumis that turned out to be fermented mare's milk, an assortment of rye breads, slivers of salty ham and saucers of large grey caviar eggs which were topped up as I tucked in. At lunch and in the evenings the ice-cold vodka that helped to wash down the caviar was poured by a waiter sporting a pistol stuck down the back of his trousers.

The end of the second day was scheduled as a big event, with a number of Mr Kulibaev's fellow ministers coming to dine. We were briefed that one was the Vice-President, Mr Ishingarin, who had been in charge of Russia's entire railway network in the days of the USSR. The table ran the length of the room and was fully laid. A Russian apparatchik sat on one side of me and a pleasant-looking Kazakh on the other. The latter's formal introduction was to say he was the state executioner, and things got off to a shaky start through a pidgin-English conversation about upgrading oil refining to improve the efficiency of imported car engine designs. It was hard for the old Soviet-era technology to keep pace – hence the terrible pervading smell of benzine, which was added as a quick fix. All the little grey-haired Russian wanted to know was if I could organise a place for his son at Harvard.

Being some distance down the table I didn't pay attention to what was going on at the top as the evening progressed and, the Russian having gone silent, I just tucked into the caviar when not in conversation with the executioner, washing it down with vodka and kumis. Suddenly Mr Kulibaev raised his hand and, pointing at me, barked something as a command. The translator sidled round the table and murmured in my ear, 'The Minister says you have said nothing.' Rising slowly to buy time while mentally searching for a relevant contribution to the evening's discussion, I spotted a giant TV screen behind the Minister's chair, featuring Torvill and Dean silently pirouetting on skates. The idea sprang to mind of using sport as a get-out and I started off, with pauses for translation, by stating that my mother had, surprisingly, once been married to a Tsarist cavalry officer who had been a formidable horseman in show-jumping circles and was even thought of highly by Tsar Nicholas himself. I got no further. Kulibaev threw his chair back, marched round the table and gave me three ferocious hugs. It was like being squeezed by a bear. Returning to his place, he raised a glass and commanded everyone to stand as he announced a toast to the horses of the steppe. He then launched into a long speech about how he and President Nazarbaev's friendship had started when they grew up together in a state orphanage. Aged 14 they'd gone out on to the steppe to manage a herd of 400 horses, with Nazarbaev one day vowing he would rule Kazakhstan – and eventually that had come to pass. Historically, the country had supplied the cavalry horses for all the Russian Tsars' armies, with the animal becoming the spirit of the nation. Then, after a few more toasts, he sat down. It was obvious that he was bored by the unending oil talk, and I'd inadvertently stumbled on to a subject much closer to his heart.

Mr Kutsuzawa was highly amused by the event, but the oil men and the Russians weren't. The minister left soon after, but they didn't. A couple of new faces appeared and a grilling began. From the tone of the questions it was clear they were alarmed by my apparent knowledge of Mr Kulibaev's background and private interests. Did I know more than I was letting on? Next morning I was woken early by yet more questioners who began asking for clarification on Paul Rodzianko, who they seemed to think was involved in the ill-fated Tsar's last Duma. Luckily I'd read Paul's biography, *Tattered Banners*, not long before and was able to explain that it was his Uncle Michael they were confusing him with. Paul had been a cavalryman pure and simple. At this one of the more friendly interrogators said that all Russian history books had been 'tidied up', with knowledge relating to the former era heavily edited.

Later that morning a minibus arrived and took us to Mr Kulibaev's one-time Soviet Politburo office. The heavy décor was similar to that of the *dacha* but with an entire wall featuring a topographical map of the world. The Minister's desk was at the end beyond a long table and supported a wonderful gold telephone assembly comprising a group of statuettes of leaping horses. We were invited to sit while further oil pipeline talks took place. Fortunately for me, all the Kazakhs' Russian conversation was repeated in English before being translated into Japanese, so I began to pick up on what was under discussion. Kazakhstan wanted to preserve its new state of independence from Moscow. Its vast Caspian basin oil reserves were landlocked, with three ways of being piped to market – north to Russia, west through Iran or east across China and Manchuria to the Sea of Japan. We were there to discuss the possibility of Japan financing the building of the oil pipeline across China. When the growing Islamic fundamentalism was raised as a concern Mr Kulibaev explained that the President had entered into a mutual defence agreement with Israel to contain the threat, but he was equally worried about China's questionable trustworthiness. The ground shook in Alma-Ata when Beijing tested A-bombs and there was presently only one international crossing point, at which trains had to change wheel bogeys because of the different track gauges. Dealing with Moscow was not on the cards.

During a pause for coffee, Kulibaev beckoned me to come and sit at his desk while he made a call. He had a long and very heated conversation, which ended with a slamming down of the receiver. With furious eyes he looked at me and growled 'Tehran!' It was like having a fleeting glimpse of Genghis Khan in the flesh.

After coffee it was announced that we were going on a tour of the city with Kulibaev, the nation's one-time pugilist champion, as our guide. His humour quickly returned, and all sorts of jokes were cracked as to how things had worked better under Communist rule and the current problems being a result of free market enterprise. The bus slowed momentarily beside a flight of steps leading up to an imposing building, which he explained was the city's synagogue. Next stop was something called 'The White House', where we disembarked outside a huge stone building in the centre of a large open space surrounded by flagpoles and entered a door guarded by ceremonially dressed soldiers. From there we were ushered on through a vast hall containing more flags and sentries into an impressive office, to be welcomed by Vice-President Ishingarin. While Mr Kutsuzawa and his translator were invited to enter a further inner sanctum, the Danes and myself were left to study another faded wall map of the world depicting the potential pipeline routes.

The last day arrived and as we were about to head for the airport Mr Kulibaev asked me to stay on and come with him hunting foxes with eagles on horseback up in the mountains. But the invitation was intercepted by the Danish principal, as my job of nursemaiding Kutsuzawa was not over. On returning to Germany we were to rest up at Baden-Baden while his report on the trip was digested in Tokyo, and my role was to keep him occupied in the interim. From the plane window the steppe slid by below, with occasional remains of defunct collective farm complexes, half-buried in drifting sand, clearly visible. Passing over Lake Balkhash it appeared as wide as the English Channel, with just distant shorelines to be sighted as we crossed the huge expanse of water. To the north all was a swirly rust colour, clearly badly contaminated from mining, while fishing fleets could be observed to the south scattered about on a sea of inky blue that stretched to the horizon.

From Frankfurt we drove to Baden-Baden, to spend three days getting bored stiff and having my amateur diplomatic skills tested to the limit as endless calls were made to Japan. The only respite was in the evenings, when visiting the casino and a spa. One day I forced him to come and look over the castle, only to discover it was awash with Christie's personnel setting out rows of Louis Vuitton trunks, stuffed animal heads, giant cuckoo clocks and sculptures of German nobility – all for auction. The Baron, it seemed, was having a tidy-up. I was very taken with a larger-than-life marble head and shoulders of Kaiser William and left a bid, but fortunately our flight to London coincided with the sale day and I heard nothing more.

16
Hong Kong and the Dublin High Court

O n my return home the usual routine of forestry work in Ireland and ceramic production at Pentridge fell back into place. While taking time out to visit my sister at Oranmore, she suggested I join her on an expedition to Hong Kong for Easter Week as her husband's band, De Dannan, would be out there. I was fixed up to stay with a senior judge with weak legs and a tendency to lose his balance when partying. Accidents often happened and sometimes involved other tables at restaurants but because of his senior position on the bench nobody ever seemed to mind or notice. One day he took me across to Macao as, on hand-over the next year, Beijing was promoting him to be in charge of legal matters between the two ex-colonies. His wife explained it was because he had a skill in sorting out problems caused by the sons of high-ranking Chinese when they overdid things at the gambling tables.

We were accompanied on the hydrofoil by Pat Davitt, whom I met for the first time but with whom a unique link existed. Both our grandfathers had, at different times, been guests of Count Leo Tolstoy at Yasnaya Polyana in the Russian backwoods, to discuss ways of advancing social emancipation initiatives in Ireland. Pat's grandfather had been Michael Davitt, the legendary 19th-century one-armed Land Leaguer, who had lost a limb as a child when chained to a cart down a Northumbrian mine. Rendered unable to work and therefore a burden to impoverished immigrant parents, he'd been sent back to Ireland, where he'd prospered, eventually becoming deeply involved in the emerging political movements of the late Victorian age; while Shane had visited much later, in 1906. During a walk around the remains of a Portuguese cathedral in the now Chinese city, I learned from the judge that capitalising where possible on the non-aligned aspect of the Irish Diaspora was proving to be an effective way of penetrating the Chinese business world.

The week went well, with a lot of fun being had at the expense of a

Chicago priest who, on the saint's feast day, gave a sermon at Mass on how St Patrick had devoted his life in the fifth century to bringing peace between Catholics and Protestants. As we downed Bloody Marys in the Sacristy afterwards, the subject had been revisited with humour and much leg-pulling, though the event was a revelation of how Irish Americans tended to have only a tenuous grasp of the old country's long history. The Governor, Chris Patten, took to attending the various St Patrick's Association gigs, confessing that he was reduced to doing so because his entire administration had gone on leave for the seven days the band was in town.

Back in London, things were not going well with the fraud case, and all progress had ceased. It was discovered that the solicitor who'd been appointed to handle affairs in the UK was actually in a state of suspension, and should not have been present or involved. After a tip-off that something wasn't right at the firm's offices, a sympathetic staff member unlocked a basement storeroom, full to the ceiling with jumbled files, some relevant to the case, some not. Time was short and, as everything was earmarked for imminent incineration, as much as possible was hastily bundled into two taxis. Sorting out the paperwork threw up some surprises. Nearly every file had a legal aid application certificate attached and we had files relating to a number of cases, some of which had been abruptly discontinued. Checking the dates on the certificates and the names of the lawyers claiming remuneration for work done, generally stated as 'perusal of documentation', it became clear that the Legal Aid Board facility for financial assistance was being massively abused. Lining up the files across the floor, sorting them into cases and then cross-referencing the certificate dates against names, there were a few instances where individual lawyers had claims totalling 25 hours or more on up to five different cases for the same 24-hour period. Generally the charge for 'perusal' had been £500 per hour, with even the suspended solicitor proving to have been a busy boy.

It was all exciting stuff and shortly afterwards the trial started in Dublin's High Court, where I was called as a witness once the Plaintiff had stated her case. The Bank of Ireland was out to defend its man and had engaged a top criminal barrister, who listened to my evidence, given over a two-hour period. In the afternoon cross-examination began and lasted for two and a half hours, during which time boredom crept in from the endless repeat questioning. In the end I started to ask questions of my own and this eventually caused the defence barrister to fall silent.

The trial ran for 19 days in total and had become a war of attrition between the counsel for the Defence and the Plaintiff's lawyers. Hers were running on a massive gamble that she would win and be able to recover accumulated fees from the opposition through the bank's culpability. If the judge found against her there obviously wasn't going to be any cash to pay legal fees, but that had been the risk worth taking. After months of deliberation the judge found in her favour, the lawyers got their fees and the original deposit money was returned from somewhere. Because of the collusion between the Japanese and the defendants revealed in the translator's faxes there was no obligation to return it to Tokyo. Damages were awarded and the judge then went on a holiday to Spain, taking with him a forensic accountant's valuation of the fraud impact for perusal, but he came home in a coffin, dying unexpectedly aged 52 at his villa. No other judge was prepared to take on the job of assessing damages, as all the relevant papers had been mislaid in Spain, and the case, which had run from 1990 to 1997, was left to fade quietly away. It was a relief as the woman's life seemed to be a continual succession of dramas, and though the experience had been very educational, from a personal viewpoint I was happy to bow out of the picture unrewarded, as something much more exciting had begun to emerge up in Ulster.

17

The Ulster Canal Machinations

ᕲ᠊ᔕᘘ

Meeting fee demands to educate two children at boarding school took quite an effort and required careful handling of timber sales, which were beginning to come on-stream. Much else had been happening in Monaghan. In 1994 the IRA had called a ceasefire and, in response, a group of local county councillors decided to meet with their opposite numbers in Northern Ireland to discuss bridge-building ideas that crossed the juridical divide. The gathering in one room of officials from Counties 'Armagh' and 'Tyrone' in the North and 'Monaghan' from the Republic was ground-breaking and a first for most, but went off well, with the decision made to use the natural basin of the River Blackwater as a focal point round which to work. It spread across the three counties and represented the perfect non-confrontational initiative, with issues common to all in the areas of tourism and environmental protection. A detailed study involving input from everyone took three years to pull together and was eventually launched in 1997 at Castle Leslie, the geographic epicentre of the project, under the title of 'The River Blackwater Regional Partnership'.

A unique element lay buried at the heart of the undertaking: restoration of the derelict 55-mile canal that stretched across the heart of the Province, straddling the infamous border in four places. The concept was only touched on in the study, but the restoration of the Ulster canal, lying as it did roughly 50:50 in each jurisdiction, was confirmed as being absolutely vital, to be pursued over the longer term. There was nothing else with sufficient sustainability to win the day in breathing life where it was so badly needed. The subject immediately caught my attention – it just felt right and reminded me of the day when, aged seven, I'd walked along its towpath listening to my grandfather describe the water-borne society that had once existed.

With the dramatic change of government in the UK and the arrival

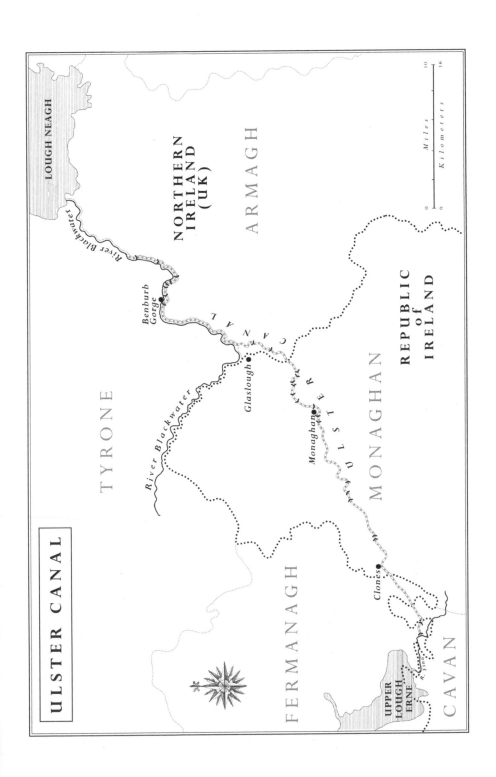

ULSTER CANAL

LOUGH NEAGH

NORTHERN
IRELAND
(UK)

ARMAGH

TYRONE

River Blackwater

Benburb
Gorge

Glaslough

Monaghan

REPUBLIC
of
IRELAND

MONAGHAN

Clones

FERMANAGH

UPPER
LOUGH
ERNE

CAVAN

Miles

Kilometers

of Tony Blair it wasn't long before the incoming administration's task of responding in a meaningful way to the IRA's second ceasefire began to take shape. The new Secretary of State for Northern Ireland, Mo Mowlam, embarked on an effort to persuade the warring parties to enter into discussions on forming some sort of workable peace accord: starting with talks in separate rooms, then the same room and eventually at the same end of the same table.

The developments at Stormont were monitored closely from Pentridge through a unique source, in the hope that an opportunity to promote the canal project might arise. A technician who had once worked at Galway's *Connaught Tribune* had a pass giving him unrestricted access to the Stormont basement, where he had the job of servicing the coffee-vending machine – a vital area of the building during the deliberations upstairs. Whenever thorny points concerning cross-community issues erupted – an insoluble impasse threatened or a movement towards breakthroughs glimpsed – there tended to be a surge downstairs for refreshments while the facts were excitedly mulled over by aides and advisers. Ears flapped. Comparing the information gleaned with the nightly announcements to the media by the Sinn Féin spokesman was riveting, and it wasn't long before the Irish Department of Foreign Affairs had an operative manning a desk nearby.

As the dust began to settle, with the promise of improved relationships across the socio-political divide, the moment seemed right to start pushing the canal project as a non-confrontational initiative, and I hosted a dinner at Castle Leslie for its introduction to motivated individuals from the more deprived counties of mid-Ulster. The evening was going well until news came that a riot had broken out in the village and a mob had set fire to the pub at the castle gates. All the roads were closed and the invitees were trapped in the castle for the night. I had two particularly important guests who had taken a risk on venturing south across the border and didn't feel comfortable facing a Gardai checkpoint, who asked for a way of escaping back to the safety of Northern Ireland. The only answer was to quickly organise and then lead a convoy through the estate forest and across the border into South Armagh.

By 2000 the North–South Ministerial Council was in place as the political interface between Stormont in the North and Dublin in the South. As it was based only 12 miles away in Armagh City I soon got to know both chairs, Tim O'Connor for the Republic and Dr Henry Smyth for the Six Counties (North). Both immediately saw what the reopened waterway had to offer in the form of a large-scale employment project, with sustainable long-term benefits. Drawing their attention to a recent article printed in the 28 July *Daily Telegraph* featuring a photograph of the wild girl I'd met in Bilbao and branding her as the new ETA leader, I gave an account of the restaurant conversation there. It included my off-the-cuff summary that a guerrilla war has a limited life and must eventually enter the political sphere to avoid running into the sand. The success of the Spanish evening had left me with a sense of confidence, and I felt comfortable looking these two senior diplomats in the eye when broaching the canal project as something for them to really get their teeth into.

Factors brought about by the Good Friday Agreement began to bed in with time, and a Boston-based columnist called Smoki Bacon, accompanied by her cameraman husband, visited Ulster on a fact-finding tour. They made contact as they wanted to compile three short documentaries covering the background history of 'The Border People', 'The current social differences' and 'Where future calm might lie', with the film footage to be broadcast in New England. We met at at the St Patrick's Trian Centre in Armagh City, where a map was used to highlight the geographical significance of the 'Sperrin Gap', the portion of mid-Ulster lying wedged between two large masses of water, Lough Erne and Lough Neagh. A rough outline of events that had occurred over the last millennium was given. Focusing on what existed to be visited, the impact of Partition and its subsequent consequences, I finished on an optimistic note highlighting what the present peace accord might achieve with the help of the canal.

After quick tour of the cathedral we headed for the gorge at Benburb, where an open day was being held at the Milltown Heritage Centre. It was sited beside a flight of six locks that lowered the canal down a ravine alongside a series of waterfalls and weirs, making it one of the best places to grasp an image of the waterway as a recreational asset. A senior IRA ex-hunger-striker friend gave a superb off-the-cuff interview on how, at a stroke, reopening the navigation addressed the historical lack of investment that had so afflicted the region and was currently the big factor underpinning social tension. After a quick tour around the Victorian flax mill and its giant steam engine at the Heritage Centre's heart, we headed for Navan Fort, where the tunnel entrance from the car park to the old earthwork's interior was designed to give no clue as to what lay ahead.

The auditorium contained a recently upgraded exhibition of the ancient site and had won many important European prizes. Smoki became confused by the cases of artefacts relating to a society of significant standing dating back to the time of the Giza pyramids' construction, and needed help getting her head round the facts. The significance of the recently unearthed skull of a Barbary ape carbon-dated to 3,000 years old was particularly difficult to get across, as she'd no idea where 'Barbary' was and the concept of trade with the North African coast in such early times took even more effort to grasp. Cameras were running continually, and it was obvious a healthy documentary was in the making. On the drive back to Glaslough, where the Americans were staying the night, the talk was an endless series of questions about what to do to get the waterway reopened, and I fell asleep feeling the day's effort to expose the merits of the canal to a wider audience had gone well.

Next morning a few stops were planned to highlight more of mid-Ulster's undiscovered secrets. While we were cruising through Monaghan town I pointed out the giant royal coat of arms on the town hall pediment, where it faced towards the Crimean War Memorial, represented by a 40-ft obelisk. The replica of Miró's *Big Breasted Woman* was viewed in the museum, the unveiling story told, and then we headed for Clones. As I parked in the centre beside the old Market Cross I didn't see it at first but had inadvertently situated the car so that Smoki stepped out on to the bloated corpse of a large ginger cat with a completely flattened head. It seemed to be sporting a grin as if to say 'Welcome'. Getting her camera out while muttering 'This town needs help', she photographed it, the weather-beaten Celtic carved cross and a local character who arrived to show us around.

A quick tour of the scenic spots provided by the hill on which the town was built included the old engine sheds left by the Great Northern Railway, and ended at the Canal Stores. Hand-to-mouth restoration to save the Victorian building from total dereliction was very much due to our guide's single-minded determination and unwavering enthusiasm. The goal was to have a tearoom operation ready for the following summer. Hopefully things would lead to a full-time community centre being established, which could help draw attention to the canal and its history. As the bed of the waterway passed right by the front door the Americans were totally hooked, and filmed where barges would be arriving from, heading to, and mooring up; most importantly, they recorded a description of the impact it would have on the town. I explained how there was literally nothing else on the horizon for the otherwise geographically isolated civic backwater to inspire school leavers and youth seeking a future career of any kind. The final stop was a hilltop ring fort outside Carrickmacross, after which we said farewell.

Some time later I heard from a Boston chum that the Ulster canal and Monaghan region in general was being given a very good airing on TV. Aware that publicity was one thing but turning the restoration of the waterway into a practical and deployable initiative quite another, I embarked on a political letter-writing campaign. Attention was drawn to recent studies concerning the canal carried out by government departments covering immediate cost benefit, recovery of investment, environmental implications and long-term Tertiary Impact considerations, as all findings had consistently ended with constructive conclusions.

Visiting the Marine Institute at Ballyronan on the west shore of Lough Neagh, the in-post director told me he had set up the institute in 1969, only to watch in disbelief as the Blackwater was turned into a spate river by a large-scale cross-border drainage scheme conducted in the 1980s. The negative impact it was having on the lough's marine life was obvious to the naked eye, but the project's 'cost-benefit' report had never been made public. Working out that Lord Gowrie had been serving at a ministerial level of some sort in the Northern Ireland Executive during the period in question, I contacted him for an opinion, but he appeared to know nothing about the multi-million-pound scheme. It seemed increasingly strange to me that in the 1980s, a period when north–south political engagement was almost non-existent, a massive inter-jurisdictional operation to lower the bed of an arterial river system by 20ft had been quietly sanctioned and executed at every level without a hitch. The one area that should have caused problems, the consequential Environmental Impact, never featured as an issue worthy of consideration by any department in either government. What was very clear was that large-scale co-operation at the highest civil servant levels had been extremely efficient at executing the task devoid of political assistance, and accounting for the public expenditure had been very effectively buried. It should have been a warning then about what I might be up against, but I didn't take it on board.

The visit to Ballyronan on the west shore of Lough Neagh brought me into contact with a forceful matriarch who had built up the South Derry marina from nothing into an impressive community centre for rural crafts and educational functions. A couple of weeks later she made a firmly worded request for me to attend the official opening of the centre, as there were some important people coming and she wanted me to brief them on the Ulster canal project. I made a point of attending and at the reception I ended up unexpectedly meeting and having lunch with Martin McGuinness, the fresh-in-post Stormont Minister for Education. Introduced to him by my hostess, who explained I was 'up from Monaghan', she asked McGuinness to 'listen to what this boyo has to say' about the Ulster canal, something she had her 'tongue hanging out for'. Caught totally unprepared to give such a briefing to the person in question, I looked around for a chair while thinking up something to say that would be acceptable. Clones town's tragic history represented the perfect example of the terrible social and economic hammering Partition had inflicted on rural Ulster. As soon as I opened my mouth, having roughly composed myself enough to speak, the man's eyes narrowed and the polite smile disappeared. We both had plates of food in our hands but no move was made to eat while the lady stood by and nodded for me to keep talking. Gradually, having touched briefly on my early background west of the Shannon and a light joke about Cromwell never having been able to effectively subdue Connaught across the 'holy river', his shoulders dropped a little, indicating I had his attention, even if only out of curiosity. Cantering through the progress of the Blackwater Regional Partnership since its launch in 1997, I'd ended on where things now stood, basically at the door of the Northern Ireland Tourist Board, which sadly appeared to be interested only in promoting the Giant's Causeway and keeping visitors as far from the Republic as possible. At that point I stopped, as I was mentally spent, and there was a short pause before he spoke. When he did it was to explain that Ballyronan was actually in his South Derry constituency and that our hostess was a good supporter of his, but then went on to say he'd grasped the logic of the project and would help whenever he could. His eyes lingered on mine for a bit after that while saying nothing, and I sensed he was trying to read me in some way but failing. The moment came to an end when we were joined by a local journalist friend of his who offered to take me on a tour of east Tyrone and Derry if I could find the time.

Shortly after this incident, I was contacted while at Oranmore and asked to say a few words at an important canal conference being held at the Inishannon Hotel in Enniskillen, which Robin Evans, the MD of British Waterways, would be attending. Just before setting off from Galway I ran into a qualified ship's master who described over a series of pints in the village pub what fun she'd recently had skippering a crew sailing a converted Citroen 2CV with modified wheels and rigged with a sail so it could run on the unused CIE railway track up the west of Ireland from Limerick city to Sligo town. Her description of the countryside as they zipped along caught my interest and, noting the journey to Enniskillen lay roughly along the line of the track, I decided to leave early in order to have a good look about during the drive north.

It proved to be a day of surprises and discoveries almost from the start. The rails had not been lifted when the line had closed back in the 1960s and it appeared that something heavy occasionally travelled the route as, though rusty, they were clear of grass and briars. It was evening when I reached the hotel and found I was to be the after-dinner speaker. With half an hour before the event kicked off, a rabbit of some sort had to be pulled out of a hat. Minutes raced by and nothing remotely relevant came to mind, until I came across a large picture of a pig in the hotel corridor. Bingo, I had it, at least the beginnings of a path that could be expanded on.

While conversing distractedly during the meal I mentally cobbled the structure together, so that when the inevitable moment arrived at the coffee stage I did at least have something reasonable to offer. Describing the day I'd just had exploring miles and miles of totally unspoilt countryside, I moved on to draw a comparison between the terrain across which the Ulster canal lay and that which featured in the Burt Reynolds film *Deliverance*. The only difference was that the film highlighted a region of abundant beauty about to disappear, whereas the canal restoration would open up much the same sort of territory but currently lying derelict and unseen. The abandoned homesteads and overgrown orchards were there, the thundering white-water rapids, the isolated communities – even the music was to hand. Somebody shouted 'Squeal like a pig', signalling they'd seen the film, which raised a laugh, with Evans coming to my rescue by weighing in with the thought that, at only 55 minutes from Belfast, the Benburb Gorge alone had the potential to become a vibrant recreational hub for the city. The lock flights of the canal and the splendid Victorian flax mill had the capability of developing into a stunning community asset that, if located in the UK, would have been restored years ago.

It was a draining experience and warranted a visit to the hotel bar at the first opportunity. This led to an encounter with an odd cove who appeared to have read up a good deal on the Leslie family, as he started to talk about my great-great-aunt, Olive Guthrie, who, he declared, was 'a Covenanter'. I'd no idea what he was talking about, but bells began to ring about a photograph album of my grandfather's that contained images dated 1912 of Loyalist Ulster Volunteer Force parades on the family estate, the year when the great oath-taking of allegiance to the Province took place. As the man rambled on, images came to mind of family members either in the ranks, inspecting or presenting colours to a large gathering of uniformed men and nurses on an estate field back at home. There was a series of photographs dated from 1912 to 1914, including one of rifles being stored under armed guard in the Old Stables, which I'd converted into a dwelling as the Coachman's House. I thought it wise to keep quiet about the memory, but the meeting gave grounds for reflection during the drive back to Castle Leslie. Returning to Pentridge and digging out the album, I found a record of parading soldiers mustering on a hill. Along with the remembered images was evidence dated July 1914 of Great-Aunt Olive's personal expenses for bandoliers and slouched hats, incurred in outfitting the 1,600 soldiers featured standing to attention. It seemed to be a matter best left unexplored any further, and the album was quietly returned to its place in the bookcase.

18
A Visit from the Special Branch

⟨◦⟩

This foray to Ulster had lasted some days and, as usual, mountains of work on various fronts awaited me on return to Pentridge. Only, this time, so did Peter Storer. I'd totally forgotten about the policeman's visit back in 1982 and invited him and his associate back into the same dining room, which now sported an oak table, carpet, chairs and curtains. He reminded me I'd agreed to make contact should anything of interest pop up in Ulster and dived straight into asking for clarification concerning the circumstances of my meeting with McGuinness – word had travelled. Obviously I had technically done nothing wrong, but he found my connections and activities in Ireland somewhat perplexing. Before I could collect my thoughts properly as to how best to describe the Ballyronan incident, puzzling eye contact broke out between the two policemen, ending with one looking under the table and drawing my attention to a chicken that was tugging at the other officer's shoelaces. Hilda, one of my daughter's pet hens, was removed and the meeting terminated shortly afterwards, with an agreement for me to meet another policeman at a nearby public house in a week's time.

The King John in Tollard Royal was the venue, with Peter and a new officer already sitting at a corner table booked for lunch when I arrived. McGuinness was the topic of conversation from the start. It was clear he was still branded as a public enemy of some sort in their eyes, and the men had difficulty adjusting to his new status as a credibly elected politician. Getting a picture across of the dire social needs of east Tyrone, Monaghan and Armagh took time, but having done so I explained that, though McGuinness could also see what underpinned the problems I'd highlighted, he had no answers and, as I had, I'd been asked to talk to him. This synopsis of the event appeared to settle the policemen's concerns and Storer concluded the meeting by stating that he was retiring and moving to France, so we might not meet again.

Back in Monaghan the concept of the waterway being reopened had caught public attention, with long enthusiastic editorials beginning to appear in the local newspaper, the *Northern Standard*. This was countered to an extent in official circles by concern being raised over the threat of Zebra mussels spreading along the waterway from Lough Erne at one end to infest Lough Neagh at the other if it was reopened. The foreign interloper's origin was traced back to the ancient Tethys Sea of pre-history, and the concept of using natural predators to exercise control seemed to offer a possibility. Understanding that tufted duck and black carp both ate the infant shellfish, the idea was born to increase numbers by defending their habitat from non-indigenous grey squirrels (for the duck) and mink (for the fish), both classified vermin. Finding a practical way of hammering their numbers might be the answer.

On noticing a new sign in an office window in Monaghan town stating that it was the Ex-Prisoners' Assistance Committee office, I rang its doorbell. Some chaps emerged from a back room and, having introduced myself as someone who had also once been unfairly incarcerated but in a place unknown to Amnesty International, I went on to explain the canal project and the need to contain the Zebra mussel. My idea was to ask if the small boys in the town's housing estates could be organised into groups to compete in hunting and killing mink and grey squirrels. Keeping gibbets well furbished as a form of sport might be a novel way to channel loose energy and have idle hands constructively engaged while the Peace Process bedded in. The image of a wide-ranging new field of employment opportunities that the canal could deliver was grasped immediately, with lots of questions concerning the route of the waterway up from Clones, the four places where it crossed and re-crossed the border, the three 1839 vintage viaducts where it passed over the Finn, Cor and Tynan rivers, the 26 locks still existing and the reactivating of the marina located under a crane park almost in the centre of Monaghan town itself. All agreed that the chaos and upheaval would be dramatic but therefore highly entertaining, and the immediate impact by the large fiscal spend could not be faulted. Monaghan's current image of a stagnant social backwater could possibly be changed overnight and put on a level with the nearby

Shannon–Erne waterway, which had transformed a severely depressed region into second-home country, now with a vibrant economy of its own.

Though a tricky time politically, as a spying scandal at Stormont had resulted in the newly formed Stormont Assembly being suspended, it was arranged for the IRA leader to bring a UVF counterpart to a meeting at Castle Leslie, where the more fundamental socio-economic aspects of the waterway project would be enlarged on. As luck would have it, on the day designated Paul McCartney was staying in the castle with Heather Mills, his future bride. They were on a private visit and wished to be treated without celebrity, so had been left to entertain themselves without fuss. I'd said nothing, but when my guests arrived at the appointed time I was surprised to find that the party had grown to six and all had met beforehand. My map of the canal, which had been carefully set up on an easel, was glanced at in passing and then everyone moved to the window, shoulder to shoulder, to watch as McCartney took his girlfriend's arm while she negotiated some steps outside. As the couple made their way to the boathouse, everyone turned with comments on how all felt towards the 'Fab Four' and their music. It was quite clear that the concept of the canal and what it had to offer was already understood by everyone and there wasn't much point in preaching to the converted – much better to get back to watching what was happening on the lake. Soon there was a cry as the two were seen in a rowing boat but not making great progress. Having observed Paul ending up punting around in circles, it was suggested that the day's business was done and the meeting could conclude. The UVF commander agreed that the project was a benefit for all and had the full support of his side of 'the Divide'. Then, with handshakes all round, everyone departed.

For a while I was left to pinch myself that the event had actually occurred, but I knew it had when the Centre for Cross Border Studies in Armagh made contact a few days later. The director, an American who had somehow got wind of what I was up to, operated from Washington and spent his time between Armagh, Kosovo and the Stellenbosch Institute for Truth and Reconciliation in South Africa. He gave me a book on the Erie Canal in New York State, *The Wedding of the Waters*, explaining how George Washington had urgently needed a healthy trade and communications artery so that the newly established western states didn't break away from the eastern bloc to form a country of their own. Building the navigable connection between the Hudson River and Lake Erie had kept the emerging 'United States' literally bolted together – 'united' – at a vulnerable time in the nation's early history, before the railroads arrived. It was clear that a champion of Washington's calibre needed to be found so that the same could be done for Ireland's tourism industry.

Unfortunately the machinations of Direct Rule in 2000 led, for some reason, to the sudden but complete closure of the Blackwater Regional Partnership office, which housed and handled all the official Ulster canal documents. Though it was funded entirely by local councils, the instruction had come from an anonymous senior administration source in Belfast to have all the office papers removed to an undisclosed location. It took time and luck to find them, but after a useful tip they were discovered lying poorly stored in a disused telephone exchange building and, as the premises were unlocked, everything was taken for temporary safekeeping at Glaslough. A civil servant contact in Peter Mandelson's Secretary of State for Northern Ireland Office relayed information that the Blackwater Regional Partnership project had come to be viewed as a threat to the newly devolved government administration at Stormont, as its cross-border characteristics were too far-reaching for civil servants to handle. The fear was that success might lead to the natural expansion of the private sector to a point where it passed beyond the power of the administration to control.

Frustrated at hearing this nonsense, I drove up to the Ballyronan community centre in Co. Derry in the hope of finding a way forward. The driving force of the manageress had developed the little harbour into a proper marina, but there was no boating activity of significance, as South Derry was an historically depressed region devoid of residual wealth or industry. Even the Marine Institute set up in 1969 on the edge of the village as an outpost of Coleraine's University of Ulster to study the lough's aquatic life had recently been closed at short notice, three decades of records hastily boxed for storage, the collating staff disbanded and the director instructed to take early retirement. Apparently it was a political decision relating to the Blackwater Drainage Scheme, as nobody wanted attention to be drawn to the unfolding ecological nightmare that had been set in train at public expense. It seemed we had no friends where it mattered, though the concept of reopening the old waterway was beginning to feature in mid-Ulster community self-help meetings as the one ray of hope for social regeneration – there being literally nothing else of a positive nature to talk about.

Growing clouds of frustration dispersed temporarily when a two-termed Belfast Lord Mayor, Dr Ian Adamson, invited me to be part of a group heading to Dublin for a meeting with the Republic's Central Bank directors to discuss stimulating the private sector economy in the border regions. He was up to speed on the canal initiative and asked me to give a presentation over lunch on the top floor of the bank's headquarters on Dame Street. The Democratic Unionist Party MP, Jeffrey Donaldson, spoke about various 'all island' trade initiatives under consideration from the Stormont point of view, before my turn. A large-scale map with the waterway bed highlighted was brought in with the coffee and erected on a stand. A neat, short talk was planned drawing attention to how the Danube, straddling Europe from the Alps to the Black Sea, had acted as an active commercial corridor throughout the Cold War, but unfortunately an almighty row erupted in the adjoining kitchen, where an Italian-sounding woman began to let off steam against one of the waiters. When he was in the dining room silence reigned, but as soon as he disappeared through the swing door all hell broke loose. A junior member of the board was asked to go in and deal with the matter, but replied to his boss, 'I'm not going in there.' It was easier to tell the waiter to remain in the room.

Peace finally breaking out, it didn't take long for the salient points to be grasped by a couple of key directors with links to the European Investment Bank as well as the Republic's Department of Finance. Requests were made in coming days for more documentation in the form of reports and studies, which were forwarded, but eventually advice came through saying that the Republic's civil service sector could not cope with the scale of the project at present, thanks to the large number of socio-economic issues it touched on – the old stumbling block of no vision where it was most needed. Dining later with Dr Adamson at his home outside Belfast, I learned he was not only Dr Paisley's physician but also a close friend and confidant. This was great news, as it gave hope that the bureaucratic log-jam might eventually be loosened by 'the big man' if he could be recruited to become a project supporter. It was just a matter of waiting for the opportunity to present itself.

As I assisted my son with a gap-year project tiling a roof two months later, news came through that two planes had flown into the World Trade Centre in New York: September 11, 2001. The world changed overnight, and it was clear that America would be looking to its own for a while and distracted from projects such as the waterway. With much attention required by the Irish forests, farm and busy ceramics business that had built up at Pentridge, only sporadic lobbying for the canal could be afforded until 2006, when a new beacon of hope materialised.

Tim O'Connor was approaching retirement after six years in post at the Armagh 'North–South Ministerial Council' government interface, and asked to meet me on a one-to-one basis at Glaslough. Over dinner I was informed that he'd nursed the canal restoration through all the hoops set out in the latest EU Interreg application and the required £200 million expenditure had been approved by the European Investment Bank for inclusion in the 2007–2013 spending round. It was at the top of the list of projects to be implemented over the next seven years. On the back of this news an impromptu all-party meeting was held at Stormont to celebrate. It was a bit *ad hoc* as it was during one of the periods of Direct Rule when the Assembly was in suspension, but as an influential MP Jeffrey Donaldson gave the meeting punch with an enthusiastic speech. It was the first time I'd been in the building, and while walking along the marble-lined corridors I'd attempted to guess which of the slabs of stone had been quarried by Wyndham across the bay down in Co. Galway and would be part of the Republic. Tim's replacement at the NSMC was present at the meeting and went on from it to see the civil servant head of the Northern Ireland Tourist Board, taking with him a copy of the latest analysis report on the canal's financial viability, which had been handed out. Sighting it, the Permanent Secretary stated that the canal restoration project 'was a fantasy which would never happen'.

Nothing did – for two years. Then, in 2009, Seymour Crawford, my local TD representing Monaghan in Dublin's Dail Eireann, asked me to call at his office. There he explained that the canal had been removed without consultation from the list of Interreg projects earmarked for support and the funds redistributed, with no indication of who had made the order. He was deeply worried about the growing leadership vacuum in mid-Ulster, where there was absolutely nothing on offer to match the waterway project in scale as a 'socio-economic regenerator'. I told him how the chief of the Strategic Investment Board had studied the initiative's broader aspects and had put a team together with the goal of harnessing support at Stormont. Suddenly the group had all been head-hunted to London, leaving positions unfilled and their work on the project allowed to stall.

The brief period of inactivity that followed had been filled when the director of the Centre for Cross-Border Studies put some board-level Louis Berger Group engineers in touch because interest from America was returning. Over the coming weeks the engineers made a number of site visits and excitement began to build. A meeting with grass-roots leaders for information to be digested back in Boston at the Massachusetts Institute of Technology was requested, so I asked the IRA ex-prisoner boss to come to the Hillgrove Hotel in Monaghan to fill in the picture from his community point of view at the bottom end of the social ladder. Unfortunately a jumped-up Dublin trouble-maker with an agenda of his own got wind of the meeting, appeared and interrupted with sarcastic anti-Anglo-Irish outbursts every time I attempted to speak. Realising that the Americans were becoming somewhat confused, I withdrew to the lavatory to avoid losing my temper in public. Tommy, the ex-IRA hunger-striker, joined me to explain he was well practised in handling such situations, coached me through a de-tensioning exercise, then said he would take over chairing the event as he could see where the Americans needed to be steered. Thanks to this intervention the meeting ended up being a success, but the ray of hope that this new interest promised to bring was soon eclipsed by events in Iraq and the post-war contract distractions.

It was at that point that Direct Rule from Westminster came to an end, with powers restored to Stormont. Dr Paisley was First Minister and came to a talk I gave at Belfast's Queen's University on First World War Irish heroes, followed by lunch, during which I pressed home why the Ulster canal was such a good idea. He joked that as it started and terminated in Northern Ireland there was no security threat of gunboats sneaking up the waterway, but agreed that the financial benefits were quite clear. Then the reverend Doctor referred to the topic of my lecture, which featured the death of my paternal grandfather in 1917 while serving with the Ulster Division a year after the Battle of the Somme, a favourite subject of his. The conversation took a bit of a twist when Paisley asked how I rated Sir Roger Casement, pointing out that the Republic had recently had his face on a postage stamp in recognition of efforts made to smuggle arms to Ireland from wartime Germany. Was his hanging by the British as a traitor not justified? Momentarily the question hung in the air, and I began to wonder if the discussion was really happening, but decided it was, and stood my ground by requesting a moment's consideration had to be given to Casement's state of mind after the horrific scenes witnessed during his diplomatic posting to King Leopold's Belgian Congo. As the lunch came to an end we parted on friendly terms and it looked as if the project had finally found its champion but, sadly, it was not to be. A message came through to me some time later that even he, the leader of the Stormont Assembly, now back in action, could not budge the entrenched bureaucratic negativity facing an initiative of such merit.

The main defence by civil service opponents featured in the form of an EU rule book, closely adhered to, which dictated that only income generated by the hiring of boats could be balanced against the capital cost of restoration. The 'Tertiary Impact' benefits along this newly created development corridor, which was estimated to be three miles deep from each bank and therefore the roughly 300 square miles of 'bandit country' could not be included in the calculations, though it was really what restoring the waterway was all about. One report went further and fielded the 'disturbance of newt habitat' as a reason against the project's implementation. This negativity was shortly compounded by the Northern Ireland Environment Agency, which produced an updated study of the River Blackwater's catchment area highlighting wildlife and water-quality issues. Surprisingly, it related to only two thirds of the river's actual basin, leaving the area in the Republic unmarked and totally blank on the map – as if it didn't exist. This 'revision' was made startlingly clear when compared with the map of the river basin contained in the original 1997 report, implying that narrow-minded politics still seemed to counter geographic facts in Northern Ireland's bureaucracy and proved the existence of its rather blinkered government.

When the ash cloud of 2009 grounded all flights between Ireland and the UK, use was made of a temporarily idle helicopter to film the entire bed of the canal from the air in order to help move things forward. With two cameramen we flew north at 60 mph, following the line of the waterway as it twisted and wove round a multitude of Drumlin hills, with one clearly visible 19-mile unbroken ribbon of water snaking across the land. It was the cross-over link between the Finn and the Blackwater river-basin depressions, and still benefited from being fed by an underground aquifer which first rose up under a lough before flowing into the canal bed and pouring out over the sills of now gateless locks. The 60 minutes of flying and filming at 150 ft was compressed into a watchable 45 minutes of highlighted footage, ending with a view of Lough Neagh shimmering in the distance like an inland sea. The DVD composition was then put to work, and a visit was made to the Minister of State for Northern Ireland's office in Whitehall. Armed with a visual of the canal, expertly edited with helpful moving graphics laid over the geographic record, I thought it worth presenting the project in its entirety to Hugo Swire MP, a reasonably senior politician involved in Northern Irish matters.

Seated at the centre of an oval table, I was faced by three Northern Ireland civil servants who turned out to be interested only in looking to see if making the film had involved breaking the law in some way. Had I landed at any point anywhere without clearance? Who had financed the operation? Had public funds been used at any point whatever? I was cautioned to think carefully before answering the question. There was absolutely no interest in the DVD's content other than to query why I'd bothered to make it, and was there in fact some ulterior motive involved? 'To do such a thing out of hand' was stated as 'not normal behaviour'. I caught the train home wondering just what was the invisible wall continually blocking the one initiative capable of resolving the Partition legacy of ongoing angst. The film should have been a throw of the dice that won the day, but it appeared to be the opposite, with some other angle of attack to break the bureaucratic log-jam still needing to be found. On the journey home the sense of frustration slowly turned to determination to see the project succeed, and by the time the train rumbled into Salisbury I was feeling quite buoyant. To me it was still obvious that the waterway would one day be recognised as the all-encompassing initiative that was so badly needed. The time would come – it had to, and the hunt wasn't over yet.

19

HRH The Duke of Gloucester's Visit to Castle Leslie

In June 2010 Bill celebrated his centenary with a big bash at Oranmore. In the evening Peter Patrick Hemphill took me aside and, in a slightly tight state, confessed there was something on his conscience he wanted to clear. Back in 1962–63 he had been immersed in a difficult struggle to master the roof leaks at Tulira, his old family home in Co. Galway, when my mother had come to him asking for guidance on dealing with a great number of similar repairs at Castle Leslie. His advice had been not to saddle me with what would be an ongoing nightmare. Her subsequent action of making over the entire property to her brother came as a shock and he felt a bit guilty that he might have helped to play a part in her unfortunate decision-making. When Renville had originally come on the market she should have bought it as a perfect home in the heart of hunting country, but had left herself financially unable to; he however had found the self-contained small estate irresistible.

This unexpected confession, coming so many years after the event, rubbed salt into an old wound, particularly as that very day I'd taken the time to go and sit alone in the burnt-out shell of the old house. Left unoccupied and unloved for over a decade, it had been needlessly torched by a vandal, with all but its little chapel left roofless.

Later on, in 2010, a British-based disaster relief organisation called the International Rescue Corps asked for help in organising a reception in the Republic of Ireland. There had been two reasons for this. First, a large number of the organisation's volunteers were Irish, and secondly, the Republic's Department of Foreign Affairs had been consistently helpful in sorting diplomatic clearance issues when time getting first responders on to site was critical. The Patron, HRH the Duke of Gloucester, wished to make a visit to the Republic so that the appreciation of the support being given could go on record. I was asked if it might be possible to hold the event at Castle Leslie because of its historic Anglo-Irish trappings, and cousin Sammy agreed, providing there was no extra work-load on the staff.

The list of invitees to Glaslough went out on some sort of IRC grapevine, not only to training personnel and volunteers who'd pulled victims from ruins of cities round the globe reduced to rubble by earthquakes and suchlike, but also to the related countries' ambassadors stationed in Dublin. 'Excellencies' from Pakistan, Iran, Peru, Costa Rica, Mexico, Japan, Turkey, Ecuador and the Philippines, plus many others, arrived at the house during the morning to greet the Corps' royal patron. Almost immediately an atmosphere of hostility broke out between two groups of Iranians, with each party coming to me to complain about the other's presence. The head-scarfed Ambassadress was particularly sullen, refusing to respond to any attempts at making her feel comfortable. The co-host of the event, Lord Merryworth, took me aside and explained that the problem lay with the fact that the London-based Iranians who had flown over for the event were in the main of the Baha'i sect of Islam, while the Ambassador and his wife were members of the Shia camp.

As the morning progressed news came through that the Irish government minister expected to attend was unavoidably detained in Dublin as the Taoiseach, Bertie Ahern, had resigned that morning without warning. This meant there was nobody of sufficient status to match the Duke when it came to speech-making, which had been choreographed to take place after a tree-planting ceremony. Something original had to be quickly pulled out of the hat and luckily a neighbouring parish priest was spotted as the assembled gathering began to head towards where a young oak lay waiting. Father Sean Nolan, a man of sharp and able wit, rose to the occasion beautifully. With only minutes to compose a response to the Duke's speech on peace and reconciliation through mutual co-operation, the fundamental tenets of the IRC, Father Sean embarked on a fiery sermon about the hypocrisy of the IRA when it came to murder, forgiveness and respect for human life. He drew on the fact that the parish boundary he'd served throughout the recent decades of conflict straddled the border and had lost parishioners dwelling in both jurisdictions to the men of violence. He showed no quarter to the paramilitaries and would not tolerate them in his church. As we returned to the house the Duke commented on Father Sean's startling likeness to the unfortunate priest skewered with a lightning conductor by the anti-Christ in the film *The Omen* and asked me for clarification as to which denomination he represented, before requesting 30 minutes alone with him in the 'safe room' that had been arranged should an incident of some sort occur.

On the Duke's eventual departure for Casement aerodrome at Baldonnel, where an aircraft from the Royal Flight awaited him, there was tea and a re-eruption of the Iranian spat. It lasted until the Ambassador and his wife left but it didn't dissipate entirely, as unfortunately there were other Shia Iranians booked to stay the night. Urgent requests for room changes began to be made, as the opposing camps didn't want to be even on the same floor. We were running slightly short of accommodation, so one chap was put in the rarely used 'Room of Calm', which happened to be fitted with heavily frosted windows, designed to help victims of traumatic and psychotic disorders. It was instantly rejected on the grounds that it bore a close resemblance to a Tehran torture chamber he'd once been held in. Luckily the Print Room, even though it was temporarily without electricity, was acceptable in the circumstances. Somehow the evening's banquet and speech by the stunningly beautiful London-based Costa Rican First Secretary passed off without incident, other than the realisation that the location of her bedroom was going to need guarding. One of the party had begun to show the wrong sort of interest and it fell to me to keep him isolated and misinformed as to the castle's rooming layout while her safe exit was secured. Finally, it was all over, and as the last taxi pulled away the next morning silence descended, leaving me to wonder what the old stones of the house had made of the Republic's first official Royal Visit.

My father died peacefully in 2012 in his bed, having reached the age of 102. Minutes before his coffin was due to leave Oranmore Castle for the service in St Nicholas's Cathedral in Galway, a call came in from the Gardai Siochana. The officer stated that as 'The Commander' had been honoured with being made a 'Freeman of the City of Galway' some years before, the hearse would be travelling down Shop Street, the pedestrian precinct threading through the heart of the town, and would be escorted by a parade of institution representatives including the Irish Navy and the newly formed Association of Irish Submariners. He was then laid to rest beside my mother, whom he'd adored from the day they had first met, leaving me with more of a sense of losing a sibling than a parent. The distant father of childhood had disappeared during the ill-fated sailing trip as a teenager, but it was during the time in South Africa that a proper relationship of respectful friendship had formed. On becoming a fellow serviceman much had been shared at anecdotal level on the story-telling front, and both of us had struggled against massive odds to revive the Glaslough farm. It was sad to witness his departure, and the feeling ran deep that I'd lost not just a parent but a friend with whom much had been shared.

20
Recovering a Rolls Royce

~⁊~

Hearing the incumbent of Norris Castle, an old family pile on the Isle of Wight, wasn't well I made a point of visiting. The neo-Gothic building hadn't changed much since I'd first visited back in the late 1960s, other than for a steady advance of jungle from nearby woods and the multiplication of dead vehicles in the farmyard. A badger that had set up home under the drawing-room sofa for a period had returned to the wild, and the dusty dining-room still echoed with memories of Royal Yacht Squadron and Bembridge Ball dinner parties. During these the Round the Island Race yachts were visible from one's table seat as they battled up the Solent fighting tides, wind, marine traffic and each other; while the circular library with its unsettling acoustics had gone down in family history as the site where Uncle Jack had discovered 'Boom-Boom' music. The event had been a cousin's 21st birthday and for the evening the room had been turned into a discotheque. Jack had wandered in and remained transfixed for the evening, unwittingly sitting beside an array of speakers. The 1927 family Rolls was still there, now on blocks in the riding school, immovable but looking vulnerable to a roof leak. I found an old boat sail and covered it. A year later the old boy was dead.

As a great-nephew of the last owner of the Rolls a cousin put his hat in the ring as an interested party to acquire the vehicle, and asked the trustees for permission for me to collect it as he lived in Yorkshire. The move opened a can of worms, in the shape of a number of locals who had plans of their own. There was going to be just one chance to get it away, which required a surprise move and being prepared for all eventualities, but, luckily, the foreman of the local security firm was a car buff on-side for the caper I'd in mind. It was obvious that the small window of opportunity was closing fast, so no time was wasted in recruiting a quick-witted and physically strong accomplice in the form of my daughter's beau, a keen petrol-head. The early morning Red Funnel ferry was booked and car transporter wheel-bearings greased. An air compressor, a three-ton ratchet winch, an assortment of straps, ropes, hydraulic jacks, wheel skids, planks, briar cutters and a tarpaulin were loaded into the Discovery. I picked up Ben at the Fishbourne ferry terminal and, as we drove to Norris Castle, explained that we'd be greeted by the security chap. From then we would have about 30 minutes to load the Rolls for transportation to a place of safety. If we took any longer things might get difficult, with access routes being blocked. The car was registered as weighing two tons and the flat tyres were an unknown quantity. During the 43 years it had been sitting there, the blocks placed to take the weight off the wheels had rotted away, leaving the chassis so close to the ground that there was no space to place a jack underneath at the rear.

We connected up the air compressor and prayed. Only 20 lb of pressure was applied to the severely perished tyres, but slowly the back of the car rose, first one side and then the other. Once the front wheels were inflated the ratchet winch was attached and for the first time in 43 years the dear old thing rolled forwards. Briars the thickness of a thumb had grown right into the fabric of the rear bodywork, and had to be deftly cut as I winched all forward. The security man appeared and said a JCB telehandler to block the road exit would arrive in about 20 minutes, so we had to be quick. More frantic cranking of the winch and clipping of briars until, at last, the front wheels were nudging the trailer. Slowly the bonnet and headlights rose up the ramp and then it was the turn of the back wheels to leave the gravel floor. With just one strap attached to the rear we were off, out of the building into daylight, where the vehicle looked as though it had just been lifted from the *Titanic*'s cargo hold, with the sheen of white dust disfigured here and there by our recent scrabbling handprints. Reaching a spot where access to the public road couldn't be prevented it was game over, with us fully in possession of one two-ton 1927 Rolls. A threatened showdown moment arose when the JCB appeared, but it rattled off into the riding school and fortunately didn't re-emerge.

It being only 10.30 in the morning I suggested we walk down to the castle to take in the view across the Solent from the ramparts, and there we found a family looting party in full swing. The important stuff had apparently already gone to the salerooms, but the trustees had invited the immediate family to come and comb through remaining tat before house clearance teams moved in. Making our way through the hall to the terrace overlooking Southampton Water we came across a crowd of relations indulging in a champagne feast. Someone had raided the cellar and corks of vintage Moët were popping everywhere. In an urgent whisper loud enough for my assistant Ben to overhear, a woman asked me where I thought some Krugerrands would have been hidden. There was about £200,000 in gold stashed somewhere and she'd been looking everywhere, with no luck. I was the one person who would really know! Sadly, I didn't, but the internal passages of the building were familiar and so I'd suggested the spaces beneath loose floorboards of a certain room. This triggered a wail of despair when it was discovered that the area was closed off because blankets of asbestos had been laid down years before to contain a fire caused by the ancient wiring circuitry. I took a last wander through the old place which, stripped as it was, still held an atmosphere harking back to earlier times of great parties and much hilarity.

Dropping my helper and hero of the day at the Fishbourne ferry meant having to double back past the Norris entrance to reach the Red Funnel terminal in East Cowes. The big fear of the yellow JCB machine emerging from a side road was only allayed when the Discovery's wheels finally rolled on to the concrete apron of the terminal loading bay. A departing ferry hooted and from its bridge a tannoy announced to the dockers, 'I want that car on this ship'. A small reverse, the ramp was lowered and the Disco was waved aboard. As the chains tightened I knew the worst was over. The new worry was an obvious miscalculation concerning the weight distribution of the Rolls. A 30-mile journey lay ahead and an ominous crack had appeared in the centre of the trailer steelwork during the short run we'd just made. There was nothing for it but to go and have a pint to wash down a well-earned pasty while mulling over the problem as the ferry steamed up Southampton Water for the next hour. Wyndham, my childhood mentor, had once shown me how great weights could be moved using rollers made from scaffolding pipe, and I'd brought a selection as part of the back-up plan should the wheels refuse to turn or collapse due to rusted-out spokes. The car had fortunately rolled of its own accord, but the trailer was now in urgent need of reinforcement before we set off down the stretch of motorway that lay ahead. On disembarking a triangle of steel was created using pipe joiners to provide a central point of support four feet above the two axles. Two ratchet straps rated good for two tons each were attached to the fore and aft ends of the trailer, looped over the support and tightened. The crack closed – not completely, but it signalled that the downward pressure from the old car's wheels was being redistributed. It proved to be enough to get us home and the journey passed off without further incident. Lying in the bath that night, mulling over the day's events since the 6 am start, I had a feeling that the satisfactory outcome was entirely due to the fundamental principles of physics I'd been taught in early youth by a kind and very patient tutor.

Having sat housed in a semi-open building near the sea for so long, most of the car's mechanical parts were non-operational and in a fragile state. Just one door opened and the engine was seized solid. Again, Wyndham's instructions on how to treat wood, leather and use of thermal expansion to separate seized metal parts came into play over the following winter. He'd once taken the time to instruct me how to identify different bolt threads and use a tap and die set to repair or re-cut irreplaceable artefacts. The knowledge proved invaluable: by Easter the engine had fired back into life and the car was moving under its own power. My daughter and Ben Broad were now engaged and the possibility of using the Rolls as a wedding-day accessory became a must-have item. Over in Ireland Uncle Jack had been kept up to speed on the recent adventures concerning the Norris Rolls, as he'd known most of the family members who had owned it, and this meant updates on restoration progress were amusing to raise as he grew increasingly frail.

Because of his love of history we sometimes talked about the prospect of the Ulster canal being reopened and how it would transform the locality. As he and Shane were the only people I'd ever met who could recall the days of its active life, I made a point of giving optimistic reports of the imminence of the old waterway's restoration. It was cheating, but knowing he didn't have long I felt there was no harm in imparting the impression that its reopening was about to happen and mark the beginning of a new era full of promise.

Epilogue

Jack was now six feet under, buried in the family plot shared by his father, mother and step-mother. The comment on the church steps earlier about a possible but unlikely UK break-away from Europe, as a result of the coming Referendum scheduled for two months' time, had lingered on, and coming across my Monaghan accountant in the dispersing throng I asked for his opinion. Slowly, with a smile like the Cheshire cat in *Alice in Wonderland*, he replied that, from his professional point of view as a resident of an Irish border town, 'It would be like Christmas come early.' A crowd comprising Irish Guards, Gaelic singers, a chapter of Latin-chanting Maltese Knights still exuding a faint odour of frankincense, and various generations of tenant families were wandering about the lawn, keen to soak up the last afterglow of the old boy's life, but now a sense of unfinished business wafted through the scene.

I had first begun to sense it earlier when down by the border and, as time passed, the smuggler's proposal gave body to the concept of the UK possibly leaving the European Union in the near future. Jack and I had led very different lives through equally different ages, but we both had a grasp of the pain Partition had inflicted on the island of Ireland. The two newly created jurisdictions had suffered for decades before finally coming to terms with the legacy and the thought of the UK and Northern Ireland's 'Six Counties' separating from Europe represented a safely sealed can of worms being needlessly reopened. The ensuing political dust-storm would be horrific, with implications probably taking years to settle, during which time there would be little hope of advancing the canal project – but common sense had to prevail in the end, as the simple logic of it could not be denied for ever.

One fact I'd learned in life was that the further one looked back into the past the easier it was to understand how to plan for the future. There was usually a simple solution to the most difficult of problems, like not having quite the right tool for a job or securing a required examination pass. I'd observed endless examples in the Third World where enterprising workmen had made do with whatever was to hand to achieve desired results, whether with bamboo and wire or an ingenious assortment of spanners and screwdrivers jammed together to loosen an outsized nut. Wyndham had built my boat from the remains of an unused garden shed and I'd seen where he'd used Model T Ford door hinges to hang a door during the war when supplies were short. The secret was to keep the mind open and be prepared to think outside the box when an obstacle appeared or the required instrument was not to hand. It was the way I had been taught to think and it had worked in getting me through life so far. The Irish Border question might well mushroom into a giant conundrum if the Brexit scenario became a reality, but it need only be a momentary problem if the political fraternity kept their heads while searching for the way forward.

By the time the last guests departed, my mind had clarified as to what the mental niggle set in train hours earlier by Jim the smuggler was all about. It was as if he had been primed to remind me of the Field Marshal's instruction of years before, when he had told me to use my unique mid-Ulster social position to 'do something useful'. The more I thought about it, the clearer it was that restoration of the Ulster canal fitted the bill perfectly. Political constraints narrowing vision might cause temporary blinkered thinking, but the fact that the old waterway represented an unarguable solution to any developing constitutional gridlock could not be avoided. It had originally been constructed in order to transport flax and coal but now represented a modern-day eco-friendly step into the field of recreation. Back in the early 1960s, Terence O'Neill had seen the need for the development of all-island initiatives to underpin future economic prosperity. Reopening the canal would have been exactly what he had in mind. It might take a little longer for the project to fall into safe hands, but knowing the old 55-mile ditch was still lying there intact felt deeply comforting as I finally made my way upstairs to bed, nodding to a portrait of my grandfather on the way.